"Therefore, Choose Life . . ."

"Therefore, Choose Life . . ."

♪♪♪

An Autobiography

by

Moisey Wolf

Edited and Translated
with an Introduction and Notes

by

Judson Rosengrant

Oregon State University Press ♪♪♪ Corvallis

The paper in this book meets the guidelines for permanence and durability of the Committee on Production Guidelines for Book Longevity of the Council on Library Resources and the minimum requirements of the American National Standard for Permanence of Paper for Printed Library Materials Z39.48-1984.

Library of Congress Cataloging-in-Publication Data
Wolf, Moisey, 1922-2007, author.
  Therefore, choose life : an autobiography / by Moisey Wolf ; edited and translated with an introduction and notes by Judson Rosengrant.
     pages cm
  Includes bibliographical references and index.
  ISBN 978-0-87071-744-4 (alk. paper)—ISBN 978-0-87071-745-1 (e-book)
1. Wolf, Moisey, 1922-2007. 2. Jews—Soviet Union—Biography. 3. Jewish physicians—Soviet Union—Biography. 4. Psychiatrists—Soviet Union—Biography. 5. Jews—Poland—Warsaw—Biography. I. Rosengrant, Judson-editor and translator. II. Title.
  DS134.93.W65A3 2014
  947'.004924092—dc23
  [B]
                        2013041305

First published in 2014 by Oregon State University Press
Printed in the United States of America

Oregon State University Press
121 The Valley Library
Corvallis OR 97331-4501
541-737-3166 • fax 541-737-3170
www.osupress.oregonstate.edu

"Therefore choose life, that both thou and thy seed may live"
Devarim/Deuteronomy 30:19

Contents

♪♪♪

Foreword

"But how are the books to blame?" Those were the last, desperate words of Dr. Moisey Wolf's father, spoken just moments before he was murdered while defending his cherished library from Hitler's thugs. Then a young man of seventeen, Dr. Wolf witnessed his father's final, noble act and never forgot it.

Jews are commanded with the imperative *Zachor*! Remember! For decades Dr. Wolf held on to his memories until his granddaughter Lyubov prevailed upon him to write them down. His extraordinary experiences, now preserved in the present volume, transcend those of our smaller lives. From these stories, however, we can grow. Through these stories, we can extend our collective human memory and find meaning.

The Oregon Jewish Museum joins in this expansive, ancient, and essential endeavor of remembrance by helping to support the publication by Oregon State University Press of Dr. Wolf's autobiography. Our participation has been guided by and underscores the Museum's mission to foster dialogue about identity, culture, and assimilation, and to provide opportunities for Jews and non-Jews alike to see the Jewish experience as a paradigm of cultural survival and intercultural understanding.

Dr. Wolf's narrative opens a new window onto an often gruesome and mad historical period. His deft interweaving of historical drama and personal experience involves the reader in events of great tragedy and triumph. And it succeeds thanks to his perceptive eye with its integration of the detached regard of a trained clinician and the passion of a learned humanist.

Such stories are the vital heart of the Oregon Jewish Museum. While we embrace the new millennium as a time when technology vastly expands the ways we capture our memories and transmit stories, we still cherish the classic art of master storytelling. Dr. Wolf's autobiography draws back the curtain on a fascinating and dramatic life and invites the reader to join him in the inspiring saga of his survival. It packs into its powerful pages more tragedy, humor, horror, and delight than most of us could hope—or fear—to see in our own lifetimes, and it does so with a conviction and integrity that are no less inspiring than the saga itself. It is for these reasons that we are proud to be associated with the book and gratified that others will now have the chance to read Dr. Wolf's remarkable story in his own compelling voice.

Judith Margles, Director, Oregon Jewish Museum

Editor's Introduction

Fine autobiographies can and should speak for themselves. Given the unusual complexity of this one, however, it will be helpful to summarize its sinuous narrative and shifting background—to follow the trajectory of the author's life and identify the large-scale forces that propelled its movement. It will also be desirable, for the sake of full disclosure, to describe the particular relationship of the English edition to the Russian manuscript from which it derives.

As readers of his vivid, intimate account of it will quickly appreciate, Dr. Moisey Wolf's life was a remarkable one by nearly any measure, but not least in his devotion to his natal heritage despite profound, often wrenching historical, cultural, and geographical change that extended from Poland in the first half of the twentieth century, across the vast Soviet Union in the second half, and then in our own time to the Pacific Northwest of the United States.

Moisey (the Russian form of his name and the one we will use) was born Avrom-Moishe Wolf on April 10, 1922, in Warsaw, the vibrant, polyglot capital of the Second Polish Republic (1918-39) and a center of Jewish intellectual and political life.[1] The elder son of a lawyer and the grandson of a Hasidic rabbi on his mother's side, he was raised in Warsaw, where he attended its Zionist Tarbut Hebrew gymnasium from 1929 until 1938, while also receiving private instruction for the rabbinate. From early childhood he also spent summers and other holidays in the then eastern Polish (Volhynian) village of Cheremoshno and the embrace of the Orthodox community of his paternal grandparents and the generations of Wolfs who had lived there before them.[2] After graduating from the gymnasium with distinction, he enrolled in medical school at the University of Warsaw, completing his first year in June 1939, despite dangerously unstable political conditions in Poland at the time and a dramatic increase in official anti-Semitism that had severely limited Jewish access to higher education.

The immediate promise of Moisey's young life and that of many others would, however, come to an abrupt, certain, and terrifying end three months later with the outbreak of world war on September 1, 1939. According to secret terms of the so-called "non-aggression" pact between the Soviet Union and Nazi Germany, concluded in August, Poland was invaded almost simultaneously from west and east, with German forces occupying Warsaw in a matter of days after unprecedentedly savage bombing that took over twenty-five thousand civilian lives. The seventeen-year-old Moisey, having just witnessed the execution of his father by the invaders and hurriedly buried him, fled on foot by night some three hundred kilometers east to Cheremoshno and what had become, with the partition and annexations, the new Soviet territory of northwestern Ukraine. There he was given Soviet citizenship, thanks to the shrewd foresight of his grandfather, who had entered him in the village birth register, although as a Jewish refugee from German-occupied Poland, he would, at least in the first months of annexation, very likely have been offered citizenship anyway. Still too young for service in the Soviet Army (the draft age at the time was nineteen), he lived briefly with his grandparents in Cheremoshno and then with an aunt and uncle in the nearby town of Kovel, before resuming medical studies in August 1940 at the University of Lvov in annexed western Ukraine (Galicia).

In 1941, after the German surprise attack on the Soviet Union of June 22, Moisey, now nineteen, again fled east, this time by hastily organized evacuation train from Kovel to Stalingrad, seventeen hundred kilometers away on the Lower Volga and what seemed a safe distance from the advancing German armies. Fraught though it obviously was, his decision to leave was a fortunate one even in its immediate result, for had he stayed, he would almost certainly have been shot at once by the Germans as a potential partisan combatant. His family failed to join him, however, remaining in Kovel and the nearby Volhynian towns of Melnitsa and Manevichi. Like so many caught up in the treacherous currents of the time and unable to imagine (how could they?) the horror that would soon follow, they decided to face whatever might come on familiar ground. Yet with a few miraculous exceptions, all the members of Moisey's family were shot over mass graves some fifteen months later near Melnitsa in September 1942, after internment in, probably, the Kovel ghetto, while the Germans gathered the means to carry out their "Final Solution" in the Polish-Ukrainian borderlands. He had by an adventitious choice in the chaos of war escaped their terrible fate, but his anguish and guilt at having left them behind would torment him the rest of his life.

The safety provided by Moisey's Stalingrad refuge soon came to an end, however, with the arrival of a large German army group west of the city the following summer. Having in the meantime completed an accelerated wartime combination of third- and fourth-year studies at the Stalingrad State Medical Institute, even as he struggled to master the Russian language, and having been given, despite his youth, a commission in the Soviet army medical corps with the rest of his class, he took part in the pivotal battle for Stalingrad of August 1942 to February 1943, serving as a *feldsher* or medical assistant in an evacuation hospital. After the destruction of the German forces in the battle, one of the bloodiest in history, with combined civilian and military casualties on both sides of over one and a half and perhaps as many as two million, Moisey was assigned elsewhere in the Volga region as a hospital orderly and then, for a short time, as an acting public-health physician—"acting" since he had not, because of the disruptions of war, been able to finish his coursework and sit for the state examinations required for medical certification. Those steps would only come with another year of study at one of the country's finest medical schools, the 2nd Moscow State Medical Institute (since 1991, the Russian State Medical University), to which he was transferred in October 1944 by medical corps superiors and mentors eager to help him recover from the ravages and disorder of his young life and fulfill the great promise of his gifts.

To be sure, many people in those years suffered losses no less grievous than Moisey's, and millions of young lives were not merely ravaged but brought to a grotesque, untimely end, yet those who did manage to survive through luck and will were often sustained by those in positions of benign authority, who did what they could in acts of quiet intercession, as Moisey makes clear time and again with unstinting gratitude. For in his view—it is a leitmotif of his story and a perdurable principle of the generous, affirmative morality instilled by his upbringing—nothing is achieved without the help of others, and it would be a denial of the nature of life itself not to acknowledge it.

In November 1944, after a one-month wartime courtship, Moisey married his Moscow classmate Susanna Kozlovskaya. In July 1945 they graduated from the medical institute, and in August their daughter, Nadezhda, was born. Moisey, now Dr. Wolf, was then recalled to active duty, but since the war had ended three months earlier for the Soviet Union with the surrender of Germany, he was assigned not to a unit of the medical corps as might have been expected, but to an installation of the Ministry of Internal Affairs (MVD), the main branch of the nervously elaborate Soviet security apparatus. He served, as ordered, as the medical officer of what was euphemistically called a "filtration camp" for the interrogation of repatriated prisoners of war and others who had been trapped behind enemy lines, but what was in much more sinister reality a conduit for the country's enormous network of slave-labor sites, the infamous Gulag, to which most of the internees, if they were not executed, were sent for having "allowed" themselves to be captured or detained by the Germans.

After that brief, morally repellent duty (although he did all that he could to mitigate the hardship of those in his care), Moisey was discharged from the military and enrolled in 1946 as an intern at the Serbsky Institute of Forensic Psychiatry in Moscow. After completing his internship in 1947, he found work at a municipal psychoneurological clinic in Moscow. In addition to his duties there as a psychiatrist and therapist, he served as a public-health officer responsible for staff and community education programs, including a popular lecture series he instituted that brought writers and other cultural figures to speak to district residents about the reflection of medicine in art and literature—evidence of his organizational vision and skill and his sense, even at the beginning of his career, of the interconnection of medicine with larger social and cultural circumstances.

Yet despite that very auspicious start in civilian psychiatry, Moisey's life would soon take another abrupt, unanticipated turn. In December 1949 he was ordered to return to active duty in the medical corps and within forty-eight hours to depart, without his family, for the Soviet Far East and Vladivostok, nine thousand kilometers away on the Sea of Japan, or roughly the distance from San Francisco to Paris. The reason for his call-up and that of numerous other veterans was to bolster Soviet troop strength in the Far East in preparation for a new war on the Korean peninsula (it in fact began in June 1950, when the North attacked the South). Soviet forces would not in the end become directly involved in the conflict, and Moisey was never assigned to a field unit. Instead, he was sent another nine hundred and fifty kilometers north to a military psychiatric hospital on remote Sakhalin Island in the Sea of Okhotsk. There he remained in virtual internal exile for seven months while endeavoring, like so many in that grim time, to negotiate unscathed the treacherous terrain (but perhaps especially dangerous for Jews because of resurgent state anti-Semitism) of late-Stalinist political culture and its paranoid, or merely cynical, eagerness to add to the population of the Gulag, or worse.

In July 1950, thanks in part to the efforts of his family and military friends, Moisey was transferred by the army medical command back from the Far East to the European Soviet Union (west of the Urals) and the southern city of Rostov-on-the-Don; and then, in October 1951, to Arkhangelsk on the White Sea near the Arctic Circle, some twelve hundred kilometers north of Moscow. He would remain in Arkhangelsk, once again without his family except for the occasional brief visits they were permitted to make, until December 1955 and his discharge from the army medical corps, thanks to Khrushchev's decision to reduce the size of the Soviet military. He then returned to his wife and daughter (Susanna had meanwhile established her own career as a pediatrician) and employment again as a psychiatrist in a Moscow area clinic—the end of over sixteen years of almost constant movement in involuntary response to the vicissitudes of history and the intrusions of a Soviet state largely indifferent to individual circumstances and needs.

Moisey would work for the Moscow clinic until 1960, while also employed, after 1957, at the city's Gannushkin Psychiatric Hospital, where he remained in one responsible capacity or another until emigrating in 1992. His almost thirty-five years at the hospital, one of the Soviet Union's leading mental-health research and treatment centers, were marked by significant personal events and distinguished professional achievement. In 1957 his son, Solomon, was born; in 1962 he organized and was made head of what would become the hospital's celebrated epilepsy ward, a position he held until he emigrated; and in 1966 he was awarded the graduate degree of Candidate of Medical Sciences with a dissertation on his pioneering empirical research in the use of electroencephalography for the diagnosis of epilepsy and the determination of treatment regimes. He would become one of the Soviet Union's preeminent specialists in that field of medicine, not only as the first in the country to use electroencephalography as a diagnostic tool, but also as among the first to combine drugs with social therapy to manage the affliction. His innovations in the organization of his ward, and thereby in the treatment of epilepsy and other conditions, were remarkable for the time. They employed an approach that took much greater account of the patient's social circumstances and their impact on the course of his disease, and they entailed occupational therapy, the direct involvement of families in ward administration through parent advisory councils, the arrangement of theatrical, musical, and other social events for, and with, those in his care, and, perhaps most strikingly, the use of stabilized patients to carry out the ward's daily operations as part of their own therapy and growth—the task of psychiatrist in Moisey's holistic, deeply humane view reaching well beyond the treatment of primary symptoms.

In his role as the hospital's chief of methodology, he supervised the development of widely used instructional materials and guides and organized municipal and regional conferences addressing the preparation of nurses and young psychiatrists. He also directed Candidate dissertations; worked as a consultant in the region; authored or edited over one hundred and twenty articles, anthology contributions, and books, including monographs and handbooks on the treatment of epilepsy that are still standard resources in Russia today; and produced autobiographical and critical essays in Yiddish, a language of which he was an acknowledged master—evidence, once more, of the breadth of his interests and the power of his intellectual grasp. In 1969 his daughter, Nadezhda, graduated from the Gnesin State Institute of Music Pedagogy and embarked on a career as a pianist and composer; and in 1980 his son, Solomon, received his degree from the 2nd Moscow State Medical Institute, the same one that Moisey and Susanna had attended, and began his own residency at the hospital. In 1982 Solomon married Margarita Leytes, and in 1984 their daughter, Lyubov, was born. In 1988, considering emigration to Israel or the United States, Moisey made a preliminary visit to Portland, Oregon, and in 1990 Solomon, Margarita, and Lyubov left for that city, with Moisey, Susanna, and Nadezhda joining them two years later.

Aliyah, "going up," in the sense of emigrating to *Eretz Yisrael*—the land of Israel, had long been a cherished dream of Moisey's, one reaching back to his youth at the Zionist Tarbut gymnasium in Warsaw, a school that had given him, along with his fine general education, a superb knowledge of Modern Hebrew in anticipation of that moment of historical and individual fulfillment, as he regarded it. His decision to come to the United States instead was thus a difficult one, but, as it turned out, it too had a compelling logic, one located in Volhynia and his family's past. For, as he would come to appreciate fully only late in life after decades of Soviet isolation, Portland was the center of the first Cheremoshno diaspora, the home of two younger brothers, a sister, and a nephew of his favorite grandfather. The four had arrived in America at the beginning of the twentieth century when Volhynia and Cheremoshno with it were still part of the Russian empire. They had not only become well established in Portland but had also, in the case of the elder of the two brothers and the nephew, been prominent members of its business community. In a surprising peripeteia that brought his sinuous path full circle, Moisey was thus in the last chapter of his life in a real sense brought back to his Cheremoshno roots, however transposed. In coming to distant Portland, the endpoint of his wanderings, he had recovered an essential, long-lost part of himself.

Yet for all the narrative elegance of that individual apotheosis, the final, American stage of Moisey's life was not easy. He arrived in the United States in March 1992, a month before his seventieth birthday, not only suddenly bereft of his eminent professional standing, the material comforts he had achieved as a prominent specialist, and, most important, the sustaining sense of place and value he had derived from his work; but also, inevitably, without a clear sense of the social and economic arrangements of the new country or, in the beginning, firm control of its language and customs. That condition of personal, linguistic, and cultural disorientation is of course experienced to some degree by every immigrant, just as it had indeed been by Moisey himself once before when, as he vividly describes, he was cast up in much more arduous circumstances on the alien cultural shore of Stalingrad in 1941. Nevertheless, thanks to the power of his mind, the richness of his cosmopolitan culture and the insight and adaptability it gave him, the irrepressible energy of his creative spirit, the solace of his religious faith, and, not least, the help of friends who responded to his natural warmth and recognized his many gifts, he began to thrive even in the face of the uncertainties and difficulties of immigration and to fashion a place for himself in the new world he had entered.

Without a medical license, obtainable in the United States only after years of intensive study for which he had neither time left nor stamina, he could not of course consider practicing his profession, except as an occasional unpaid consultant. On the other hand, he could devote himself to the other domains of his spiritual and intellectual life—his faith and his literary and philological interests. In the latter regard he produced two valuable reference works, the first a Hebrew-Yiddish and the second a Hebrew-Yiddish-Russian-English lexicon; published widely in Yiddish periodicals in the United States and Israel as a critic and essayist; lectured in the United States and Canada on Yiddish language and literature; and even contributed, for new immigrants from the former Soviet Union, a regular column in Russian to the *Jewish Review* in Portland.

In 1994, thanks to the aid of a wise and generous friend, he finally realized his dream of visiting Israel, spending three weeks in Haifa with relatives of his Cheremoshno descent and a week in Jerusalem with members of the country's elite. In 1998 and 2000 his granddaughters Emilia and Julia were born, further enriching his life. In 2004, after delays and even reluctance, since it would mean returning not only to the joyful moments and significant achievements of his past but also to its most painful and terrible events, he began to work on the manuscript of his autobiography. In July 2004 his daughter, Nadezhda, died in Portland after a protracted, agonizing illness. In October 2006, his own health in steep decline, he completed a draft of his manuscript, and on February 14, 2007, he died of heart failure, survived by his life companion, Susanna (they had been married for over sixty-two years), his son, Solomon, and daughter-in-law, Margarita, and his three much-loved grandchildren, Lyubov, Emilia, and Julia.

Such then was the long, circuitous path of Moisey's extraordinarily interesting and productive life, a representative mid-century Eastern European life in many respects, certainly in the way its geographical movement and life choices were impelled by momentous events and suddenly shifting circumstances, but also a life that, like any other, was unique in its particular realization of its experience, in its sense of meaning and purpose, and of course in the persistence, in Moisey's case, of a religious faith and values that remained firmly intact, whatever the situation and however devastating the changes it brought, or great the need, during much of the Soviet period, to dissimulate, to maintain for survival a sharp distinction between his private and public selves. The resilience of that inner integrity in the face of destructive historical change is a main theme of Moisey's story and one of the ways in which it is most instructive. But of course the story is not only about the preservation and growth of an identity in strenuous circumstances; it is also to a significant degree about its secure formation within a distinctive milieu. For Moisey, that milieu was dual: Warsaw and Cheremoshno, the first a center, the largest and most robust in Europe, of intellectually disciplined, ideologically diverse, outward-looking cosmopolitan Jewish culture; and the second a vessel of the deeply rooted, inward-looking religious and ethical traditions of Jewish village life embodied in the simple, innocent, forever vanished world of his grandparents, a world described in the book with an elegiac grace that yields some of its most affecting passages. The result of that dual milieu was for Moisey's character and mode of thought an amalgam of urbane intellectual openness and skill, broad tolerance, and adaptability, on the one hand, and an unselfconscious devotion to age-old tradition and meaning, on the other. It was an amalgam whose moral strength would sustain him throughout his long life and provide the inner capacity not only to withstand the tremendous historical, social, and personal tragedies and stresses he faced as a man and a devout Jew, but also to find a way through them to great achievement, to move across a long series of perilous territorial and cultural boundaries and yet remain true to himself and his heritage and to its ancient, abiding principles.

Moisey Wolf tells this remarkable story with insightful, often eloquent anecdote, a lively sense of individual character, compelling and even harrowing drama, and yet, for all that, much humor and charm. But because the Russian manuscript he left was still a draft, still a work in progress that he had been unable to revise or correct before his death, it required not only judicious translation but also significant editorial intervention. The author was of course aware that it would, and in fact in conversation with me in his last months he instructed me with an astonishing but, as readers will see, a quite characteristic lack of vanity to "add or subtract" according to my judgment. My editorial activity was thus wide ranging, touching on every aspect of the text and extending from large-scale decisions about such matters as narrative sequence and presentation to the innumerable small-scale discretionary moves that are the basic stuff of any literary translation, but especially one between languages as distantly related as Russian and English and refracted, moreover, through Yiddish, Hebrew, and Polish. To the extent that the strands of that interwoven editorial-translational activity may be readily distinguished, it proceeded along three main lines.

1) Verifying and where necessary correcting the manuscript's various personal and other references (names, dates, public facts) to ensure conformity with the historical record and clarity and consistency in the representation of encompassing circumstances and events and their numerous details.

2) Adjustment of the structure of the narrative through the reordering of episodes that internal or external evidence indicated were in a faulty, misremembered sequence; omission of passages that were irreparably corrupt in their transcription, fundamentally flawed in their factual basis, irresolvably contradictory in their exposition, or contained sensitive personal information about living persons; and finally the selection of a title and the division of the story into four biographical periods instead of the overlapping three of the manuscript.

3) Providing endnotes to amplify Dr. Wolf's references and usages, including explanation of foreign-language phrases not glossed within the text; clarifying literary, cultural, and historical allusions unlikely to be familiar to non-specialist readers; unpacking historical or narrative implication through summary discussion of contextual matters about which Dr. Wolf was reticent; identification by birth and death date and, as appropriate, capsule biography of individuals mentioned in the various episodes; inclusion of a family tree and archival family portraits (some of which were, inevitably, not of the highest quality) to help clarify the intricate relationships on which the first part of the narrative turns; glossing of specialized medical terms; explanation of Jewish devotional practices and texts for those who may be unfamiliar with them; and the inclusion of bibliographical citations for any who might want to consult the original materials.

Dr. Wolf's individual culture, it should be abundantly clear, was both profound in its understanding of his own heritage and comprehensive in its embrace of the diverse communities within which he moved, but it was also naturally multilingual. That multilingualism has, as a fundamental part of his identity, been preserved in this edition, although with appropriate help. Thus, the passages in Yiddish, Hebrew, and Aramaic have been rendered in a YIVO Institute for Jewish Research or modified Ashkenazi Roman transliteration and provided with accompanying English translations. Similarly, Yiddish and Hebrew names have retained their original forms, which may differ from common English variants (for example, *Noemi* instead of *Naomi*), while words and phrases in Polish have been given in their native spelling with diacritics, and expressions in German have followed the conventions of that language. The transliteration from Dr. Wolf's Cyrillic of Russian and Ukrainian names, toponyms, and other terms uses a popular system with simplified endings (*-sky* instead of *-skii*, etc.) and without hard and soft signs, unless the items are found in the endnotes or bibliography, where the more detailed Library of Congress system has been followed for those who may wish to consult the original materials.

None of these manifold editorial changes or additions or procedures has, however, been allowed to distort or mute the expression of Dr. Wolf's own vibrant personality. Although the English edition is to a significant degree a painstaking reconstruction of his raw manuscript and even, as I have tried to make clear, a necessary adaptation of it, the story-telling voice remains Dr. Wolf's own and is true to his tone and emphasis and his distinctive cognitive rhythm, as I might call it, just as the story and its broad deployment are the product of his remarkable memory and his taste and judgment, and scrupulously convey the facts and meanings that he himself installed. It is Dr. Wolf's voice and articulate story, his own talented autobiography, and there should be no doubt that he is speaking in this English edition just as he himself meant to be heard.

♪♪♪

As Dr. Wolf himself might have said, nothing is achieved in isolation. I would therefore like to recognize the essential support of the Jewish Federation of Greater Portland and the Moisey Wolf Life Story Publication Committee, which launched the project and raised funds from generous donors in partial support of the work of translating and editing (their names are listed in the following Acknowledgments section) and, through the efforts of Charles Schiffman and Paul Haist, made arrangements for a reading from the translation at the Mittleman Jewish Community Center and the publication of excerpts in the Portland *Jewish Review.* I would also like to thank Judith Margles for inviting me to read from the translation at a literary evening hosted by the Oregon Jewish Museum. Literary translators, no less than other writers and scholars, have a need to step out of their scriptoria and directly engage the readers they would serve. And that may have been especially true of this book with its warmly social character, its author's embrace and eloquent articulation of many communities of time and place.

Although work on a project of this complex kind must be a largely solitary enterprise, it will also require, and with luck even receive, the substantive help and advice of others. Among those who provided such help during the book's long gestation I would like to single out Irina Mikula, who gave needed moral support and served as a tireless native consultant about unusual Russian usages and other editorial matters; Professor Amelia Glaser of the University of California at San Diego, who kindly answered questions about Yiddish; and Dr. Solomon Wolf, who with great generosity and scrupulous care shared his knowledge of the fascinating details of Wolf family history and of his father's medical career in the Soviet Union, and who provided from his own archive the photographs used to illustrate the text. I would also like to acknowledge the contribution of the late Professor Craig Wollner of Portland State University, who gave the English manuscript a sensitive reading and offered thoughtful comments about its structure and substance. And, finally, I would like to express my gratitude to Jo Alexander and Micki Reaman of Oregon State University Press for their tactful and insightful assistance with what proved to be a very complicated manuscript, and for their gracious tolerance of what must at times have been my dismaying urge to rewrite and improve. None of those mentioned here should, of course, be regarded as responsible in any way for whatever errors or confusions may remain despite their efforts. Those errors and confusions will in every instance be entirely my own.

Judson Rosengrant
Portland, Oregon

Select Bibliography

Applebaum, Anne. *Gulag. A History* (New York: Doubleday, 2003).

Freeze, Gregory, ed. *Russia. A History* (Oxford and New York: Oxford University Press, 1997).

Gross, Jan T. *Revolution from Abroad: The Soviet Conquest of Poland's Western Ukraine and Western Belorussia*, expanded edition (Princeton: Princeton Unversity Press, 2002).

Hoffman, Eva. *Shtetl. The Life and Death of a Small Town and the World of the Polish Jews* (Boston and New York: Houghton Mifflin Company, 1997).

Hoskings, Geoffrey. *Russia and the Russians. A History* (Cambridge, Mass.: Harvard University Press, 2001).

Hupchick, Dennis P., and Harold E. Cox. *A Concise Historical Atlas of Eastern Europe.* (New York: St. Martin's Press, 1996).

Mendelsohn, Ezra. *The Jews of Central Europe between the World Wars* (Bloomington: Indiana University Press, 1983).

Moseley, Marcus. "Autobiography and Memoir." In *YIVO Encyclopedia of Jews in Eastern Europe* 13 (13 July 2010). Web version: http://www.yivoencyclopedia.org/article.aspx/Autobiography_and_Memoir

_____. *Being for Myself Alone: The Origins of Jewish Autobiography* (Stanford: Stanford University Press, 2006).

Peretz, I. L. *Selected Stories*, ed. with an intro. by Irving Howe and Eliezer Greenberg (New York: Schocken Books, 1974).

Rothschild, Joseph. *East Central Europe between the Two World Wars* (Seattle and London: University of Washington Press, 1974).

Savenko, Iu. S. "Nekrolog. Moisei Solomonovich Vol'f (1922-2007)." *Nezavisimyi psikhiatricheskii zhurnal* 2 (2007): 92-4.

Service, Robert. *A History of Twentieth-Century Russia* (Cambridge, Mass.: Harvard University Press, 1998).

Snyder, Timothy. *Bloodlands. Europe between Hitler and Stalin* (New York: Basic Books, 2010).

_____. "The Life and Death of West Volhynian Jews, 1921-1945." In Ray Brandon and Wendy Lower, eds., *The Shoah in Ukraine: History, Testimony, and Memorialization* (Bloomington: Indiana University Press, 2008), 77-113.

_____. "Holocaust. The Ignored Reality." *The New York Review of Books* 56, 12 (16 July 2009).

_____. "What We Need to Know about the Holocaust." *The New York Review of Books* 57, 14 (30 September 2010).

Family Tree

Mechel + Chaya Wolf
|
Chaim + Reiza Wolf

Yeruchim + Rivka Wolf
(d. 1942)

Samuel (Sheiya) Wolf
(1881–1958)

Harry (Osher) Wolf
(1884–1948)

Charlotte Wolf-Cohon
|
Richard Cohon

Hannah Wolf-Chusid
(1888–1988)

Shimon + Esther Wolf
(d. 1940)   (d. 1940)

Blossom Wolf-Grayson
|
Jeffrey L. Grayson   Nancy Grayson Fruchtengarten

Ruvim Wolf
(d. 1942)

Yankel Wolf
(d. 1940)

Rivka Wolf
(d. 1942)

Chaya Wolf
(d. 1942)

Basya Wolf
(d. 1942)

Morris + Sophie Wolf
(1897–1981)   (d. 1987)

Berl Wolf
(d. 1981)

Mechl Wolf
(d. 1942)

Ronya Wolf + Avrom-Osher Zeltzer
(d. 1942)

Pesya Wolf + Fishel Katzan
(1909–2000)   (d. 1999)

Martin Wolf   Leslie Wolf   Maureen Wolf-Horenstein

Chaya Zeltzer
(1924–44?)

Polina Zeltzer-Krell
(b. 1926)

Dovid Zeltzer
(1929–42)

Shloyme Wolf + Noemi Raiz
(d. 1939)

Reizele Wolf
(1930?–42)

Moisey Wolf + Susanna Kozlovskaya   Libche Wolf-Goldschmidt
(1922–2007)   (1921–2011)   (1923–42)

Yankel Wolf
(1926–42)

Nadezhda (Wolf) Kozlovskaya
(1945–2004)

Solomon Wolf + Margarita Leytes
(b. 1957)   (b. 1961)

Lyubov Wolf
(b. 1984)

Emilia Wolf
(b. 1998)

Julia Wolf
(b. 2000)

Acknowledgments

During his fifteen years in Portland Dr. Wolf was regularly visited by recent Jewish and Christian immigrants from Russia, who came for instruction in Judaism and Hebrew. They were greeted by Dr. Wolf's wife, Dr. Susanna Kozlovskaya, who entertained them with lively conversation and traditional refreshments while they waited their turn to enter his study with its crammed bookshelves, day bed, and health equipment.

It was to this setting that Rosanne Royer was taken by one of the immigrants in 2006. She had told her escort about her own Slavic heritage and studies, and he had asked if she might help Dr. Wolf with the English translation of an autobiography he was writing. Royer was deeply moved by her visit: "The air in his study was close, and I had to lean in to catch the ideas and concerns that poured out rapidly, as if we had known each other for years. It did not take long to realize I was in the presence of a great scholar and survivor. To leave without offering to help would have been unthinkable."

Dr. Wolf printed a few dozen pages of his manuscript and gave them to Royer, who sent copies to two acquaintances, both specialists in Russian history, asking their opinions. They replied that the material appeared to merit publication by a university press. Such a project would, however, require funding and other support, and Royer took Dr. Wolf's suggestion to contact Charles Schiffman, then executive director of the Jewish Federation of Greater Portland, and Jerry Stern, the Portland business and community leader and philanthropist. Both enthusiastically agreed to help, and Schiffman invited Jewish community actvists to join a publication committee to pursue the project. With Schiffman as chair and Royer as coordinator, fundraising began, and after it the work of the book's editor and translator, Judson Rosengrant.

To the great sadness of the committee members and the hundreds of others who knew and loved him, Dr. Wolf passed away in February 2007, just three months after the committee was formed. He did not live to see his manuscript in print, but he knew before he died that its translation and editing were underway, and that a group of people had dedicated themselves to its publication.

Chief among those people were the members of the publication committee whose names are appended to this section. The committee is grateful for the warm hospitality of Dr. Kozlovskaya, whose enthusiasm sustained its work, while Dr. Solomon Wolf, Moisey Wolf's son and a committee member, served as an invaluable source of information for Dr. Rosengrant. The Jewish Federation of Greater Portland kindly lent space for the committee's meetings and provided initial financial assistance to the project.

It is fitting that the project has also enjoyed the support of the Oregon Jewish Museum, the foremost repository of Jewish culture and history in Portland and the state of Oregon. Under its director, Judith Margles, the Museum has evolved from a small organization into a major institution that serves many different groups as a bountiful resource. Dr. Wolf's life story exemplifies what the Museum itself offers through its own programs, collections, and beautiful facility—a fount of Jewish experience in many times and places.

It is also essential to thank the diverse community of generous donors who valued Dr. Wolf's work and friendship and helped to make the publication of his autobiography possible. They include Semion and Larissa Bakman, Yelena Baldetskaya, Alla Baram, Steve Berliner, John K. Bishof, Efim Bresler and Sofia Zalmanova, Marianne Buchwalter, Nancy Fruchtengarten, Olga and Edward Boyko, Irene (Rena) Brooks, Richard and Roberta Cohon, Carol and Seymour Danish, Brian Davis, Boris Diner and Serafima Osadchaya, Mihail Elisman, Reva and Jack Falk, Kim Feuer, Olga Gavrilova, Elena Goldstein, Lila and Doug Goodman, Nancy Griffith, Gloria and Jeffrey Hammer, Sue Hickey and Sheldon Klapper, Holman's Funeral Service, Erwin Horenstein and Maureen Wolf Horenstein, Rabbi Daniel and Carol Isaak, the Jewish Federation of Greater Portland, Zinovy and Ada Kane, Rabbi Joshua Katzan, Naomi Kaufman Price, Nina Khatayevich, Oleg Kulkov and Sylvia Zhivotinsky, James Lafky and Madeline Nelson, Lev and Galina Leytes, Ruth Leytes, Daniela Mahoney, Maxwell Martel, Elizabeth and Ruben Menashe, Artemiy Miheyev, Pesya Nusinova, Vilen Oganyan and Lyuba Kazakova, Jeffrey Olenick and Amy Shapiro, Luisa and Boris Polansky, Sidney Resnick, Rosanne Gostovich Royer, Sergey and Eugenia Samarchyants, Anna Schpitalnik, Simcha Simchovitch, Rochelle Simon, Laura Starushok, Eydil Stelmakh, Jerry and Helen Stern, Semen and Galina Taycher, Leslie and Janice Wolf, Martin and Cornelia Wolf, Solomon and Margarita Wolf, Lyubov Wolf, Susanna Kozlovskaya, the Yiddish Culture Club of Los Angeles, and Min Zidell.

Before his death, Dr. Wolf asked that tribute be explicitly paid to those who gave him and his family special help and friendship throughout his years in Portland. Although he has written about many of them in the book, they are named here again in deference to his wishes. First among them are Jerry Stern, the Portland philanthropist, who is much beloved by those who know him and by the many others who have benefited from his generosity, and Charles Schiffman of the Jewish Federation of Greater Portland, who, as Dr. Wolf put it, "gave him back his Jewish soul" by helping to arrange opportunities for him to write, lecture, and take part in religious services. Others who played important roles in Dr. Wolf's years in Portland and whose treasured friendship he wished to have remembered were his aunt and uncle Pesya and Fishel Katzan; his cousins Martin and Cordelia Wolf, Nancy Fruchtengarten, Jeffrey Grayson, Erwin and Maureen Wolf Horenstein, Leslie and Janice Wolf, and Richard and Roberta Cohon; his friends Yasha and Maria Berenshtein and Mihail Elisman; Lilka Maisner and Sidney Resnick, leaders of Yiddish literary clubs in Los Angeles and Hamden, Connecticut; and Paul Haist, editor of the *Jewish Review* newspaper, and the paper's city editor, Deborah Moon. Dr. Wolf also wished to thank Alex Mikhaylov, David Summer, and Warren and Shirel Dean, who were his students and frequent visitors, and Anya Brichak and Zhenya Snegur, who were his caregivers in his final years and who in fact endeared themselves to the entire Wolf family.

Dr. Wolf was a frequent contributor to Yiddish language periodicals, and often spoke at international conferences on Yiddish-related matters. In doing so he acquired other friends and admirers, whom he also wished to acknowledge. They include the editors Moshe Shklar of *Kheshbn* (Los Angeles), Israel Rudnitsky of *Toplpunkt* (Tel Aviv), and Boris Sandler of *Forverts* (New York). The name of Dr. Wolf's favorite poet, the renowned Simcha Simchovitch of Toronto, was also frequently on his lips.

Thanks from the committee on its own behalf are also due to three people who contributed to the earliest stages of the project: Natalia Birger, who produced a rough translation of an excerpt from the manuscript to assist with the fundraising effort; and Alan Kimball of the University of Oregon and Daniel Waugh of the University of Washington, professors of Russian and Central Asian history, who gave encouragement and advice on how to proceed with the project itself. Finally, our gratitude goes to the project's superb fountainhead, Dr. Moisey Wolf himself, who was an inspiration to us all. By the end of his life he was worn down by illness and cumulative hardships. Nevertheless, his mind remained sharp and his will, indomitable. He continued to write and teach and inspire until the end. While his achievements as a psychiatrist, scholar, and spiritual teacher will easily stand on their own merits, his amazing story brings all the parts of his rich life together against the background of major events of the twentieth century. Now that people around the world will be able to read Dr. Wolf's story in Oregon State University Press's publication of Dr. Rosengrant's exquisite translation and edition, we realize that what we sadly thought of as the end was perhaps not really the end at all.

For the Moisey Wolf Life Story Committee
Steve Berliner, Richard Cohon, Mihail Elisman, Jack Falk,
Gloria Feves Hammer, Nancy Fruchtengarten, Paul Haist,
Professors Zinovy and Ada Kane, Priscilla Kostiner, Judith Margles,
Naomi Kaufman Price, Rosanne Gostovich Royer, Sura Rubenstein,
Charles Schiffman, Jerry Stern, Lyubov Wolf, Leslie Wolf, Martin Wolf,
Maureen Wolf Horenstein, and Dr. Solomon Wolf.

"Therefore, Choose Life . . ."

♪♪♪

Author's Preface

𒊹 𒊹 𒊹

Among the philosophical reflections of the *Pirkei Avot* is the observation that there are three times when we are compelled to act against our will: "*Al korchacha ata nolad, al korchacha ata chai, v'al korchacha ata met . . .* " ("Despite yourself you were born, despite yourself you live, and despite yourself you die . . . ").[1] That is true as a general principle, to be sure, but besides those three times, there may be many other occasions when we are forced to act not as we might like but against our will. And not because someone has made us do so but because of the circumstances we face—because a duty requires it, or because our love for another person does.

Thus it has been with this story of my life and my roots. But before I proceed with it, let me consider for a moment two occasions when I acted "despite" myself, the second of them helping to explain how this book came into being.

The first occasion was in 1973, when my then sixteen-year-old son, Solomon—may he be healthy and happy till 120!—was seeing me off on a trip to the Caucasian mountain resort of Kislovodsk. We were standing on the steps of a railroad car and quietly talking. Nervous, I was avidly smoking. Just as the train was about to leave, my son said, "Papa, either you quit smoking right now, or else I'll start right now." Many people had tried to persuade me to quit before. And I myself had been convinced in the almost thirty years I had smoked of the need to put an end to that pernicious habit. But I had never been able to stop for more than a few days. This time, however, I threw away the still lit cigarette, gave the pack to my son, and began . . . to suffer. My struggle with the desire to smoke tormented me for a long time, but the image of my son with a cigarette always kept me from succumbing. Many years have passed since then. In that time I have experienced a great deal, and there have been many bitter situations in which I could easily have returned to that bane, but I never put a cigarette to my lips. Thus, despite myself, I performed something like a little act of valor, not only protecting myself from potential complications but also saving my son from that harmful narcotic. He has never smoked. I thank you for that, beloved man!

The other "despite" took place just a few weeks ago.

For many years my son and my friends had been urging me to write my

3

autobiography, the story of a long life filled with many tragic circumstances and a great deal of varied experience, and to provide an account of my roots, of those ancestors who left a deep imprint on my soul and to whose memory I have returned again and again. I myself regarded and still do regard the enterprise with skepticism. I am well aware that descendants rarely avail themselves of such documents, and for me personally the effort of memory will entail great anguish as I return to the tragic events in my life, for it would be impossible to tell my story without them. When a son of the famous Russian memoirist Sergey Aksakov was asked to write about his father, he warned, "*De mortuis aut vere aut nihil*": "Of the dead, either the truth or nothing."[2] Of my own ancestors I too am obliged to tell the truth.

I was led to pick up my pen by my beloved granddaughter Lyubov Solomonovna, who from the day of her birth (December 25, 1984) to this one has taken unto herself the best qualities of our ancestors. Here is what happened. She had asked me many times to "do my duty" and leave behind my memoirs, but I always found a way to avoid carrying out her request. But this time, just before she was to depart on a tourist trip to Israel, she said in a coaxing voice as we were making our farewells, "Grandpa, promise that you'll sit down today and start writing, and send me what you've written in sections and I'll see if I can translate it into English." I am unable to say what came over me then, but despite myself I blurted out, "I promise." She smiled, kissed me, and said, "I believe you. You have always kept your word."

In view of my advanced age, I am thus obliged to sit down and write while there is still time.

Part One

⸙⸙⸙

1922–1941

Ancestors

♪♪♪

"Ve'eilu toldot b'nei Noach"
"Now these are the generations of the sons of Noah"
Bereishit/Genesis 10:1[1]

From time immemorial, the study of genealogy has played an important role in preserving the identity of the Jewish people and in constructing its history. There are numerous genealogies of Jews in the Bible—in the Torah or Pentateuch, in the Nevi'im or Prophets, and in the Ketuvim or Hagiographa. Reading them, you are constantly amazed by the memory of the people, by the generations that were first passed down orally (for in the beginning there was no writing) and then through transcription of the ancestral names—the children, grandchildren, and great-grandchildren—who lived both before the Captivity (Bereishit or Genesis 5:6-32, 10:1-32, 25:1-18, 36:1-43, 46:8-27) and after the Exodus from Egypt. The second book of the Torah, Sh'mot (literally, Names, but known in the English Bible as Exodus), is so called because the first words of that extraordinarily interesting account of the beginnings of Jewish history read, *"Ve'eilu sh'mot b'nei Israel habaim mitzraima"* ("Now these are the names of the children of Israel, which came into Egypt"). A list then follows, totaling just seventy people. Yet despite the harsh conditions of slavery, those seventy rapidly multiplied. By the end of the four hundred years of the Captivity, they numbered six hundred thousand. And in the various sections (*parashoth*) of the Torah, their genealogies are enumerated again and again, with a final listing of the tribes occurring in the Divrei Ha-Yamim, or 1 Chronicles, Chapters 1-9.

Over the centuries of our doleful modern history, there were in every Jewish community (*kehile*) specially mandated scribes (*ba'alei pinkas*) who kept a genealogical record of every member of the community: date of birth, death, circumcision, *bar mitzvah,* and marriage beneath the *chuppah* or traditional wedding canopy. The information was entered in special books called *pinkassim,* which were preserved in the synagogues with meticulous care, since the entire history of a family could be reconstructed from them.[2]

During the Holocaust, in which six million Jews were murdered and their cultural treasures destroyed, many of those books were lost. Accordingly, one of the first tasks of the new State of Israel was to establish the Yad Vashem Holocaust History Museum and memorial site in Jerusalem, where work continues to this day on restoring the genealogies of all the Jews who perished.[3] As for Jewish genocide in the Soviet "evil empire," the genealogies of its victims have yet to be restored, although there has been talk of a Ukrainian museum for the memory of the victims of Babi Yar in Kiev,[4] where work will presumably begin on restoring the genealogies of the Jews killed after the Nazi invasion, as well of those who were executed or died in the torture chambers of the Gulag.[5] Is the talk accurate? Only time will tell.

I hope that this brief digression on Jewish genealogy will escape the reproach of any who may take an interest in my life, for the story of anyone's life consists not only of his past and his present but also of his future—not only of his ancestors but also of his descendants: his children, grandchildren, and even subsequent generations.

My knowledge of my own ancestors and relatives is incomplete and may, I am afraid, contain many errors, the result of several objective and perhaps even subjective factors. There were many of us children and grandchildren and even great-grandchildren. The time of our childhood and youth was happy and carefree. Our interests and love were confined to our attachments to our parents, grandfathers, grandmother, and, to a certain extent, Great-grandmother Reiza, who passed into the next world at more than a hundred years of age, when I was about five.

My great-great-grandfather Mechl Wolf moved early in the nineteenth century from Warsaw to the prosperous eastern Polish village of Cheremoshno, which at the time had a population of one thousand, including thirty-seven Jewish families.[6] There he acquired a large property. But since Jews were not allowed

to own land in the Russian empire, of which Poland was then a part, Mechl entered into a private agreement with the landowner and, relying on the latter's word, signed not a purchase contract but a lease.[7] As long as Mechl and the landowner were alive their agreement stood, but after their deaths it became the source of protracted litigation and much distress for both Mechl's son Chaim (my great-grandfather) and his grandson Yeruchim (my grandfather). From Grandfather Yeruchim, I learned that Mechl had led a respectable life after his move to Cheremoshno, although

Mechl and Chaya Wolf

he was by nature a merry, life-loving man and very successful at cards. He was married three times. His first two wives having died of different illnesses, he took his third wife, the twenty-nine-year-old orphaned spinster *mume* (Aunt) Chaya, when he was seventy, and lived with her another thirty years, during which time she gave birth to a daughter named Maria. Maria in her turn gave birth to a daughter named Chava, whom it was my good fortune to meet, since she and I attended the same Hebrew gymnasium in Warsaw.

Mechl Wolf's first wife was survived by their daughter, Sarah, and his second, by their two sons, Chaim and Moishe. The line from which I, my daughter, my son, and my son's children descend is, as I have already mentioned, that of Great-great-grandfather Mechl's first son, Chaim. Chaim, as Grandfather Yeruchim told me, was a man of resolute will. All his life he contended in court with the son of the landowner from whom Mechl had acquired their property, since the landowner's son, citing the contract, endeavored to prove that the purchase had indeed been only a lease. Great-grandfather Chaim was married to Great-grandmother Reiza. He lived with her almost fifty years, producing four sons and six daughters. The two middle sons, my great-uncles Sam (Sheiya)

Harry (Osher) Wolf)

and Harry (Osher) Wolf,[8] left Cheremoshno for America in 1903, settling in Portland, Oregon, in 1905, where their grandchildren and great-grandchildren live to this day. The eldest son, my grandfather Yeruchim, and the youngest, my great-uncle Shimon, remained behind with Great-grandmother Reiza the rest of their lives, since she would permit neither to leave: "I won't allow it, and that's final!" Despite their mature ages, they both yielded.

Till the end of her days Great-grandmother Reiza would refer to my grandfather Yeruchim as *der kleyner* or "the little one." If for some reason he was delayed on business, she would gruffly ask my grandmother, "Riva! *Vu iz der kleyner?*" ("Where is the little one?"). I remember her very clearly from the time I was four, or perhaps even younger: a white-haired old woman with exceptionally fair skin and contrasting pink cheeks who would sit next to the tile stove on a chair specially adapted for her use. She sat with her eyes closed and appeared to be asleep and to see and hear nothing. In fact, she

Reiza Wolf

was wide awake. If I or another of her great-grandchildren happened to disturb the way her things were arranged, she would shout in a fierce voice, *"Sheygets! Shoyn zol vern alts in ordnung!"* ("You Gentile rascal! Put everything back where it was this instant!") No one ever thought of disobeying her.

She was especially strict with me. Whenever I did something wrong she would shout, *"Vos vet fun dir oysvaksn?! Nor a ganev!"* ("What will you turn into?! Nothing but a thief!") That terrified me. I would run to my grandfather or mother in tears and ask if that really was to be my fate. Great-grandmother Reiza died in an accident at the end of 1926 or the beginning of 1927. Since at the time there was no electricity in my grandfather's house where she also lived, the rooms were lit with kerosene lamps arranged chandelier-style. On the fateful evening a lamp chimney fell down and broke. Great-grandmother Reiza immediately got up from her chair, found a spare chimney, put a stool on top of the table, climbed up onto a chair and then onto the table and the stool, and attempted to put the new chimney in the lamp. Exactly what happened then is unclear, but it is certain that she lost her balance and fell, striking her head on the floor. She died the next afternoon. She was, it was said, just twenty days short of her 103rd birthday. She was buried in the Jewish cemetery of the nearby town of Melnitsa, where her favorite daughter, *mume* Freyde, lived.[9]

Great-grandmother Reiza was survived not only by her four sons but also by six daughters (my great-aunts): Hannah, Freyde, Beyla, Rivka, Esther, and Liba. Hannah emigrated, also with Great-grandmother Reiza's blessing, settling in Portland, where she lived in the home of her brother Harry before marrying Morris Chusid.[10] I managed to make the acquaintance of the latter's son, Michael. The only things he knew of his own paternal ancestry were that he was named after his great-grandfather and that the latter had a large carbuncle—a benign growth—on the crown of his head. Hannah died at the age of one hundred and is buried in the cemetery of the Shaarie Torah congregation in Portland.

Among the buildings on Grandfather Yeruchim's property was the modest home of his brother, Shimon, and Shimon's wife, Esther. Shimon was different from the other three brothers. He was short, skinny, and half-blind. He had as a child suffered from trachoma, which had completely scarred the cornea of his right eye. As a result he studied little, and poorly when he did. Among the hired workers on my grandfather's property was a glazier, and Great-grandmother Reiza ordered him to teach Shimon his trade. Shimon soon mastered it and took his teacher's place. I can still see him with a broad box on his bent back as he made his way around the streets of Cheremoshno crying, "Glass! Glass! Who has a broken window? Who has a broken window? Glass! Glass!" No more than three or four people a day ever needed his services or responded to his call.

Curious by nature, I often ran to his so-called workshop to watch him work. He did so very deliberately. With a folding ruler he would measure the length and width of the frame into which he was to install the glass. He would intently measure it many times, more even than the proverbial seven, each time stopping to scratch his beard and say, "*O, Gotenyu! Oy vey!*" ("Dear God! Woe is me!") And then after further lengthy consideration, he would lay his ruler on the glass and draw his glasscutter along it, after which came the most interesting part. Placing the pane of glass with the cut line over the edge of his workbench, he would press down, breaking it exactly as required. Then raising his eyes to heaven, he would say with obvious relief, "*Ribono Shel Olom! Got tsu danken!*" ("Master of the universe! Thanks be to God!"). Using brads and a special putty to secure the glass, he would then put the frame in a box for "repaired items." He got a pittance for his labors. So he could feed his family, Grandfather Yeruchim and especially Grandmother Rivka gave him regular help. He also received a fixed sum of dollars twice a year from his brothers in America and from his eldest son (and my father's first cousin), Morris Wolf, who had left for Portland in 1913 at the age of seventeen.[11]

And since I have mentioned Morris, let me say a few words about him before continuing. Refusing the help of his already prosperous uncles Sam and Harry, Morris had shortly after his arrival taken a job in Portland pumping gas by hand at a service station. He worked very long hours and was paid just two dollars a day for that tiring work. His wages were insufficient for renting a room, so he lived and slept in the shack next to the gas pump. He worked at that job for a year and then after his eighteenth birthday joined the army. After serving three years, obtaining his citizenship, and putting aside a decent sum, he received his discharge and returned to Portland. There he bought a gas station in nearby Vancouver, Washington. He worked the station himself, pumping gas and living just as he had before.

Within two years, he bought up all the stations in Vancouver with the money he had saved. He also bought a house, married a beauty named Sophie, and continued to develop his business. He started his own firm, the Wolf Supply Company, a large auto parts and tire store that included an auto repair shop. In 1932 the company was split into Wolf Auto Parts and Wolf Radio and Electric. In 1952 the companies were recombined in a single enormous enterprise known as Wolf Supply Company, with an inventory in the millions of dollars. In time, Morris became so successful that he bought a condominium in Hawaii, a winery, and a hotel, and even founded his own Portland investment bank.

Early on he had begun to send a sum of money twice a year to his parents and the brothers and sisters who had remained behind in Cheremoshno. Just before the beginning of World War II in 1939 he sent his parents and other family members the documents needed for immigration to the United States. Unfortunately, they arrived too late. Cheremoshno had already passed into Soviet hands, making departure impossible, and the family was murdered by the Germans after their invasion of Soviet territory in 1941.[12] In 1965 Morris turned over control of Wolf Supply Company to his younger son (and my first cousin once removed), Leslie. Leslie and his brother, Martin, and their sister, Maureen, are well and living in Carmel, California, and the Portland area.

In 1979 when Morris learned of our existence—that is, of my and my family's—he responded warmly and immediately invited us to join him. To our great regret, he died in 1981 at the age of eighty-four before we were able to leave the Soviet Union. Six years later his wife, Sophie, died too. Both are buried in the cemetery of the Portland Reform synagogue Beth Israel. From the time of my arrival in Portland I have visited the graves of Morris and Sophie three times a year to say Kaddish and the *El malei rachamim* over them.[13] It is a time to pray for their repose and to express my sorrow and remember not only Morris and Sophie but also all my relatives who were killed by the Germans and buried in mass graves in the forest near Melnitsa. I will return to that sorrow in detail later in my story.

To complete the account of the family of my great-uncle Shimon, let me add that, besides Morris, Shimon and Esther had four other sons, Berl, Mechl, Ruvim, and Yankel, and three daughters, Rivka, Chaya, and Basya. Berl was married to Sheindl, who bore him two children, Itsik and Zlata. Berl operated a cattle business and was considered one of the richest Jews in the town of Povursk, ten kilometers from Cheremoshno, and he too helped his mother and father, as needed. In 1942 he was shot in a mass execution of Jews and thrown into a common grave together with my brother, also named Yankel. Berl witnessed Yankel's agony. Berl was himself badly wounded in the hip but pretended to be dead and at night crawled with great effort out of the mass grave. A peasant he knew gave him refuge, but his wife and their two children were killed and buried along with the others. Buried in the same grave were his brother Mechl and Mechl's wife, his brother Ruvim, and his three sisters.

Upon discovering in 1977 that I was alive, Berl sent me a letter from which I learned for the first time the details of the tragic fate of my brother and the rest of my family. I have kept all of Berl's warm letters, so full of bitter memories.

No less tragic was the fate of Shimon and Esther's youngest son, Yankel. Of all of their children, he was the most literate and refined, a handsome, well-built man, friendly and kind and devoted not only to his parents and his brothers and sisters, but also to the rest of his kin, including us. He never married. He perished at the hands of Soviet thugs after the 1939 partition of Poland and the Soviet annexation of eastern Poland and Cheremoshno.

Because the new Soviet authorities forbade correspondence with the residents of foreign countries, thus cutting off Morris's help, Yankel, in order to provide for his mother and father and his siblings, continued to manage a windmill he had previously purchased. He operated it himself without hired labor and performing with his own hands all the hard work involved in adjusting the vanes and millstones, storing the grain, and unloading the flour. For that work he received by agreement with the local farmers a certain portion of the milled flour. Nevertheless, the Soviet authorities considered him a *kulak* who had been exploiting the labor of others.[14] Unlike Grandfather Yeruchim, who had given the local agricultural committee all his files and the keys to his personal and real property, Yankel failed to turn over the windmill in time. One morning he was arrested. In jail (in the version provided by the investigator) he became ill with typhoid and died in custody. His body was never returned to his family and his place of burial is unknown. From grief, his mother, Esther, fell into a deep depression, refusing to eat, and died a month later. Soon afterward Shimon became seriously ill too. His son Mechl and eldest daughter, Rivka, took him to my father's elder sister, Aunt Ronya, in the nearby city of Kovel.[15] The medicines and efforts of the best doctors there failed to save him. Gasping for breath, he died in my arms. He was buried in the Kovel Jewish cemetery in the summer of 1940.

Shimon and Esther's other children, Mechl, Ruvim, and their daughters, were, as I have already mentioned, killed by the Germans and their Ukrainian henchmen, just as were my mother, my brother Yankel, my sister Libche and her husband, my sister Reizele, and Grandmother Rivka and Grandfather Yeruchim—all of them in a mass execution of Jews on September 23, 1942,[16] as confirmed by the 1977 letter from Berl, who after his own miraculous survival and the war lived out the rest of his life in Germany, passing away in 1981 in Frankfurt, where he is buried in the city's Jewish cemetery.

Such are the roots of the Wolf family, some members of which I knew only from accounts about them, while others were people with whom I was directly acquainted and will not forget for the rest of my days.

My Immediate Family

♪♪♪

I thought that writing about those close to me, about those who were there beside me and whom I had known for so many years and who had become part of me and had largely shaped my destiny—I thought that writing about them would be far easier than writing about those who were more distantly related. In fact, it has been far harder. Numerous details are right before my eyes. All of them seem important and it is very difficult to select from among them those that will truly interest any who might one day have the patience to read my story to the end. And so I beg you, dear reader, not to judge me too harshly!

I knew both my grandfathers, Yeruchim Wolf, my father's father, whom I've already had occasion to mention, and Shloyme Raiz, my mother's father, about whom I am now writing for the first time. Grandfather Shloyme was a rabbi (and a Cohen or direct descendent of Moses' brother Aaron, according to tradition). He lived a good distance away in Zwoleń in central Poland and rarely visited us.[1] His first wife died before I was born. She was survived by two daughters, Noemi, my mother, and Hannah, and a son, Yosele. By Jewish law a rabbi may not serve unless he is married. For that reason, Grandfather Shloyme soon remarried. His second wife bore him three daughters, Gittel, Yoheved, and Tsipora. His second wife was very jealous and envious and ruled in her home, oppressing the children of Grandfather Shloyme's first wife. She was opposed to his continued relations with his married daughters and with his son from his first wife. That was another reason why he visited us so rarely.

Grandfather Shloyme looked like a village elder, or like the various depictions of the Russian folk hero Ivan Susanin.[2] His face was hidden by a long white beard and drooping mustache, neither of which he ever trimmed. From his temples hung white sidelocks or *payot*, and from under his equally white eyebrows gazed sad eyes that always seemed preoccupied. The rest of his scalp was shaved and his high forehead was covered with deep horizontal furrows. On the back of his head sat a black velvet yarmulke that he never removed, not even at night when he slept. Before going out, he would put on his *shtrayml*, a traditional black velvet cap trimmed with expensive fur. Wrapped in a long woolen *tallis*, the fringed shawl worn by devout Jews during prayers, its *ateret* or top edged with gold (the mark of a rabbi), he would quietly pray for a very long time. But if he had to pray from a pulpit while performing the role of *chazan* or cantor, he would do so in a loud and resonant baritone. Grandfather Shloyme ate little, and wine touched his lips only when ceremony required it. When there was no one to talk to, he occupied himself with the study of devotional books.

He was emphatically strict with us children, demanding righteous adherence to all the precepts of the Torah. If one of us fell ill, however, he would come and pray silently by the bed of the afflicted until the recovery was complete. Then he would depart in silence. On the other rare occasions when he simply came to visit, he would call me over to him, sit me on his knee, question me to see if I had learned the weekly chapter of the Torah, and then feel the hair on my head to see if it was too long, and curtly ask my father why I was not wearing *payot*. His encouragement was restricted to his putting his hand on my head and saying, first in Yiddish and then in Hebrew, "*Nu, nu, zol zayn in a guter sho. Yivorechecha Hashem v'ychuneka Letorah, Lechuppah ulmaisim toivim*" ("Well, then, good luck. May God preserve you, raise you in the spirit of the Torah, and grant that you survive until your *chuppah* and do good deeds"). I was required to say "*Omeyn*" ("Amen") and kiss his right hand. With that the blessing ended. Then it was the turn of my little sister, Libche. Placing his hands on her head, he would whisper something for a long time and conclude with, "*Got zol zayn mi dir un gey gezunterheyt*" ("God be with you, go in good health"). Last came my little brother, Yankel, whom, like me, he had circumcised himself, and for whom he had especially tender feelings. He would take him on his knees, press him to his breast, and pet him. Then he would put a new *kippah* or yarmulke on his head, the only gift he ever brought.

Not only I but all the other children regarded him with timid respect, although (may he forgive me for saying so) without any particular affection. Only my paternal grandmother Rivka, herself a rabbi's daughter, took any pleasure in him. The two were bound, I think, by an important event that had taken place long before and that colored her regard for him—but more of that below. Before his arrival, she would prepare two rooms for "his holiness": a bedroom and a reception room for his votaries (Hasidim) and for prayer. He did not speak to or take the hand of women to whom he was not related, including Grandmother Rivka, who adored him, but would instead bless them from a distance. "*Yesimeich Elohim k'Sore, Rivka, Rochl, v'Leya. Got zol shtendik zayn mit dir, mit dayne kinder un kinds kinder, Omeyn, veOmeyn*" ("May God make you like our ancient mothers

Sara, Rivka, Rachel, and Leah. May God abide with you always and with your children and your children's children. Amen and Amen"). If any woman came to him to consult about *shailes* (questions of Jewish law) or personal matters, she would have to put her questions in a *kvitl* or note and communicate with him through the *shames* or synagogue beadle or sexton. He would stay no more than a week with us and then, seen off in a procession of all the Jews of Cheremoshno, he would depart for home. Grandfather Yeruchim's attitude toward all that was amiable enough, although a skeptical little smile did always seem to flicker behind his mustache.

Of my mother's other relatives, her half-sister Gittel often used to visit us and became good friends with my father's younger sister, Aunt Pesya,[3] just as did Sheindl and Miriam, the daughters of my mother's sister, Hannah. Sheindl and Miriam's father, Baruch Zuckerman, had died of typhoid when both girls were very young, so they lived mostly with us. They emigrated to Jerusalem in 1937. Homesick, Sheindl came back to visit Mama and us in 1939, but failed to leave in time. The Germans invaded Poland and she perished in a death camp, along with her mother, Grandfather Shloyme, and the rest of their family. In 1977 I found Aunt Hannah's younger daughter, Miriam. She was still in Israel. As she told it, she had worked very hard her first years paving a highway in Haifa. Then

she married a very good man named Zulya. They opened a small auto-repair shop that provided a decent living and allowed them to raise three children. I last saw the family in 1994 when I visited them in Haifa. In 1997 their only son, the well-known Israeli gynecologist Ari Klein, died suddenly of a massive heart attack. A year later Miriam died at the age of eighty-four, and in 2001 her husband Zulya died too. Both their daughters, Aviva, an artist, and Leah, are still alive. Their children (Miriam's nine grandchildren) still live in Israel. Aviva's oldest daughter, Tamara, is married and a teacher. We call each other from time to time.

Noemi and Pesya

My relationship with my grandparents Yeruchim and Rivka Wolf was very close. Their personalities were very different, but they loved each other till very old age and the end of their days. Grandmother Rivka was strict, serious, and demanding, and brooked no opposition. Having grown up in the family of a rabbi, she was, unlike Grandfather Yeruchim, very devout. She insisted that we observe all the Jewish traditions and dreamed that one of her grandsons would eventually follow in her father's footsteps, since he had produced no sons of his own. When we misbehaved, her punishment was to take away our favorite pastimes. Nevertheless, she loved us very much, and no one but she had the right to insult or say bad things about us. She took care of the youngest and would buy us treats and give us presents on holidays.

Grandfather Yeruchim was a man of the mildest temperament and very kind. We never heard a harsh word from him about anyone, and he expected the same from us. He could not bear it when Grandmother Rivka punished us, but he did not dare defend us when she was around. But when she was not, he would try in every possible way to ease the punishment. If one of his grandchildren got sick, he would remain by the bed, the distress apparent in his face. He remembered our foot and head sizes and for holidays bought us shoes and caps that always fit. He was a great organizer of games and loved to joke. His favorite amusement was something called "The beard that never sleeps." He would pretend to be asleep, the end of his beard resting on the edge of the table. We were supposed to grab it, although we never could. At the slightest touch, he would catch our little hands, roar with laughter, and kiss us. He did not care about money or wealth. Grandmother called him a spendthrift, and if it had not been for her, we would

Yerukhim and Rivka Wolf

not have had half of what they earned through their labor. He was a religious skeptic. Although he observed all the traditions and prayed with comical fervor, there was frequently a little smile on his lips expressing resigned doubt about Grandmother's requirements. He loved her very much and always emphasized her wisdom and righteousness to us, and he obeyed her in everything as the "commander" of the household. And she looked after him like a little boy till the end of her days. He was careless about the way he dressed and never went out without allowing her to inspect him first.

Grandmother Rivka liked to tell about how she and Grandfather Yeruchim were married. In those days, marriages were arranged by the parents, who did not ask what their children thought or wanted. Grandmother and Grandfather were married when she was fifteen and he was sixteen. She saw him for the first time just before going under the *chuppah*. She sat covered by her bridal veil and surrounded by her girlfriends, who with the help of a *badchen*, or specially engaged wedding entertainer, were singing laments for the loss of her maidenhood. Although the event took place in the middle of winter, the bridegroom was required to bathe in a ritual pool or *mikveh* before presenting himself to his bride. After bathing, Grandfather, accompanied by the traditional witnesses, went to his bride, lifted her veil, and gazed at her for the first time. Whether because he was nervous or had rushed in the cold after stepping out of the pool, he had not dried himself properly, and at the solemn moment of his first look at his bride, drops of water trickled down his nose. But Grandmother kept her poise, and, using the handkerchief with which she had been drying her tears, she dried the water on his nose, gave him a big smile, and modestly looked down. It was a sign that she was pleased with him. And he, after moving a few steps away, suddenly turned and went back to lift her veil again, gave her a smile just as big, and puckered his lips, thereby kissing her for the first time, albeit from a distance.

They lived well. As the eldest son, Grandfather Yeruchim had inherited from his father part of a Warsaw building and the Cheremoshno property. I was four when I was brought from Warsaw to Grandfather Yeruchim and Grandmother Rivka to recover from a bout of scarlet fever that had been followed almost at once by diphtheria. Here is what I remember from that and other visits.

Grandfather Yeruchim and Grandmother Rivka had two large wooden houses of their own with sheet-metal roofs (a sign of prosperity): one for themselves and the other for guests, that is, for their children and grandchildren who came to visit in the summer. On Grandmother's orders, the second house accordingly belonged to us—to my father, mother, and us children. But when any of the other children and grandchildren visited at the same time, the guests were on Grandmother's orders lodged in both houses. No one felt cramped. Each of us had enough space. My own place was a separate room in the threshing barn, which had been divided into two parts. The right side, dark since it had no windows, was used for storage: hay, wheat, millet, winter fruits, vegetables, Passover dishware, barrels with pickled beets and cucumbers, and jeroboams of homemade raisin wine. The left side, bright with windows looking out onto the garden and a field, was divided into five rooms. I occupied the middle one with Aunt Pesya, whose job was to keep an eye on me, especially at night, when she would give me milk to drink if I woke up, or cover me up again if I kicked the blanket off in my sleep. From then until the end of her days, I subconsciously identified her with my mother, and she treated me like a son. I loved Aunt Pesya very much, and as will be seen, she would long occupy an important place in my life.

In the attic of his own house Grandfather Yeruchim had built a pigeon loft. He was very fond of pigeons. He was convinced that they were the cleanest, noblest creatures, noble because "they have no bile," as he put it, and quickly get used to whoever feeds them and respond to that person with gratitude. They live in pairs and love each other all their lives, never changing partners. As Grandfather often said, "People should follow their example."

He instilled that fondness for pigeons in me too. I developed such an interest in them that I soon put aside all my other childhood and later youthful pastimes. I fed the pigeons three times a day. They had big appetites and ate everything we ate in our home, along with every kind of grain. Whenever I visited Cheremoshno on vacation, the pigeons would sense far away that their benefactor had returned. They would fly to the window in groups and vie with each other to peck at the glass. Spring was their time of romance. It was an amazing spectacle. The male, distinguished from the female by a crest, starts to court her. While she is eating he walks around her cooing and prevents any other suitor from approaching. He often covers her with his wing and they unselfconsciously touch each other's bills. Then they build a remarkably soft nest together in which she lays a pair of eggs every six weeks. The most intimate moment—impregnation—takes place in seclusion, away from human sight. While the female sits on the eggs, the male continually walks around her, truculently cooing. She leaves the nest only for very short periods to eat. During that time he immediately takes her place, remaining on the eggs until she returns. After two and a half weeks, a pair of blind, naked, helpless chicks is hatched to be warmed and fed by their father and mother in turn. Both parents teach the chicks to fly, first in the attic and then beyond after nudging them outside. With that, their parental duties come to an end and a new cycle begins. The next year the chicks repeat all they have been taught by their parents or have been endowed with by nature.

I am unable to pass by another "warm" spot in my memory of my grandparents' home: their immense cellar, which was in essence a kind of refrigerator. Every year toward the end of winter Grandfather and Gricko, *der shabbes goy* (the Gentile who did the work forbidden to Jews on the Sabbath), would fill the cellar with ice brought from the nearby lake. They placed it in layers, covering each layer with sawdust, up to eight layers thick. That method made it possible to maintain near-freezing temperatures in the cellar until the following winter, and thus to store perishable foods all year round, including earthenware jugs of milk and sour cream.

That ice cellar also served as a personal resource for me. Whenever Grandmother forbade me to eat until I had said my prayers, I, following Grandfather's covert gestures, facial expressions, and hints, would go down to the cellar and consume a layer of sour cream. When Grandmother discovered the theft, she would raise a great fuss. She knew perfectly well which "cat" had consumed the sour cream, but, evidently feeling that she too was to blame, she never punished me for it. On the contrary, she would wake me the next morning and, while I was still in bed, give me after a *brocheh* or blessing and some "brown" milk, that is, milk that had simmered all night on her Russian stove and then been mixed with cream and sweetened.

Besides the buildings already mentioned, Grandfather had a large barn with three cows and, unfailingly, a calf. The cows provided our whole family with a year-round supply of fresh milk, sour cream, hand-churned butter, cottage cheese, and, in the summer, even ice cream, which Grandfather would make right before our eyes, to our enormous delight.

In the yard behind the houses there was also a large coop with numerous chickens and ducks and a pair of turkeys, while across the road in front of the house extended an enormous orchard (one kilometer long by seven hundred meters wide) containing a great variety of fruit and nut trees: apples, pears, plums, and even chestnuts. There was also a pond with leeches, crayfish, and frogs, the last of which filled the orchard with a loud orchestra of sound on early summer evenings. In spring, the trees were covered with blossoms, and in summer the nectar of the ripening fruits filled the air with a divine fragrance. The orchard was patrolled by hired watchmen and by Grandfather himself, who often spent the night there. In the middle of the orchard was a large thatched lean-to to shelter the watchmen from the rain. But as I recall, it never rained in Cheremoshno in the summertime. The watchmen would build fires to warm themselves or to boil or roast various kinds of food.

It was not long before Grandfather gave in to my pleas to go with him to spend the night in the orchard. He would lay me down next to himself, hold me to his breast, and in a low voice sing a Yiddish lullaby. I would pretend to be asleep, but as soon as he started to snore, I would quietly creep out of the shelter and go over to the fire. I liked to warm myself by it and gaze at the moon and stars. I was fascinated by the question of how night changes into day, and I promised myself that I would catch the very instant of that magical transformation. But the harder I tried to stay awake, the harder it would be to keep my eyes open, and after a time I would fall asleep by the fire. The watchmen would then put me back beside my grandfather. And when he woke me the next morning, the sun would already be up and brightly shining.[4]

Grandmother Rivka was a very hard worker. She was busy from early morning till late at night with household chores and with us. She bathed and dressed us, changed our clothes when necessary, and taught us common sense, along with elementary morning prayers and basic rules of hygiene. She did all the cooking and baking herself. She would not trust Gentile women to do it—"What if they touch the food with their *treyf* (non-kosher) hands or put something *treyf* in it?"—nor would she allow any of her daughters or my mother to enter the kitchen when they were there for the holidays. "Your time will come soon enough," she would say.

Grandmother Rivka would begin preparations for the Sabbath on Thursday evening. She set the dough to rise in a large wooden tub after lightly kneading it, and then got the various ingredients ready, along with separate dishware and utensils for dairy, meat, and fish. On Friday she rose at dawn to light her Russian stove and make an enormous quantity of onion and poppy-seed griddle cakes, which we would gobble down after dipping them in fresh sour cream. Her face damp with perspiration, she would continue to work all through the morning. Then at noon, flushed and still clad in her sweaty work clothes, she would proceed to the *mikveh* that Grandfather had built in the yard with help from his American brothers, so that his mother Reiza and bride Rivka would not have to go so far for their ritual baths in honor of the Sabbath. After bathing, Grandmother would retire to her room to dress, eventually appearing before us utterly transformed—a majestic queen in a magnificently cut black silk dress trimmed with a snow-white lace collar and cuffs. Protruding from one of the cuffs was the small handkerchief she used to dry her tears during prayers and her ardent conversations with God. Resting on the tip of her nose were her gold-rimmed Sabbath spectacles (so she would be able to keep a sharp eye on us during prayers), while her head was covered by her elegant black Sabbath wig topped with a charming white lace cap. She would then seat herself by the window, open her *siddur* or prayer book, sometimes upside down, since she was barely literate, and start to pray.

Just as she had been taught as a child, she murmured first sentences of the *siddur* from memory in Hebrew. Then in a prayerful tone came her heartfelt conversation with God in Yiddish, "*Got fun Avrohom, Itschok un Yankev bentsh mich mit mayn man, mit mayne kinder un eyneklech lekoved dem shabes koydish*" ("God of Abraham, Isaac, and Jacob, bless me, my husband, my children, and my grandchildren in honor of the Holy Sabbath"), followed by her personal grievances to and reckonings with the Omnipotent and Omnipresent. Grandmother talked to Him in a dolorous sing-song, as if speaking to a close friend or relative. She repeated all the worries and cares she had accumulated over the previous week and asked Him in what way she had sinned before Him, before "God the Just and Forgiving of all sins." She wept, frequently beat her breast with her fist, begged forgiveness, and asked for health for her husband, children, and grandchildren, naming each one. And then her requests would assume the form of pleas: "*Gotenyu! Du muzt undz helfn! Du muzt undz gebn koyech tsu dinen dir, tsu ibertrogn ale undzere tsores; Leyg nit op oyf vayter, shik a refue sheleyme tsu dem krankn un gib chochme tsu mayne einiklech zey zoln geyn in dayne vegn, vi es fodert fun dir dayn dinst Rivka. Omeyn, v'omeyn selo!*" ("Dear God! You must help us! You must give us strength to serve you and endure all our troubles! Don't put off your help till tomorrow. Send a blessing for recovery to so and so, who is sick, and give wisdom to my grandchildren, so they may follow your way, as your servant Rivka begs of you! Amen, Amen!") After that Grandmother would wipe her eyes and kiss the *siddur*, bringing her conversation to a close. And then with a nod and a beckoning gesture, she would call each of us over to her (each with bated breath), kiss each of us on the forehead, and give each of us her blessing, barely moving her lips. Then she would let the other grandchildren go but, since I was the oldest, she would keep me behind for an important errand.

"Now," she would say in a quiet voice, "let us go and perform our *mitsve* (good deed). You'll collect and distribute *lechem laaniim* (bread for the poor)." She would then give me a large basket with three loaves of challah and a list of five well-off Jews, from each of whom I was to obtain another loaf. "Then," she would continue, "you'll distribute the loaves to the poor using the other list," adding by way of instruction, "Wrap each loaf in clean paper and leave it on the porch or beside the door so that no one will see who brought it."

I had long been tormented by three questions about that procedure, and one day I could no longer restrain myself and I timidly asked, "Grandmother, why am I the only one who has to carry out this *mitsve* every Friday?"

"Because you're the oldest and God Himself has chosen you. It isn't proper among Jews to ask, 'Why me and not another?' A Jew must ask, 'If not me, then who?'" And—imagine!—I understood and never again questioned that it was my duty.

"But Grandmother, why do I need to get challah from the other Jews? After all, we always have more after the Sabbath than I get from them! Why can't you just give me whatever is needed?"

"Because," Grandmother answered, "every Jew has to perform this *mitsve*. And if any should forget, then you'll remind them."

"But Grandmother, why do I need to place the challah by the doors of the poor so no one will see who brought it?"

"So that you won't shame or offend the one to whom it has been given. Let him think that God Himself has sent challah for the Sabbath."

There are some lovely lines in the "Princess Sabbath" by the nineteenth-century German-Jewish poet Heinrich Heine: "The tranquil princess, pearl and flower of all beauty, fair as the queen of Sheba, Solomon's bosom friend."[5] Our grandmother was that Princess Sabbath incarnate. Not only did she do everything she could to provide the Sabbath table with all the heart could desire, but she was in her transformed aspect and in her demeanor and gestures a radiant princess.

She was the first to light the Sabbath candles. She would put her arms around them three times and then, covering her eyes with her palms, recite the prayer. And when she uncovered her eyes again, it would seem that a surge of light had filled the entire room. Whenever they were present at the table, her daughters

Ronya and Pesya and my mama would follow Grandmother's example and repeat her gesture, although for some reason their prayers never seemed to produce quite the same luminous effect.

All that was not enough for Grandmother, however. In addition to Sabbath light, she required Sabbath music. After blessing the candles, she would add, "*A gut shabes*" ("A good Sabbath"), and then turning to Grandfather, she would say, "*Nu*, Yeruchim, *vos hosty zich fartracht? Di kinder zenen doch hungerik!*" ("Well, Yeruchim, what are you daydreaming about? The children are hungry!")

And Grandfather would commence the prayer of supplication addressed to the angels who, according to legend, accompany every Jew from the synagogue on Friday evening: "*Sholom aleychem, malachey Hashores, malachey elyon, mimelech Mal'chey Hamlochim Hakodesh Boruch hu.*" ("Peace be with you, ministering angels, messengers of the Most High, the Supreme King of kings, the Holy One, blessed is He.") It was a prayer of hospitality consisting of four stanzas and ending with a farewell wishing the angels peace as they departed the house on their long journey home. Grandfather sang it with a particular rapture, swaying from side to side and making us sing along with him while he conducted with his hands, so that the prayer was turned into a kind of divine oratorio. And Grandmother, beaming with happiness, paid close attention to see which of us sang the most expressively. At the end, she would intone the angels' farewell reply: "*Halevay in kumendikn shabes zol zain nisht erger vi haynt*" ("God grant that the next Sabbath shall be no worse than this one"). And then, lifting her eyes to heaven, she would say, "*Omeyn, Gotenyu*" ("Amen, Dear God").

Only then would Grandfather, dressed in his long silk Sabbath frock coat with snow-white cuffs showing from under its sleeves, get up from his place, stand erect, raise a silver goblet, and, with his eyes closed just like Grandmother, intone, "*Borey pri Hagofen*" ([Bless you, God], "who created the fruit of the vine")—the prayer blessing the wine. Then with special feeling and an ardor not usually found in him on ordinary days, he would sing the *kiddush* (the consecration of the Sabbath). And then, after sipping the wine, he would pass the goblet around clockwise to everyone at the table.

After that he would go around to all the children, place his hands on their heads, and recite a prayer: for the boys, "*Yesimech Elohim k'Efraim u'Menashe*" ("May God bless you, as he blessed Ephraim and Menashe"); and for the girls, "*Yesimach Elohim k'Sara, Rivka, Rachel v'Leya*" ("May God bless you, as he blessed Sara, Rivka, Rachel, and Leah"). As soon as Grandfather had concluded his blessing, we would run off in a noisy *gevald* or tumult to see who would be first to wash up. Grandfather would intone the *brocheh* or blessing: *"Hamotsi lechem min haorets"* ("Blessed art Thou, our God, who brings forth bread from the earth"). Each of us was required to repeat the prayer in a low voice after Grandfather, but say *"Omeyn"* in a loud one, and then tear off pieces of challah and pass them around to everyone at the table.

Thus did the Sabbath meal begin. I have never in my life eaten anything more delicious than the dishes Grandmother prepared. Nor can I recall anything more joyous than that Sabbath meal. How painful now to think that it has all gone, and gone, it may be, forever. How much I want my only son and his children to preserve that holy tradition!

Though barely literate, Grandmother was very wise and fair. She tolerated our mischief and very rarely resorted to corporal punishment. She loved me very much and often said that she was spoiling me. In fact, she required more of me than of her other grandsons. And she gave me a good spanking twice.

The first time was after I had taken ten *groschen* and gone over to the neighbor's yard and bought a sunflower from him. Returning home, I started to tease the other children with it, holding it out to them and then jerking it away when they tried to grab it. They began to yell, howl, and cry. Grandmother immediately came outside, and after determining what had been going on, she ordered me in a severe voice to come over to her. I refused. She came toward me and I backed away, eventually reaching the ladder to the barn roof. Thinking that she would not come after me, I quickly started to climb, but she came right up behind me, catching me just as I was about to reach the top. Seizing my leg in a fury, she started to pull me down. When we were back on the ground, she led me over to the porch, stood me between her legs, and began to interrogate me.

"Where did you get the sunflower?"

"I bought it!"

"Bought it? From whom? With what money? Where did you get the money?"

"From the neighbor. For ten *groschen*. I found it."

"Where did you find it?!"

"In the dining room under the table," I mumbled.

"In the dining room under the table?!" Grandmother said indignantly. "You don't find money under tables. That money belongs to all of us, and children have no right to take it without permission, let alone spend it as they like. After all, the same sunflowers grow in our own garden. And why didn't you share it with the others instead of teasing them?!"

Silence.

"Have you nothing to say?! Pull down your pants at once!" And without waiting for me to do so, she placed me on her knees and started to spank me. It didn't hurt, but it was very humiliating. All the children who were standing around us began to laugh and yell, "Give it to him, give it to him! The little thief! The little thief! He found it! He spent it! Let him know! Let him know!" From the humiliation of it I ran to Grandfather, who comforted me a long time but in the end said, "You should listen to your grandmother. You mustn't insult her."

The second episode was even more disgraceful. It was summer. We—some boys from the neighboring yard and I—decided to go for a swim. Without saying a word to our families, we set off for a deep pit that had been dug for a *mikveh*. It had proved impossible in the end to obtain running water for it, but the excavators hadn't closed in the pit, which the rain had filled to the brim with muddy water containing every sort of noxious creature. It was there that we decided to swim. One of the boys pushed me into the water without waiting for me to get undressed. I struggled and then suddenly turned over on my back and started to sink. The other boys began to scream and yell. A worker who happened to be nearby pulled me out and took me back to Grandmother. Upon seeing me in such a sorry state she first removed my wet clothes, wiped off all the mud, washed me, and put dry clothes back on me. And then an interrogation began about why I had gone off without first asking permission. After giving me a spanking, she said sternly, "You're still little and shouldn't go swimming anywhere unless there's a grown-up with you, and all the more in a filthy pit. And remember this! Only swim where the water is clear. Never go in where you can't see the bottom."

I have had many occasions to recall that phrase. After I became an adult, a husband, and a father, I made numerous mistakes from taking part in dubious affairs without heeding the consequences—without considering whether or not I could see the bottom.

Grandmother did not, as a rule, mean to single out any of us grandsons. She tried to be strict and kind with each of us in equal measure. But all the same everyone noticed her special treatment of me. It came, I think, from the fact that, being quite vain, I tried to please her, especially in observing all the Jewish traditions and learning by heart all the prayers and the weekly chapters of the Torah. I was very fond of her praise and presents. And she took great pride in telling everybody what a "gifted" grandson she had.

There was a Jewish blacksmith in Cheremoshno named Reb Chaim. He was short and stout and very strong. He could straighten horseshoes with his bare hands. His wife had died and he had no children. He refused to marry again, since "you couldn't find another like her in the whole world." No one looked after him. He cooked for himself and washed his black clothing, which remained just as black. His face too was always black from the coal dust embedded in his skin. Only the whites of his big, always smiling eyes remained clear and shone with a kind of inner goodness. Besides that, he was, of all the Jews who lived in Cheremoshno, the most knowledgeable in matters of religion, the Talmud, and Holy Scripture. On the Sabbath he read the weekly chapter of the Torah, precisely observing the tropes—the musical notations for each word—and never erring. The Jews of Cheremoshno respected him for that, but because of his permanently filthy state, they avoided him. Our grandmother, however, felt sorry for him and held him in high regard. She always invited him for the Sabbath evening meal and fed him on other days, as well. It was he whom she chose to be my vacation teacher. I myself doubted that I could learn anything from such a grimy old man. But he came to instruct me every day, and what a wonder it turned out to be! And then once during *minhah* or afternoon prayers at the synagogue, he called me up to the Torah and announced that the first part of the chapter for the next Sabbath would be read by "*Sloymes zynele Moyshele*" ("Shloyme's young son, Moishe"). He then put his dingy *tallis* on me and, in a voice that permitted no objection, commanded, "Read!"

Anxiously, since it was the first time in my life, I chanted the first part of that week's chapter of the Torah, following the ancient Hebrew tropes just as Reb Chaim had taught me. Grandmother, standing in the doorway of the women's section, beamed with delight.

Later that summer as Grandmother and I were saying goodbye before my return to my parents in Warsaw for the start of the school year on September 1, she put a little purse of money in my pocket and said, "Now don't spend this. It's for a return ticket. Anything could happen along the way, and if it does, then buy another ticket and come straight back." To that admonition she added, "Don't forget to pray and continue studying the weekly chapter of the Torah, as Reb Chaim has taught you. Remember that you're protected by *der Ruach hakoydesh* (Holy Soul) of Rabbi Dovid, my father, and by the good name—may he live to be 120!—of your grandfather Rabbi Shloyme. You have no right to shame them and must follow in their footsteps."

It was clear from that touching farewell that Grandmother had already decided that I would be a rabbi. And I might have been, had not my worldly father already enrolled me in the Warsaw Tarbut Hebrew gymnasium, of which he was a founder and trustee.[6] All the same, Grandmother held tightly to her cherished dream. At great expense to herself, she engaged for me in Warsaw a well-known, kind-hearted rabbi named Eleazar Maisel, who came to our house every day after I got home from the gymnasium and instructed me in the *Yahadut* (the body of Jewish religious lore), the *Halacha* (the rabbinic law pertaining to the performance of the rites), and so on—all the knowledge required to receive the *smichut lerabanut* (recommendation by the Chief Rabbinate for the office of rabbi). After assuring himself that the additional studies would not interfere with my excelling at the gymnasium, Papa consented to them, and my rabbi instructed me for nine years—until the beginning of World War II in 1939. Rabbi Maisel perished in the Holocaust in the Warsaw Ghetto. It is to him and the wise counsel of my grandmother that I owe whatever knowledge I gained in my youth. May their memory be blessed by my children and grandchildren.

It was because of Grandmother Rivka too that my father married my mother. But to tell the story of that event, which after all made the subsequent history of our family possible, I will need to return to Warsaw and the situation in Poland in 1918-21.

As is well known, those years gave rise to a new epoch in the life of Russia and the states within its domain. After the 1917 revolution and the collapse of the Russian empire, a multilateral civil war began, with much Polish and Ukrainian territory passing back and forth between the Reds and the anti-Communist Whites, and between the Reds and the various national factions fighting for Ukrainian and Polish independence. As the different sides advanced and retreated, many blamed the Jews for their failures, and a number of vicious pogroms were carried out in western Ukraine near Cheremoshno by the anti-Soviet forces of Petliura and Makhno and by the pro-Soviet Cossacks of Budyonny's First Cavalry Army.[7] At Grandmother's urging and taking advantage of the fact that an apartment belonging to a relative was available on Krakowskie Przedmieście Avenue in Warsaw, Grandfather, Grandmother, and my father's sisters, Pesya and Ronya, hurriedly moved to the capital.

There was, however, another reason for Grandmother's decision to go. She was, as Aunt Ronya later explained to me, worried about her youngest son (and my future father), Shloyme. Her first son, Leyzer, had at an early age been captivated by revolutionary ideas and gone underground, where he had disappeared without a trace, most likely having been killed. Her second son, Dovid, had one winter fallen into a snow-covered well in the orchard and frozen. He was dead when they found him. Broken-hearted by the loss of her first two sons, Grandmother was constantly depressed and anxious about her surviving one and kept him close by for a long time. He was, according to Aunt Ronya, a very handsome and well-bred young man, to whom everything came easily. He was self-taught and very well read, thanks to the substantial library left by his brother Leyzer. In addition to Yiddish, he knew Polish, Russian, German, and Hebrew, and was very drawn to Zionist ideas and burned with a desire to emigrate to *Eretz Yisrael*—the land of Israel, or Palestine. But he pitied Grandmother's suffering and yielded to her demands, even though he was not religious. A main concern of Grandmother's during World War I, when Poland was still part of the Russian empire, was that he would be drafted into the Tsarist army and either killed or lost to her forever. In January 1915, therefore, Great-Grandfather Chaim wrote to a relative in Warsaw (I do not know his name) and told him about the tragedies that had befallen his son Yeruchim and daughter-in-law Rivka, and about their fears for their youngest son. The relative replied at once and even came to Cheremoshno, where he persuaded Grandmother to let him take her son back to Warsaw. He promised to treat him like a member of his family and support him, to let him use the apartment on Krakowskie Przedmieście, and, most importantly, to help him pass the entrance examination for the law school at the University of Warsaw, where the relative's cousin was the dean. As a student, young Shloyme would be exempt from military service. The relative was prepared to take the rest of the family too, but Grandmother declined that offer. The relative kept every one of his promises. In 1920, two years after the birth of the *Rzeczpospolita Polska* or Polish Republic, my father completed his studies and obtained his degree. Using his connections, the relative found him a place in the firm of a prominent attorney, where after a nine-month apprenticeship he earned the right to open his own law office.

Arriving in Warsaw herself in early 1919 and finding her remaining son healthy, Grandmother grew less anxious and even started to languish from having so little to do. But then an urgent new worry emerged; her son was twenty-five and still unmarried. In those days, that made him an old bachelor. Grandmother decided to find a solution.

Judging from the partial accounts of Aunt Ronya, Grandfather, and Grandmother herself, the events unfolded this way. Grandmother got in touch with various male and female matchmakers, who offered candidates to her and my papa, praising their merits and distinguished parentage and producing photographs of them. But my papa, who was opposed in principle to such sight-unseen acquaintanceship, in the end refused every matchmaking overture. So Grandmother set off to different synagogues, looking in the women's sections for beautiful maidens, engaging their mothers in conversations dear to her heart, and learning indirectly whether the daughters might be ready to marry a very good, very talented young man who was sure to become a successful lawyer. For a long time those inquiries failed to produce the desired result. Then Grandmother learned that a Zwoleń rabbi, Shloyme Raiz, had recently moved to Warsaw as a temporary replacement for a colleague who had emigrated to Palestine, and that he had a daughter who might be just what she was looking for.

The next day Grandmother dictated a *kvitl* or note in which she laid out certain questions about the *kashres* or dietary laws with respect to dishes and utensils: for example, what if meat spoons fall into a dairy saucepan? Since Rabbi Shloyme Raiz did not speak to women, Grandmother went to his kitchen in search of "someone" who might give her *kvitl* to the rabbi. And in that she was very fortunate. She was met by a "remarkably beautiful and friendly young woman with an angelic smile." The young woman exchanged greetings with Grandmother and asked what had brought her to their home. Grandmother told her and gave her the *kvitl*. The young woman said that *der shames* or beadle was with her father and a Jew who needed advice on a very important matter. When the *shames* came out, Grandmother could pass her *kvitl* and the rest of her questions to the rabbi through him. Grandmother required no more. She continued to talk to the nice, modestly dressed young woman. The latter was very well disposed to Grandmother too. She revealed that her name was Noemi, that she was twenty-four, that her mother had passed away, that her life was not much fun, and that she was still unmarried. When Grandmother asked in astonishment why, Noemi turned away and began to dry her eyes. Grandmother said to her, "*Veyn nisht mayn kind. Got vet dir tsushikn dayn bashertn un mit groys mazl vestu bakumen dayn por. Magst fregn bay dayn heylikn tatn un er vet dir dos eygene zogn. Got is mezaveg zivugim.*" ("Don't cry, my child. God will send you your destined one. Ask your saintly father and he will confirm it. Matches are made in heaven by God.") Grandmother kissed her, and the young woman left the room. Not waiting for the *shames*, Grandmother quietly opened the door and departed too.

Schloyme Wolf

She came home very excited. She was sure that Rabbi Shloyme's daughter had been chosen by God himself for her only surviving son. But how to proceed so that God's plan would be fulfilled, she was less sure. The first task was to persuade the future bridegroom to make the young woman's acquaintance. Would he like her? That she would like him Grandmother had no doubt, but would her father, the rabbi? And would the latter give his consent? These questions tormented her so much that she was unable to sleep. Grandfather immediately recognized that something was wrong. Unable to withstand his persistent questioning, she told him whom she had met and the circumstances, along with the

thoughts that were churning within her: "Yeruchim, *zog vos tit men? Vos tit men?*" ("Yeruchim, tell me, what is to be done? What is to be done?") As a matter of firm policy, Grandfather never risked taking any decision upon himself, and he was even less inclined to do so this time. Usually in difficult times he would comfort her and say that God would help her, and that the morning is always wiser than the night: "*Men darf nisht zorgn, Got vet rign in der morgn*" ("Don't fret about it, God will tell us in the morning"). But this time he said nothing and grew thoughtful too.

Finally Grandmother called in her only son. She said that she had a secret to share with him, but that he must first promise to grant one request. He promised. Grandmother then asked him to repeat her visit to the rabbi and raise with him the same questions of ritual that two days before she had failed to ask because of certain circumstances. And at the same time, let her son "take a look" at the one who had captured her heart. "*Ich shver zich bay Got, az du vest gornisht farlirn un efsher epes gefinen*" ("I swear by God that you will not lose anything but may perhaps gain something"). This time my father did as Grandmother asked without resisting. The time needed for him to carry out the errand and return home seemed like an eternity to her. Suppressing her anxiety, she first waited by the front door and then tried to occupy herself with work, but everything kept falling out of her hands. When the door opened at last and she saw the beaming face of her son, Grandmother knew that God had answered her prayers. Over dinner my father said that on the Sabbath he would henceforth go only to the synagogue where Rabbi Shloyme and, he added significantly, his daughters worshipped. It was there at the synagogue that my mother's and father's first wordless encounters took place. He secretly passed her his first love letter, to which he received a modest but encouraging reply the following Sabbath. They met in secret after that. And then my papa proposed and my mama anxiously accepted. The next question was who would tell her father and how it would be done.

The son raised that worrisome question first with his mama. After lifting her eyes to the ceiling and intoning a heartfelt "Thank the Lord," she replied, "*Zorg nisht zynenyu! Mir veln epes tsutrachtn.*" ("Don't worry, my son! We'll think of something.") The next morning after breakfast she announced to Grandfather in her typically peremptory way, "*Her mich oys mayn liber man! Morgn baym davnen, zolstu opgebn sholem dem rov un farbayt im bentshn undzer hoyz—mir zenen doch noch fremde—deser tsu der erev-shabesdiker vetshere. Gey nit op fun im azoy lang biz eer vet nit tsuzogn, az er vet kumen.*" ("Listen to me, my beloved husband. Tomorrow you'll go to the rabbi at the synagogue, greet him in peace, and invite him to come to bless our home—since we too are strangers in the city—and best of all to come for a Sabbath supper. Don't leave until he promises to do so.")

Grandfather did as Grandmother instructed, but the rabbi said that he never went out on the Sabbath. If his blessing was required, however, he could certainly come on Monday or Thursday, the days when the Torah was read at the synagogue.

Grandmother was very pleased and diligently made preparations to entertain the rabbi "properly," at the same time coaching Grandfather on how to approach the main question: the betrothal of the rabbi's unmarried daughter, Noemi, to their son.

And Grandfather too carried out Grandmother's instructions to the letter. After the *birkat hamazon* or after-meal blessing, Grandfather initiated a "family conversation": how did the rabbi like his new place, did he need anything, and how were his children doing? And then, as if in passing, he slapped himself on the forehead and exclaimed, "I almost forgot, you have a beauty of a daughter to marry off! And we have a son . . . I think you know him. He comes to worship at your synagogue every Sabbath. You called him up for the reading of the Torah several times and for the *Maftir* (additional reading from the Nevi'im or Prophets), and even honored him with praise. How would you look upon, um, um, a marriage between our two children?"

Grandmother had been standing in the doorway the whole time intently listening to the most important part of the conversation, in case Grandfather encountered any obstacles or needed any help.

There was a long silence. Then the rabbi raised his eyes and the index finger of his right hand to the ceiling and said, "Your crystal chandeliers, silver candlesticks, and fine china make me doubt that I would have the wherewithal to provide my daughter with a suitable *nadn* (dowry). As *mechutanim* (in-laws), you would be above my means."

At which point Grandmother, who was still standing in the doorway of the next room, cried in a loud voice, "Yeruchim, *shoyn bald kum tsu mir!*" ("Yeruchim, come here to me!") My grandfather was so startled by the interruption that he went over to her at once. Grandmother removed a string of pearls from her neck and said, "*Gib dos iber dem rov—a matone far zayn tochter Noymi un zog im, az kayn nadn darfn mir nit un ale chasene—hetsoyes nemen mir oyf zich!*" ("Give the rabbi these pearls as a gift for his daughter Noemi, and tell him that we don't need a dowry and that we'll take all the wedding expenses upon ourselves.")[8]

Grandmother said it all so loudly that there was no need for Grandfather to repeat her words. He went over to the rabbi, gave him the pearls, and asked, "*Ir hot gehert?*" ("Did you hear?"). The rabbi nodded, put the pearls in his pocket, offered Grandfather his hand, and said, "*Zol zayn in a mazldiker sho*" ("May the lucky hour come to pass").

Although her life had been full of worry and distress, our heroic grandmother had in this matter triumphed completely. Aunt Ronya told me, and my mother confirmed it with gratitude, that Grandmother had bought shoes for the bride and gold rings for both the groom and the bride and had hired a seamstress, who spent a month making not just a wedding gown and other dresses for Mama but also a wedding veil and even a velvet cover for her *chuppah*. Grandfather assumed all the expenses of the ceremony (the *badchen* or entertainer and the musicians) and paid for the wedding supper too. Thus began a new link in the Wolf clan: Papa, Mama, and all of us.

Like everything else in their lives, my parents' love for each other was reserved and unassuming. Yet all our relatives held them up as an example for their own adult children.

Moreover, Grandmother Rivka treated Mama differently from everyone else and always spoke of her with respect, praising her quiet nature, her goodness, her lack of pretension, and above all her wide reading and learning—her general and her Jewish literacy. Mama always went to synagogue with her and rendered her every honor, showing deep respect and sincere love. She helped Grandmother to prepare the festive table, and immediately after her, and just like her, she prayed over the candles for the health of Papa and later on the rest of us. And Grandmother took obvious pleasure in all that.

Aunt Ronya and Aunt Pesya often asked Grandmother why she spoiled her daughter-in-law so much and never said a harsh word to her. "She's no angel!" they would point out. To which Grandmother would invariably reply, "You don't understand anything. You're my children. If I should offend you or say something unkind to you, you'll forgive me—you're my daughters. But she isn't my own, and she suffered a long time from her stepmother. If I offend her, she'll always remember and may never forgive me. And that will affect the life of your brother and his family." *"Fregt nisht keyn narishe kashes! Zol aych Got lib hobn, vi ich un der tate hobn aych lib."* ("Don't ask foolish questions! May God love you as your father and I love you.") With that the conversation usually ended. Ronya and especially Pesya became very good friends with Mama. When Mama got pregnant with me after Grandmother and Grandfather had returned to Cheremoshno thanks to the improved political situation under the new Polish government of Marshal Piłsudski, a protector of the Jews, Pesya stayed behind with her in Warsaw and for two years helped first with the housework and then with me.[9]

I was born on the twelfth day of the Hebrew month of Nisan in the year 5,682, or April 10, 1922. My *brit milah* or circumcision was performed, as I have said, by Mama's father, Grandfather Reb Shloyme. In keeping with Jewish custom, I was named after ancestors—Grandfather Shloyme's father, Avrom, and, to respect her feelings, Grandmother's father, Reb Moishe—and entered in the birth register as Avrom-Moishe. That cumbersome dual name followed me for many years and would produce not a little awkwardness.[10]

My earliest memory is fragmentary and comes from when I was about three. I am in Papa's arms and wrapped in Grandmother's woolen shawl, through a small slit of which I am looking out at the world beyond. It is an early spring morning. The sun is not yet up, although the edge of the sky near the horizon has begun to turn pink. Papa is carrying me somewhere. He walks with long strides and is in a hurry. From time to time in answer to my questions about where we are going, he tenderly tries to explain something, but I am unable to understand.

Other hurrying men start to catch up with us, many of them carrying their own children wrapped the same way I am. They join Papa and speak about something I cannot understand. Then they all stop by the door of the synagogue and silently wait for something, their eyes turned toward the luminous edge of the sky, which grows pinker and pinker. Out of the synagogue comes my grandfather, Reb Shloyme, wearing his large *tallis* and carrying a Torah scroll. After him shuffles the old *shames* with a tray on which lies a large *shofar* or ritual ram's horn. And suddenly, with the first beams of the emerging red sun, the Jews joyfully begin to pray. The *shames* presents the *shofar* on the tray to one of the Jews, who blows on it with all his might, his face turning red. Frighteningly loud voices then cry out—the loud praying of the Jews. Many rise three times on the tips of their toes with their arms stretched toward the sun and chant something in words that I am unable to make out. They joyfully offer each other their hands, and some embrace and even kiss. Papa takes me over to Grandfather, who puts his hands on my little head and prays with animation. Then we slowly return home.

I continued to wonder about that mysterious dawn gathering by the synagogue. It was only a year or two later that my father explained that it had been a *Kiddush* or *Birkat Hachama*, or Blessing of the Sun, which Orthodox Jews observe every twenty-eight years.[11] Unfortunately, the next two times it occurred, in 1953 and 1981, neither I nor my son nor any of the millions of other Jews in the godless Soviet empire could celebrate it.

After that event there is a gap in my memory of a year or so before another event occurs that is also linked to my dear papa. I am in a hospital. I am lying on a cot in a ward. And Papa is lying next to me on a mattress on the floor. Why he could not bring a second cot to the ward, I am unable to explain to this day. Several times in the night he gets up to give me medicine or something to drink or to adjust the covers. And then one beautiful morning he dresses me and takes me home in a *britzka*.[12] Mama greets me with a baby in her arms. She puts the baby in a baby carriage and rushes to Papa, kisses me with tears in her eyes, and tries to set me on my feet, but I am unable to keep my balance and fall down and start to cry.

That second event also needs an explanation.

Mama and Papa were unstinting about increasing their family. I'm not sure they observed all the other commandments, but the first, "be fruitful and multiply," they held sacred. Every year and a half to two years a new family member appeared in our home. In December 1923 my sister Libche was born,

Noemi with Moisey, Libche, Yankel, and Reizele

and a year and a half later came another sister, the only blonde in our family, Leah, who died of a terrible infection at a very early age. I barely remember her, and what I do recall is vague. Then in September 1926 my brother, Yankel, was born, followed a few years later by my sister, Reizele. Soon after Yankel's birth and circumcision, I fell ill with scarlet fever complicated by diphtheria, as I have already mentioned, with a large abcess in my throat. The illness was grave, according to family stories. There was no alternative but to put me in a hospital and stand watch over me twenty-four hours a day. Papa came at night. Only his heroic efforts and those of the doctors prevented my death, which after Leah's would have been a terrible blow to my parents.

After I was released from the hospital, Mama and Papa sent me in the company of Aunt Pesya to Grandmother and Grandfather in Cheremoshno to regain my strength, as I have also mentioned. Soon after I had recovered, Papa came to visit me almost every month in summer and winter, bringing me various toys and taking me around to all his aunts (my grandfather's sisters) to show them what a "fine job" I had done in Grandmother Rivka's care. I returned to Warsaw a year later.

I remember Papa clearly only from when I was six or seven. He was tall with broad shoulders, and had long wavy hair combed straight back, which emphasized his high, wide forehead and large, rather mournful eyes with precisely curved eyebrows and long, dark lashes. He had a sharp, slightly elongated nose, and his symmetrical face was edged with a carefully trimmed black beard with light-brown flecks. He took meticulous care of the beard to preserve the shape he had given it.

Papa spent the better part of his day in court on behalf of his clients. Coming home at night, he embraced and kissed Mama (and naturally Grandmother, if she was there) and us children. At dinner, Mama sat next to him on his right, while the rest of us sat on his left. He often held Yankel, the youngest at the time, on his lap, awkwardly feeding him some favorite dish with a spoon. After dinner, he would ask Mama in a quiet voice about her health and ours and the events of the day. He compensated for the lengthy speeches he had to give in court with taciturnity at home. He rarely rested, however. After examining the day's mail, he would read two newspapers, *Przegląd Polski* (*Polish Review*) in Polish, and *Der Moment* (*The Moment*) in Yiddish. In the 1930s, his last decade, he also read another Yiddish paper, *Yedie Achrun* (*Latest News*), if I am not mistaken. After that he would open his large briefcase containing the documents to be discussed the next day in court or at other proceedings. He never shared their contents with us and did not like us to ask about them. He was very scrupulous with his clients and always frank about the likelihood or unlikelihood of a positive outcome. People therefore trusted Papa and had confidence in him. He always charged poorer clients less than his standard fee.

After I turned seven in 1929, Papa enrolled me in the only Hebrew-language gymnasium in Warsaw, an institution of which he was a founder and trustee, as I have said. Admission was not easy, and the cost of instruction was quite high, from fifteen to thirty-five *złotys* a month or more, depending on the family's means.[13] Beside the high cost, there was another commitment: the parents and other members of the student's family had to speak Hebrew with him at home. When anxious parents with no knowledge of the language asked, "How shall we speak it if we don't know how?" the answer was, "Your student will teach you."

Tarbut students were required to wear summer and winter uniforms with billed caps. During summer vacation we were taken to a camp in the nearby countryside, where we were taught the history of the struggle of European Jewish youth for the liberation of *Eretz Yisrael*—the history of the *Hashomer Hatzair* (Young Guard), the *Hehalutz* (Pioneer), and Betar movement.[14] We were given paramilitary training—*al hamishmeret* (standing guard), archery, and blowing reveille with a *shofar*, along with formation, mess, and taps "for rest and sleep." We were also taught the Jewish national anthem and other Hebrew songs, many of which I remember to this day and have passed on to my son. Those activities all cost money, and even though the Jewish community subsidized them, they were still beyond the means of poorer Jewish families.

In addition to a variety of general education subjects in Modern Hebrew, we studied Jewish religion, Hebrew literature, the history of the Jewish people, and the geography of the land of Israel, as well as Latin and either German or French. Only the Polish language, Polish literature, Polish history, and Polish geography were taught in Polish. Discipline was strict. After a recess, everyone had to be seated three minutes before the beginning of the lesson. When the teacher appeared in the doorway we had to stand up and wait for his permission to sit down. Marks for homework, answers on the blackboard, and behavior were recorded in daily reports that parents had to sign after reviewing them. Even so, there were occasional lapses: making fun of defenseless teachers or the collective cutting of classes (especially on April 1).

It is with a feeling of enormous gratitude that I recall the remarkable gymnasium teachers Israel Schwarz (Hebrew), Shaya Laier (Latin), and Nochum Guberman (mathematics), the last of whom devoted his days off to walks in the woods with us and to remarkably interesting impromptu lectures on the history of the Jews in Poland and in Warsaw in particular. And the Erlichs, husband and wife, who taught Polish language and literature and German language and literature, respectively. And, finally, the one-armed, invariably enthusiastic Baruch Roiter, the Tanach or Bible teacher, whose inspired lectures and readings from the prophets began the moment he entered the doorway. He never called us to the blackboard. He would go over to a student and quietly ask him something, and it would be clear to him from the answer how well the student had prepared the lesson. His marks were always fair and never provoked any objection or complaint. In 1947, my former classmates the Barzilai brothers, who had by a miracle survived the Holocaust, visited me in Moscow and told me that during the mass execution of Jews in Warsaw, after all those who had been able to had gone into hiding, Baruch climbed to the roof of a building and with a megaphone began to recite the prayers *"Eli, Eli lama azavtani?"* ("My God, my God, why hast thou forsaken me?"),[15] *"Lama yomru hagoyim ayey eloheyhem?"* ("Why ask the gentiles, where is their god?"), and *"Nekoim nikmas dam avodecho Hashofuch!"* ("Revenge the spilt blood of your servants!"). Seeing him, a German thug shot him, and Baruch fell dead from the roof.

Besides the regular gymnasium curriculum there were various clubs or societies. I took part in the choral, dramatic, and debating societies. Mock trials were often organized in the last one, and I played the role of an attorney. At home, Papa would help me to shape my arguments for the defense. In the third year, students were encouraged to join one of the Zionist organizations. My own preference was the *Hashomer Hatzair*, and until my last year I took an active part in all its programs.

I was lucky enough to be in court for one of my father's speeches for the defense. It was my last year at the gymnasium, when students usually decided with their parents what they wished to do and to which university or institute they would apply. I do not know if Papa wanted me to take up his profession, but once he asked me, "Would you like to go with me to court and listen to a case, to the prosecutor's presentation and my rebuttal?" I jumped for joy, since I had long dreamed of such a thing. Papa sat me down in the courtroom and then disappeared into another room, on the door of which was a sign that read, *Lokal adwokacki* (Counsels' Chamber), and below it, *Wstęp Wzbroniony* (No Admittance). After a few minutes, a man came out whom I did not recognize at first. It was Papa, but transformed. He was wearing a long black robe with a large lilac bow at the neck. Visible in one its wide cuffs was the edge of a white handkerchief. Pinned where the breast pocket would have been was a silver name plate of the sort given to all law-school graduates on graduation night. Inscribed on it were the words, *Jurysta Pan Sz. Wolf* (Mr. Sh. Wolf, Jurist). It seemed to me that even Papa's hair looked different. When the presiding magistrates entered the courtroom, everyone stood up, but Papa held his head in a particularly proud way. During his examination of the accused and the witnesses, his rebuttal of the prosecutor, and his replies to the magistrates, his voice, usually soft, was loud and confident. I was especially enthralled by his summation for the defense. Much of its substance—a deft compilation of paragraphs from the *Zarząd królestwa polskiego* (Adminstration of the Polish Realm)—was beyond my grasp, but how he said it, his facial expressions and his gestures, and the way he addressed the *wiele szanowany Pan Sędzia* (greatly esteemed Mr. Magistrate) simply amazed me. It seemed like a dream. Only when the other people in the room responded with loud applause, which was discouraged in court, did I come to. Papa was blushing. He wiped large beads of sweat from his face and brow with his handkerchief and then slowly resumed his seat. He covered his eyes for a few moments, and when he uncovered them, I saw their usual slightly mournful expression again—he was my everyday papa. The judge then ruled to postpone the case for a month, and I no longer remember what its outcome was.

We walked home in silence. Papa was evidently still in the courtroom in his mind, and while I squeezed his hand with barely concealed delight, I was also afraid to disrupt his train of thought. It was only when we were sitting at the table at home that he turned to me and asked in Hebrew, "*Nu, ma tomar li yakiri?*" ("Well, what do you think, dear one?"). I mumbled something in half sentences and then repeated them, since I was unable to make an intelligible reply. Papa put his arm around me, drew me closer, and seeing the tears in my eyes, said, "*Ma kara, chadal!*" ("What's the matter with you—enough of that!") adding the famous phrase of Theodor Herzl, the founder of the Zionist movement, "*Im tirtzu ein zo agada*" ("If you will it, it is no dream"), meaning, in this case, "If you truly wish it, then you can be a lawyer too."[16]

I really did very much want to follow in my father's footsteps, but unfortunately things do not always turn out the way we want them to. There are also circumstances, sometimes harsh ones, that are beyond our control.

In 1935 Marshal Piłsudski, the first prime minister of Poland, died. His death was a particular loss for Jews. The anti-Semitism that he had managed to hold in check flared up again with even greater virulence, thanks to the support of the gang of Nazi thugs who in the meantime had come to power in Germany under the mad Hitler (may his name be cursed for all eternity!). As a result, there were anti-Jewish pogroms in many Polish cities. The newly elected members of the *Sejm* (the lower house of the Polish parliament) enacted a menacing anti-Jewish law reducing the quota for kosher meat, which severely affected the daily lives of the overwhelming majority of the Jewish population. Enacted too were new restrictions on the admission of Jewish children to state gymnasiums and universities, and a so-called *numerus nullus* rule that banned Jews completely from certain academic departments, including the law schools. In the departments to

Moisey and Noemi Wolf, 1936

which Jews were still permitted to enter, special rows of seats, painted yellow, were set apart where "students of the Jewish faith" were required to sit during lectures. As a result of these measures, many Jewish students left Poland for foreign universities. Others entered the Jewish (Yiddish) Pedagogical Seminary in Wilno (now Vilnius) in Lithuania, which at the time was part of the Polish Republic. Others chose to leave for British Mandate Palestine, which, according to the Balfour Declaration of 1917, was to become "a national home for the Jewish people."[17] Young men and women making that last choice had to be at least eighteen and willing to submit to a year of *hachshara* (preparatory training) in a *kibbutz*, where they would also learn a manual skill. Sheindl and Miriam, the daughters of Mama's sister, Hannah, had emigrated to *Eretz Yisrael* in that way.

I too dreamed of *Laalot Artza* (returning to the land of the ancestors). All the more since my cousins were already established there, as was one of Grandfather's nephews, Shloyme-Mordche Tenenboim. The latter had lived in Jerusalem for many years, where he was a professor at the university. But I was only sixteen and too young for *hachshara,* and Grandmother, Mama, and even my Zionist papa were categorically opposed to that impulse anyway. After extensive discussions within our family and the circle of Papa's closest friends, it was decided that the best option for me under the circumstances would be to enter medical school, which was still open to Jews.

I graduated from the Warsaw Tarbut Hebrew Gymnasium in June 1938. Since I had passed the *matura* (the state examinations given after graduation from secondary school) with distinction, I had the right to enter the university with no examination other than an essay on Polish literature. I wrote in the allotted four hours an essay on the great nineteenth-century poet Adam Mickiewicz and his *Oda do młodości* (Ode to Youth).[18] The examining professor, named Rudolf Marczinski, hesitated for a long time over what mark to give me, calling me back for a second oral examination, unlike the other students. The topic of that second session was Mickiewicz's brilliant epic *Pan Tadeusz* and the character Jankiel Korczmar and his zither playing.[19] In the end, the professor gave me a five, the highest mark, and that September I began my first year of medical school at the University of Warsaw.[20]

The year proved to be a difficult one. The political situation in the country was growing tenser with each passing day. Anti-Semitic articles had begun to appear in the newspapers with ever greater frequency, as had belligerent calls from anti-Semitic organizations. A wave of pogroms against Jews rolled

Noemi and Libche, 1930s

through the country, and skirmishes between Jewish and Polish students were becoming increasingly common. As a gesture of protest, the Jewish students refused to sit on the yellow "ghetto" benches assigned to them; during the lectures we remained standing, which angered the Polish students and professors. Many wealthy Jews, overcoming various obstacles, managed to emigrate. Grandmother and Grandfather's youngest daughter, my favorite Aunt Pesya, had already left for Portugal in 1937 with the rest of her family. Papa, held back by Grandmother's unwillingness to give her permission ("Where will you go?"), could not bring himself to follow Pesya's example. The academic year thus passed without any particular joy, and even though war did not seem imminent, the majority of Jews felt dread in their hearts. They were most afraid of new pogroms and of a repetition in Poland of the *Kristallnacht* of the German Nazis.[21]

It was therefore with great relief that my mother, my brother, my sisters, and I (Papa was to join us a little later) left Warsaw at the end of June 1939 for our Edenic haven—for Cheremoshno and Grandmother and Grandfather. Visiting them at the same time were Aunt Ronya and her three children: Chaya, born in 1924; Polina, born in 1926; and Dodik (Dovid), born in 1929. Ronya's husband, Avrom-Osher Zeltzer, had, like Papa in Warsaw, been detained in Kovel, where he and Ronya made their home.

Ronya and Avrom-Osher Zeltzer

Libche with Polina and Chaya

That summer in Cheremoshno I experienced an entirely new feeling: first love. Its object was Aunt Ronya's elder daughter, the vivacious, mirthful, witty, imaginative, passionate Chaya. That romance deserves its own story; here I will say only that it was a revelation, a new creation of the world that completely changed me, depriving me of sleep, thrusting into the background all my other enthusiasms and attachments, and turning me into a dreamer and versifier, a user of words that I had never used before and that seemed to come out of nowhere. And it seemed to me too that Chaya was changing before my eyes and shared my feelings. Grandmother noticed our relationship and disapproved of it: "It's too early. Your time will come soon enough! And you shouldn't anyway, since she's your cousin. Nothing good will come of such games." Aunt Ronya pretended not to notice anything out of the ordinary: "They're just bored." But when her husband, Avrom-Osher, arrived, he took Chaya and then me to task, rebuking and trying to shame us. In the end he said, "I forbid it! I'll send for your papa today and tell him everything. Because of you," he continued, "we'll be forced to leave tomorrow." But kind Grandfather Yeruchim hugged his favorite granddaughter, smiled behind his mustache, and whispered in her ear, *"Shrek zich nisht mayn kind. Er bet aych gornisht tun, un zol aych voyl bakumen."* ("Don't be afraid, my child. He isn't going to do anything, so you do whatever you like.") And he winked at me the way he did when Grandmother would punish me for not saying my prayers. Chaya and I eventually learned to be more circumspect about the expression of our platonic attachment and to go off by ourselves whenever the grownups were busy with their own things or away.

There was a second obstacle, however: Chaya's sister, Polina. She was only a year and three or so months younger than Chaya and very attached to her. Whenever we attempted to slip away, she would make a fuss, cry, and threaten to tell Grandmother. Her parents spoiled her terribly and had instilled in her

Moisey and Chaya

the belief that she was more beautiful and intelligent than Chaya. In fact, the opposite was true. She was a poor student, spoke with a lisp, and was in short a tedious little creature. I was supposed to bring about an improvement in her bad marks over the summer, and that in some measure saved us, though it was necessary to indulge her and each time to think up new ways to placate her and send her off somewhere. Their brother, Dodik, on the other hand, was a remarkable boy. He had spent more time with our family than with his own and was very attached to our little sister, Reizele. He played various games with her and looked after her. My sister Libche didn't bother us either, since she had her own fish to fry. One of her teachers had begun to court her very early and she married him at the age of seventeen. And my little brother, Yankel, a shy, kind, obliging, and, unlike me, always obedient boy, spent every day helping Grandfather in the garden and the orchard. Mama, my mama who understood everything and was aware of my early sexual maturation, took quiet joy in the relationship. As I learned afterward, she wrote of my "gallantry" in a letter to Papa. He responded by not responding at all.

My youthful romance with Chaya lasted two years, until my hasty escape to Russia after Nazi Germany invaded the Soviet Union on June 22, 1941. But we'll return to that tragic event soon enough.

We were expecting Papa's arrival, but he kept putting it off. And then on August 16 Mama received a telegram from him, quickly followed by a letter with instructions to send me back to Warsaw by September 1 to resume my university medical studies, but for her and the rest of the children to remain in Cheremoshno, since the start of the non-university school year would be delayed for a month. Although they were alarmed by that news, Mama, Grandmother, and my Chaya (or Halka, as I called her after the opera of the Polish composer Stanisław Moniuszko[22]) put me on the morning train to Warsaw on August 25. Papa met me at the station with a grim smile quite unlike his usual one. When we got home he informed me that the political situation in the country was unstable, that Polish army reservists had been called up, that there had been a meeting of the German foreign minister with his Soviet counterpart, and that an agreement, the Molotov-Ribbentrop Pact, as it came to be known, had been signed defining the conditions of mutual non-aggression in the event of war, among various other undisclosed points, as would quickly become clear. That war would soon break out was thus not out of the question. Nevertheless, Papa tried to be calm about it, assuring me that there was really nothing to fear, since the Polish army was very strong, and the other countries of Europe, and America too, would help, so that Poland would certainly prevail and keep the enemy out of Warsaw.

Alas, less than a week later the world was given convincing proof that the claims for the Polish army's invincibility had been empty propaganda. On September 1, 1939, Hitler's forces began their invasion of Poland. The terrible repeated bombardment of Warsaw and many other cities in the country produced widespread panic, along with arson, looting, and the murder of Jews. The German hordes seized the Baltic port of Gdansk (Danzig) on the second day of fighting and then crushed the Polish advance guard in Sopot to take control of the port of Gdynia too. The surviving Polish remnant retreated east toward the Soviet Union. On September 27, ten days after Soviet troops had, in keeping with the secret terms of the Molotov-Ribbentrop Pact, occupied Polish Ukraine as far west as the Bug River, German motorcyclists entered Warsaw and, with the help of Polish fascist traitors, took control of all the state institutions and marked the most properous Jewish shops and large buildings with swastikas.

A few days later, German *Quartiermeister* or quartermasters appeared in our building too. Shouting *"Verfluchtene Jude"* ("Damned Jews") in a rage, they ordered Papa to vacate the building in two days and to present himself to the newly organized *Judenrat* or Jewish Council. Black with grief, Papa replied that he would obey the order. But two hours later they came back and started to smash the dishes and throw precious clothing, furniture, and whatever else came to hand out the window. Papa embraced me, his hands shaking in fear, and kept saying in Hebrew, *"Lo livkot, lo litsok. Rak lishtok, sheket vesheket!"* ("Don't cry, don't yell! Just be still!") At one point during the looting, two hulking thugs went over to Papa's library and started to tear apart the books on the shelves. Papa couldn't bear it anymore. He went over to the case, leaned back against it with his arms spread wide in defense of the remaining books, and said in German, *"Aber was für ein Schuld tragen die Bücher?"* ("But how are the books to blame?").

One of the Germans, staring wide-eyed at him and turning as red as a lobster, shouted, "*Raus, du verfluchte Schwein!*" ("Out of here, you damned swine!"). Papa froze, his legs as if paralyzed. The German took his pistol out of its holster and shot him in the chest. Papa fell down, bleeding heavily, and then stopped moving. Overcome with terror, I ran outside and started to scream. Without stopping, those passing nearby on the sidewalk muttered between their teeth, "Shut up, Jew boy, or they'll do the same to you!"

They had murdered my papa and gravely injured me and all the others. And soon, along with six million other Jews, they would murder the rest of my family too.

New Ordeals and a Refuge

$$\int\int\int$$

That night a few of Papa's closest friends and a relative, one of the dwindling clan of Wolfs still in Warsaw (the old had died, and many others had either left in time or for large sums had bought birth certificates and identity documents and changed their names, residences, and ethnicity), helped me to bury him in the main Jewish cemetery on Gęsia Street (now Mordechaj Anielewicz). We put a marker on the grave and quietly dispersed. Taking me aside, the relative gave me one hundred *złotys* and advised me to leave the city at once with a group of other Jews who would be guided by a trusted Polish friend of his. He would tell the friend about me and my connection to him. I ran home, got an extra set of underwear and some food, put on my student overcoat, and ran to the address of my relative's friend. A group of Jewish men had already gathered there with their wives and children. I entered a room in which four or five men were sitting around a map and intently discussing something. The oldest shot a glance in my direction. I realized that he was the one to whom I should introduce myself. He silently nodded, thereby indicating his consent, and asked me to wait outside. He said he would come out in a few minutes and give us the instructions we needed before we set off on our journey. As soon become clear, it was to be a long and dangerous one, for the Germans had occupied the western and central parts of Poland, including the cities and towns we would have to pass through to reach the Bug River to the east and Soviet territory. We would therefore move only at night and mainly through the forest. The route had been worked out down to the smallest detail. The group would be led by *Pan* Marczinek, whose only distinguishing feature was a scar on his right cheek. We would have to obey him and not argue along the way or lag behind but try to help each other as best we could. He would have a first-aid kit with him, if needed. If everything went as planned, the trip would take ten to twelve days. At a certain place on the west bank of the Bug a boat would be waiting to take us to the other side. After that, everything would depend on the Soviet border guards and whatever we might be able to say on our own behalf.

Everything turned out more or less as anticipated. The journey was arduous. It was very hard to cover fifteen kilometers through the forest every night, and on the last nights, twenty kilometers. It was especially hard on those with small children. Everyone was obliged to take a turn carrying the infants. With great effort, the more intrepid among us obtained bread and drinking water for the others along the way. It was no easy thing to see to personal needs or to find a safe place to sleep during the day. But those hardships were far less painful than the terrible memories each of us carried inside. I cannot say how it was for the others, but the anxious thought never for a moment left me of how I would tell Mama, Grandfather, Grandmother, and the others how Papa had been killed, or how I would look them in the eye as I explained how I had run from the building, leaving my murdered father lying on the floor, or how we had buried him. Even now after the nearly sixty-five years that separate me from those events, a sharp pain stabs my heart as I recall them, and it is hard to breathe and I am forced to stop writing.

Oh, God! Why did I ever yield to my granddaughter, Lyuba? May she never know such sorrow. Why did I ever agree to return to those tragic days? For she, and any others who may read my story, will share my pain and suffering too!

After the ordeal of that nearly two-week journey and an eight-hour interrogation at the Soviet border post, I arrived in Cheremoshno around three in the afternoon, filthy, much thinner, with sagging cheeks and torn and filthy clothing, and without any warning, since the Polish telegraph service had stopped working and its Soviet counterpart was not yet in operation. Grandmother and Mama were the first to see me. I did not have to say anything; it was obvious from looking at me. They started to scream and tear their hair and clothing. "Oy! Oy! Oy! Why am I alive! Why am I alive!" Grandmother cried over and over again. "Where is

Shimon and Esther Wolf

he?! Where is he?!" The two unhappy women grabbed and shook me and then collapsed in a swoon. Everyone—Grandfather, Aunt Ronya, Avrom-Osher, and all the children— came running. They put something between Grandmother's and Mama's teeth to keep them from choking and splashed cold water in their faces. The shock affected everyone. Then they all gathered round me, hugged me, wept, and said something, though I do not remember what. I later awoke in bed in clean underwear. The only ones who had kept their heads despite the lacerating emotion were

Grandfather and Ronya. Silently, bent with grief, they cared for Grandmother and Mama, cooked the meals, covered the mirrors and chandeliers with black material of some kind, and fed the youngest. The next morning we all took our shoes off and got down on the floor to sit *shiv'ah*. By Jewish law, after the death of one of the seven first-degree relatives—father, mother, son, daughter, brother, sister, or spouse—the survivors sit on the floor without shoes and eat only small amounts in a partial fast. As a rule, neighbors help during that time. No fewer than ten Jews pray for the repose of the deceased, while children who have reached the age of twelve (Libche and me in this case) say Kaddish three times a day. The sons and daughters of Grandfather's brother Shimon were a great help in that time of terrible grief.

Meanwhile, the new Soviet authorities had begun to show what they were capable of, and Grandfather had been prudent in his dealings with them. He had taken the chairman of the newly established village council all his keys and deeds, along with an affidavit stating that he was voluntarily surrendering to the council everything under his control. In return, the council assigned plots from the property to Grandfather and our family and allowed us to keep two cows and enough grain, flour, fruits, and vegetables to last until the next harvest.

Grandfather had managed to address another important matter, as well. Availing himself of the fact that the chairman of the village council was a friend of ours, he had obtained from him a new birth certificate stating that I had been born in now Soviet Cheremoshno and not in Warsaw, thereby ensuring automatic Soviet citizenship for me and preventing my being returned to Poland.[1] Grandfather's friend, in a complicated and dangerous time, also submitted a petition on behalf of the village council requesting that I, as the "son of a Cheremoshno villager," be admitted to the recently reopened medical school of the University of Lvov, an action that made it possible for me to continue my studies.

But as the Russian proverb says, when calamity comes, open the doors wide. Letters stopped arriving from Pesya in Portugal. The link with Grandfather's brothers and Shimon's son in America was also severed. And then Yankel, the only remaining provider in Shimon's family, was arrested and killed. Shimon's wife died of grief, and Shimon too died soon afterward, as I have recounted earlier. Grandmother and Grandfather helped them as much as they could, as did Grandfather's sister Freyde in Melnitsa. Ronya went back to Kovel with her family, taking my Chaya with her. I missed her very much and dream of her even now. In those times of grief, she turned serious. She stopped laughing, making witty jokes, and playing amusing tricks. She began to help Grandmother and especially to comfort me. We talked for hours about how things would be for us in the future, and she swore that she would never leave me. When she finished her last year at the gymnasium, now turned into a Ukrainian ten-year school by the Soviet authorities, everything would be decided. She had already told her parents, who rebuked her and said, "First finish school—if you're allowed back—and then we'll see." Grandfather helped with that too. He obtained appropriate birth certificates for all three of them—Chaya, Polina, and Dodik—along with petitions from the village council. Because of the September invasions, the start of the school year had been postponed two months, while classes at the University of Lvov had been delayed until January 1.

When Chaya, Polina, and Dodik finally did start school, it became clear at once that their ignorance of Ukrainian would make it very difficult for them. Aunt Ronya asked Mama to send me to them: "He isn't doing anything and we need him." I went, although as it would later turn out, it was not merely to help the children with their schoolwork. Ronya and Avrom-Osher had promised to help Mama financially, and they did so with generous hands, taking upon themselves the expenses of Libche's early marriage.

In those first months, many Jews fled from German-occupied Poland to what had become northwestern Soviet Ukraine. One day, one of them, Mechl Goldschmidt, Libche's former teacher, called the village council, which had the only phone in Cheremoshno, and asked them to tell our family that he would call again the next day at the same time. And he indicated that his pupil, Libche Wolf, should answer the phone. The news was met by us with joy. When Mechl learned of the terrible grief suffered by our family, he hurried to us the next day to take an energetic part in the solution of various complex family problems. One evening he asked Libche to go for a walk with him and proposed to her. She came back radiant with happiness. Together they went first to Grandmother and Grandfather and then to Mama to ask their permission. While giving it in principle, all three asked them to delay the wedding until after the period of mourning for my father had ended. The delay, however, proved impossible for reasons beyond anyone's control, for a new disaster would soon be visited on Cheremoshno.

By order of the supreme administrative body of the Soviet Union, the Council of People's Commissars, the village was declared a firing range, and all its residents were given a month to relocate to Bessarabia, where homes and plots of land had been reserved for them.[2] Those not wishing to go to Bessarabia would receive monetary compensation for their homes and plots but would within the same period have to move with their families to other places of their choice.

Our family was thus suddenly faced with the question of where to go. Ronya was prepared to take in Grandmother and Grandfather in Kovel. There was a similar response from Grandfather's sister Freyde in Melnitsa, with whom Grandmother was on very close terms. Grandmother liked the idea of moving to Melnitsa better, since a synagogue and *mikveh* were very close to Freyde's home. She also did not want to depend on her son-in-law, Avrom-Osher, who was half-Gentile and not very particular about the kosher way of life and the observance of Jewish customs, nor requiring them of his children either. "Better for them to visit me than for me to be a millstone around his neck," she said, summarizing her decision.

As for my mother and my brother and sisters and me, the decision was considerably more complicated. Mama refused to move to Kovel, since Ronya's house was too small for all of us. "It's enough," she said, "that Moishe's there. He'll probably marry Chaya." Libche's fiancé, Mechl, offered a solution. "What's the problem?" he asked. "Everyone can come to me in Manevichi.³ My parents and I have a spacious apartment. If you don't like it, my sister and her husband will give you and Yankel and little Reizele half of their newly built house, and Libche and I will move in with my parents instead. You needn't worry about that. They will love her and she will be a blessing to them in their old age," he concluded.

All that would have been fine, had not a legal obstacle immediately presented itself. In order to move to either residence in Manevichi, we would under Soviet law have to prove that we were related to Mechl. The only solution was to register his and Libche's marriage, and that was done at once. Of course, since the period of mourning had not ended, there was no wedding, nor was there a *chuppah* or even a traditional celebratory supper, although Mechl promised that they would make up for that when the period of mourning was over. At the end of March 1940, the dispersal, or rather breakup, of our large, close-knit family took place. Grandfather and Mama, after receiving meager compensation for our dwellings and property, departed for different, if nearby places. At the time, no one thought that we would be separated for long. The breakup, however, proved to be the beginning of the end.

But for the time being, at least, we seemed to be better off than many other people we knew. Mechl, as he had promised, provided everyone with decent living arrangements. During *Shavuot*, or Celebration of the Weeks, in the spring of 1940, a very modest wedding took place, shrouded in unspoken mourning with only the closest relatives there, yet without Grandmother and Grandfather, who would never recover from the loss of their son.[4]

Mechl was appointed head of the methodology section of the Manevichi high school, and Libche suddenly revealed business abilities. The Manevichi Municipal Trade Directorate (*Gortorg*) put her in charge of a small dry-goods shop. She managed her responsibilities very well and was able to hire Mama as the shop cashier. Grandmother and Grandfather led a quiet life in Melnitsa. Grandmother ate little, frequently fasting, and lost weight. She went to the synagogue three times a week until the Soviet authorities closed it, and silently prayed and wept. The last months she would visit a *moshav zekeinim* or home for the aged, taking challah and other baked goods left over from the Sabbath. Ronya and Mama often visited her and Grandfather. He had changed drastically, becoming worn and withdrawn, replying to questions only in brief monosyllables, refusing to go out, and rarely visiting the synagogue. As I realize now, he had from the time of my father's death fallen into a deep depression. Occasionally, he would make a sudden visit to Kovel, but most of the time he just sat in a soft chair at home, dozing or silently swaying from side to side with his eyes closed.

My own circumstances had become a good deal more complicated too. As I noted, I had at Aunt Ronya's request and with Mama's approval gone to Kovel to help my cousins adapt to their new Soviet school, where the subjects were taught in Ukrainian instead of Polish. I really did help them, especially Chaya, who, although restless, was the most capable of the three. Uncle Avrom-Osher started to treat me better and gradually acquainted me with his commercial ventures. To keep the Soviet authorities from harassing him, Grandfather had earlier secured a document stating that Avrom-Osher had, before the 1939 partition, worked for a scrap-collection cooperative. On the basis of the document (and a sustantial bribe), the new Soviet trade authority assigned him the same kind of work. He did not do it himself, however; rather, he hired someone else to obtain the required quantity of rags (two metric tons per month), paying triple, in that way fulfilling the socialist work plan and earning official recognition for himself as a "production expert" (*otlichnik proizvodstva*).

Meanwhile, Avrom-Osher continued to conduct the real business that had occupied him under Polish rule. I am unsure what to call it. Perhaps the best name would be "foreign currency trading." He had before the 1939 partition many clients in Kovel to whom he sold various kinds of currency (dollars, tsarist gold rubles, pounds, Reichsmarks, Serbian dinars, etc.) at a profit after obtaining it at a discount. The business had become illegal under Soviet rule, however, and he was afraid to engage in it close to home, since everyone was watched and none of the new buyers could be trusted; there were too many informers and secret agents among them. But even in the most intractable of circumstances, Jews have always found a way. About two hundred kilometers southeast of Kovel in the city of Rovno lived a distant relative of Avrom-Osher's who worked in a bank and who was thus much less vulnerable to exposure, since foreign currency transactions were his and his boss's official duty. And that was were I came in. Twice a month Uncle Avrom-Osher would put on my feet special double-soled hiking boots and hand me a copy of *The History of the Communist Party of the Ukraine* and a train ticket to Rovno. There I would be met by one of the relative's two sons, who would greet me warmly and escort me to their home. The next day I would return to Kovel wearing the same boots. It is not hard to guess what was hidden in the soles that followed the boots to Rovno and back. But I never asked how much there was or what it might be worth. Judging by my uncle's happy demeanor, by the increasing cordiality of his treatment of me, and by the fact that he stopped chiding his elder daughter about her attitude toward me—judging by those signs, it might be concluded that whatever the sum was, he was quite pleased with it.

All the same, that life was starting to grate on me. The situation was aggravated by the fact that the opening of the University of Lvov medical school had been postponed again and again, and for two very simple reasons. The Soviet authorities had been unable to provide the university in time with professors and instructors who knew both Ukrainian and Polish. Nor were they able to supply the necessary textbooks; the University of Kiev had allocated a certain number but only for the first-year course. Finally, at the end of August 1940, all the prospective medical students were summoned to Lvov. The dean of the medical school gathered us together and announced that since strictly medical subjects were not taught in the second year (I had already completed my first year in Warsaw, as mentioned earlier), the first semester would be extramural, and then, after examinations, those who scored the highest would be assigned dormitory space and allowed to continue full-time study as medical students. At the beginning of February 1941 I passed the examinations in biochemistry, physiology, "historical materialism," and Latin with the highest marks, and was enrolled full-time and assigned dormitory space.

Was I happy with that development? Yes and no. Yes, because I was tired of the idle life of a tutor in my aunt's home. Polina was a bit slow. It was necessary to explain the same things over and over. She would answer every critical comment with a howl and complain to her parents that it was my fault because I had explained poorly. The spoiled favorite of his parents, Dodik was a lazybones too and not shy at all about not wanting to do any homework. The departure for Lvov released me from those burdens.

At the same time, the change in my established routine was less than smooth. First, Lvov was two hundred kilometers from Manevichi, and the possibility of frequent visits to Mama, my sisters, and my brother was thus curtailed. When I was in Kovel, a week had not passed without my seeing at least one of them, and every two or three weeks I would visit them all in Manevichi. I missed Grandmother and Grandfather very much and, it goes without saying, Chaya. Being ill-adapted to life on my own, it was not even clear to me how I would feed myself. The food in the student cafeteria was neither tasty nor filling. Moreover, the study conditions were very poor. In the room I was assigned there were also three Ukrainain students, who despite the strict prohibition against anti-Semitism (at least in the pre-war years) let me know who I was whenever they could, albeit in veiled form. There was no shower. To wash you had to go to the municipal bath, something I was completely unprepared to do. The only good thing was the lack of strict discipline and attendance taking. That allowed me, in addition to holidays and other days off, to make occasional overnight trips to Kovel, returning the next morning. Uncle Avrom-Osher helped with that by paying for the train tickets and covering my pocket expenses.

I just barely made it through to the end of the semester, which ended on May 31, a month earlier than usual because of a newly instituted program requiring that one month of the summer vacation be devoted to work at one of the region's newly organized collective farms.[5] In return for a "contribution" to the dean, however, I had managed as "the eldest son of a seriously ill mother" to forgo the joy of working on a collective farm and was thus able to arrive in Manevichi on June 1 with excellent marks in my course record book. While in Manevichi, I went to see Grandmother and Grandfather in Melnitsa and then returned to Kovel for the rest of the summer. Aunt Ronya and Uncle Avrom-Osher and the three children were glad to see me. A few days after I got back, Grandfather came too for an extended visit to see Ronya and us children.

Chaya and I intensified our preparations for her final examinations and the ensuing party. The latter took place the evening of June 21. Chayechka was in great form. She made me dance the whole time and proudly introduced me to all her friends. The party ended around one. We returned home holding hands and then strolled for half an hour along a nearby boulevard. The night was clear and warm. The moon seemed to be shining with a special brightness and smiling just for us. Everywhere around it was peaceful and quiet. Nothing foretold disaster. After kissing to our hearts' content, we turned in.

Less than two hours later that calm was shattered. Loud explosions and a terrible rumbling brought us all outside. Everyone understood. War! It had begun with the German invasion of Poland less than two years before, and now it had come to Soviet Ukraine. In half an hour the voice of the subsequently famous radio announcer Yury Levitan informed the world of the sudden, perfidious attack of Nazi Germany on the Soviet Union.

A few hours after the attack began, all railroad, telephone, and telegraph links with Manevichi and Mama and the children and Mechl and Libche were severed. Every two or three hours alarming communiques were broadcast that "despite the valiant resistance of the Red Army," which "has inflicted mortal blows" on the enemy, "German forces have occupied . . ." It became ever more obvious that the enemy was advancing at a rapid pace. A disgraceful evacuation from Kovel of the families of the valiant Soviet commanders and their subordinates began. They shamelessly emptied the stores and even the pharmacies. All the available passenger and freight trains were commandeered for their exclusive use, since the valiant commanders were in fact in full retreat. Then on June 25 the local radio station announced that an orderly evacuation of civilians would take place, as well. Over the next two days freight trains consisting of twelve boxcars, each one capable of holding forty people and overflowing with mostly Jewish families, pulled out of the station at four-hour intervals.

On the first day of the announced evacuation, I asked Ronya and Avrom-Osher to get their things ready in order to evacuate with everyone else. But they just could not bring themselves to take such a step, which would have meant leaving Grandmother and Grandfather, who had decided that if they were going to die, "then better to do so at home." And none of them really believed the Germans would be so monstrous as to kill all the Jews, one after another. Grandfather suddenly came to and said, "I saw them in the First World War. They didn't kill Jews then." Chaya and the other children had no objection to leaving but said, "We're not going anywhere without our parents." The local radio station announced that the last train would depart the next day, June 27, bringing the organized evacuation to an end. My turn had come. It was an agonizing decision, but the fact that the route lay east through Manevichi where Mama and the children and Libche and her husband lived, and that the train would stop there for at least a half hour, gave me the strength to decide to leave and to look for them and perhaps to take them with me, if they had not already left on their own. Along with a small knapsack containing the most essential articles and documents, I also took a small packet of photos I had prepared over the preceding days and the silver watch Grandmother had given me at my *bar mitzvah*. At the time she had told me to keep it with me "so you can sell it or trade it if you're hungry and have no money for a crust of bread." Even on that joyful day she had foreseen that there might be such a time in my life. And as it turned out there was.

The parting was extremely painful. Grandfather, silent and trembling, held me to his breast. Large tears rolled down his face from his dulled eyes. Aunt Ronya wept and moaned. "What shall I tell Grandmother and your mama? They will curse me," she said. Uncle Avrom-Osher and Polina and Dodik wept too. But Chaya, holding me tight, only said through her tears, "What am I to do?! What am I to do?! What will become of me without you?! What will become of me without you?!" Dodik refused to say goodbye at all and sank into a corner and howled.

I left for the station early the next morning. A crowd of Jews was already waiting there, but the train was slow to arrive. Half an hour later Chaya came running with a parcel of boiled chicken, challah, and a small package of sugar. From the pocket of her dress she took a hundred rubles that her father had sent for me. Like many who were saying goodbye, we embraced and stood with our heads bowed and silently wept. It was not until late in the afternoon that the locomotive pulled into the station with its boxcars. Agitated and grabbing hold of their small children, pushing and shoving each other and sometimes scrambling over the heads of old men who had fallen in the crush, those in the throng forced themselves into the boxcars. Chaya gathered herself and, bitterly sobbing, said her last words to me: "They must be going crazy at home. They'll think we left together." And then she ran off, glancing back several times. And I, as if turned to stone, remained standing where I was. And then I suddenly felt a powerful shove in my back. Shoving me again, a red-haired Jew shouted ominously, "Blockhead, the train's pulllng out, but what are you doing?! You're standing there dumbstruck! It's not going to wait for you!" He shoved me again and then dragged me with him and pushed me up into a boxcar . . .

It was only later that night that I realized the enormity of what was happening and of my own situation. I was on the right-hand side in a front corner of the boxcar in a space that was already half taken up with bundles of some kind. The train crept along at a snail's pace. The passengers who knew something about it explained that the slow pace was in case there was an air raid. If there was one, the train would have to stop at once, with the passengers taking cover under the boxcars, and the younger and stronger of us running toward the plane.[6] The train arrived in Manevichi at five the next morning. It was announced by loudspeaker that it would continue on its way in an hour. I jumped from the car with the knapsack on my back and ran to the house where Mama and the children lived. A sign had been nailed to the door: "Everyone's in the forest." I ran to Mechl and Libche's home and found the same thing. Distraught, I turned to some passing Ukrainians. Without stopping or looking at me, they muttered in reply, "*Usi zhidi davno vtikali. De voni, tilki bis vidae*" ("The Jews all ran away long ago. Where they are, the devil only knows"). And in fact all the nearby houses belonging to Jews were empty.

What was I, a nineteen-year-old boy, to do? The train would leave in twenty minutes. Hanging my head like a beaten dog, I returned to my corner of the boxcar, my mind tormented with guilt and self-reproach: "I should have left on the first train or else stayed behind in Kovel. I would have found them then, or they would have found me. I would have made them leave with me. If they wouldn't leave, then I would have stayed . . . until the end . . . and not tried to save myself." (As Polina, who miraculously survived, later told me, Mama had in fact come to their house and had berated them for letting let me go off on such a long, unknown journey by myself.) At the same time, hopeful thoughts also flashed through my mind: "Perhaps they went east ahead of me. Perhaps I'll find them there." And then thoughts of self-accusation and self-reproach would coming rushing back. Those thoughts stayed with me for many, many years afterward. Somewhere in the depths of my soul they haunt me to this day.

Part Two

♪♪♪

1941–1955

Dubovka. A Collective Farm. A Hospital. A Factory

$$\int \int \int$$

The air in the boxcar was foul. Not so much from the baking sun as from the fact that instead of the forty that had been announced, there were more than fifty people in it, including several small children and nursing infants. The poor mothers looked after the children the best they could, and the infants' unwashed diapers dried in the boxcar. The only time you could get water to drink or fill a bottle to take with you was during the stops to replenish the locomotive's own water and fuel. By the third day most of the passengers had, like me, consumed all the food they had brought with them. Buying more (whatever you could carry: some rolls, a loaf of bread, a tin of herring, a hundred grams of butter, a couple of pieces of candy) proved to be very difficult. By the third day of the war, the still free part of the population was already experiencing shortages from the collapse of the transportation network and the lightning-fast German occupation of the Ukraine and its unharvested crops. As a result, the Soviet authorities introduced strict rationing of basic foodstuffs, a system that would continue even after the war, until 1947. Toward the end of our journey, the only food available came directly from peasants, who brought it to the stations to sell for large sums or barter for scarce items or goods. It was in that way that I traded the silver watch that Grandmother Rivka had given me.

We were attacked several times by Messerschmitts as the train moved east. A few minutes before their arrival a heart-rending rumble and then a thunderous roar were heard. Screaming and swearing in a panic, people took refuge under the stopped train, shielding their children with their bodies. Machine-gun fire ripped through the train, but, thank God, no one was hurt during the week-long journey. We arrived in Stalingrad on July 3.[1] The Stalingraders knew we were coming and greeted us warmly, "with bread and salt," as the Russian expression has it. Buses were waiting to take us to hotels, where we were provided with clean underwear, towels, and a bar of soap. Finally, we could wash our clothes. Then we were given a nourishing meal and informed that those in charge would come to see us the next day to decide what to do with us in the immediate future. For the first time in that week-long ordeal, I lay down on a clean, soft bed and at once fell into a deep sleep.

The next morning an official from the Stalingrad municipal council arrived, gathered us in the hotel's movie theater, and told us that in three hours buses would take us to the town of Dubovka, some fifty kilometers north of Stalingrad on the Volga. There we would be lodged in rest homes for a week. "You'll rest, regain your strength, and put yourselves in order. A representative of the regional committee of the Communist Party will meet with each of you there. He'll get better acquainted with you and assign you to various enterprises, according to your abilities. The responsible authorities will also assign you private quarters. At the enterprises, you'll each be given an advance of two-weeks' pay to get you back onto your feet. Write down the address of the council and the number of my office, in case something doesn't seem right to you. I'll always be ready to listen."

With that his presentation ended.

The buses arrived on time and in forty-five minutes had taken us all to Dubovka and our rest homes. My bus stopped at one called *Red Dawn*. We were registered four to a room, summoned to the dining hall, given supper, informed of the meal schedule, and advised "not to go anywhere without a companion." The next morning after breakfast, a young man of medium height with a pale, expressionless face, watery blue eyes, and a mouth full of stainless-steel teeth came to see us. He wore a uniform without any insignia of rank on its red collar tabs and introduced himself in a long, incomprehensible phrase as "Comrade Trendyakov, your security adminstration plenipotentiary." He was accompanied by another man in civilian clothing. Comrade Trendyakov introduced him. "This comrade is an interpreter who knows all the Slavic languages. Whatever you don't understand, he'll translate."

Over the next several days following that brief introduction, the interpreter called us one by one into Comrade Trendyakov's office with the, at least to me, unfamiliar phrase "Special Section" on its door. On his desk lay a stack of folders, each marked "Personal File" and containing a multipaged personal questionnaire in two languages (Russian and Polish) with numbered questions. All the questions had to be answered. The last section read, "Everything I have written is true. I have been warned that providing false information is a criminal act." And then a space for a signature.

I should add a background detail here. There had been several Poles in the boxcar with us, former Communists who, after their liberation from Bereza Kartuska, the infamous Polish political prison, were fleeing the Germans too.[2]

They had not been allowed to join the All-Union Communist Party of the Soviet Union and were subject to careful scrutiny, lest there be any "Mensheviks," "Trotskyites," or "infiltrated" provocateurs among them.[3] They had kept mostly to themselves on the train, discussing their humiliations and other experiences after their liberation. The oldest of them had urgently instructed the others on how to conduct themselves during their interrogations, although at the time it had not been quite clear to me why. "The main thing is to say, on the one hand, how bad living under the Polish yoke was, how the capitalists mocked the working class and the Poles mocked the Jews, and, on the other hand, how good it has been under Soviet rule, adding something, obviously, about the depravity of the damned Fascists." But now I was beginning to understand a good deal that until then I had not: Grandfather's "voluntary" surrender of all his property and his keys to the newly appointed Cheremoshno council chairman, the death of Shimon's son Yankel in custody, the division of Cheremoshno's peasants into *kulaks* and the poor, my grandfather's "amendment" of our vital records—all of it was consistent with the Polish Communist's recommendations.

Nevertheless, a lot of what he had said then was new to me and beyond my grasp. What were Mensheviks and Trotskyites and what did he mean by interrogations? Why was it necessary to say how bad it had been under the "yoke" of Polish authority and "how good it had become" under the Soviets, when in fact so much had changed for the worse? But when the perspiring refugees whose last names began with the first letters of the alphabet started to come out of Trendyakov's office and glance around in alarm even as they described their conversations with the "security administration plenipotentiary" as "amicable," it finally dawned on me, and I was able to appreciate the full significance of the warning offered in the boxcar by the long-suffering Polish Communist.

And then it was my turn. I will not to the end of my days ever forget the "amicable" conversation conducted by Comrade Trendyakov with the student Avrom-Moishe Wolf. The interpreter and I entered the office together. Comrade Trendyakov was sitting at his desk and was so absorbed in reading material in a file that he "didn't notice" our coming into the room. Unable to bear the long pause, I coughed. Only then did Trendyakov, still reading, indicate the chairs with his hand. We sat down. After fifteen or twenty seconds and a deep sigh, he put down the file and turned to me. "Here's a questionnaire. Fill it out, as indicated. The comrade interpreter will help you. I'll step out for a moment and then we'll have a talk."

I began to fill out the questionnaire. I could give exact answers in only a few cases. The rest of the questions, such as those regarding my "social origin," or whether I had any "party memberships," giving the name of each, or had taken part in "counter-revolutionary activities," or had ever been "convicted of a crime," naming the statute, or what the "address of my next of kin" was, or if I had "foreign ties," etc., left me bewildered and dismayed. The interpreter, noticing my state, moved closer and began to reassure me, advising me simply to draw a line next to any question I did not know how to answer.

Trendyakov returned an hour later and resumed his place behind the desk. After quickly looking over what I had written, he put the document down and began to question me. "Well, how are you getting along, Avrom-Moishe Shloymovich? How do you like the rest home? How are you feeling? Do you have any complaints?" Receiving positive replies from me on the first two accounts and learning that I had no complaints either, he picked up the questionnaire again and examined it more carefully. And then he fixed his watery eyes on me, gave me a sardonic smile, and asked in astonishment, "How is it that there are more blank spaces here than answers? What's the matter with you? Can't you read Russian? But that's what the interpreter is for. But you were a student at the University of Lvov! Your conduct is not good, not good, Avrom-Moishe Shloymovich!" And he asked about the questions next to which I had drawn lines. Anxious and with tears in my eyes, I started to mumble something in broken Russian. Seeing my confusion, he smiled with his stainless-steel teeth and started to reassure me.

"Now, now, it's all right. My goodness, what a mama's boy!" And then with a frown, he abruptly returned to his official tone. "Listen, Avrom-Moishe Shloymovich! We know all about you—about your Grandfather Yeruchim Chaimovich and how he acted in a Soviet way. We know that the Germans killed your father, and that your sister and mother have been doing honest work in Manevichi. We know everything. The only thing we don't know is how to use you. You seem to be educated, but you don't have any skills. I just went to the Party regional committee to consult with them about you. Here's what we've decided. The best thing will be to send you to the *Leninist Truth* collective farm. It's a prosperous farm. A good harvest has ripened. They need your help. All the peasants are at the front. Only old men and women and youths remain. They need your help! They need it! They need it! And you're the son of a villager!" he said, giving that last phrase an ironic twist, as it sounded to me. "You'll lodge with

Elizaveta Ivanovna. She's a very kind-hearted woman. Her husband was killed in the 1940 Finnish war and her two sons and son-in-law have volunteered for the front.[4] She'll receive a ration from the collective farm for your workdays. After the harvest, you'll probably return to Stalingrad to continue your studies." And with those encouraging words, which fairly flew out of his metallic mouth, our conversation ended.

Elizaveta Ivanovna did indeed prove to be a very kind-hearted woman, pleasant-looking and talkative. Our first evening together she told me about her hard life. Her husband had been arrested in 1937 and given ten years for "careless words," and then sent from prison straight to the front, where he had been killed. Her two sons had been drafted into the army. And her daughter lived in Siberia and very rarely wrote.

Like all the other collective farmers, Elizaveta Ivanovna received for her own work ration a loaf of rye bread every two days, a liter of milk once a day, a kilogram of millet once a month, and half a kilogram of molasses every two weeks. Everything else she grew in her own garden. She also had some chickens and rabbits.

"Now I'll get a supplement for you," she happily observed.

"Well, how is life on the collective farm?" I asked my new landlady.

"Tomorrow you and I will go out to help with the harvest and then you'll see," she replied with a noncommittal smile.

On July 15 I got up at seven and washed with cold water that Elizaveta Ivanovna had brought from a nearby spring, just as she would every morning. On the table were a glass of milk and a hunk of bread. Beside them was a note: "Eat and drink as much as you like. I'm glad to share what I have. I'll be back soon." I have never eaten or drunk with such relish. Elizaveta Ivanovna soon returned and told me that she had just seen the chairman of the farm and made all the arrangements. He had authorized a supplement for my share. "A cart will soon be here to take us to help harvest the rye. It's already overripe, but there hasn't been anyone to bring it in, you see. So many men have been sent to the front," she added sadly.

It was already very hot outside, with the sun beating down. Around nine an odd-looking cart pulled by two oxen stopped in front of Elizaveta Ivanovna's house. It had lattice side panels and was called an *arba*, as I learned from the collective farmers. It was only with a tremendous effort that I kept from laughing outloud or otherwise expressing my wild astonishment. A barefoot youth with tousled blond hair came to the door and yelled, "Vanovna! Hurry up with your *panych* (little Polish guy). The sun's already scorching!" We quickly gathered our things and climbed into that splendid folk contraption, and the youth commenced his song to the oxen consisting of two phrases, *tsob-tsob* and *tsabe-tsabe*, the first of which meant "to the right," and the second, "to the left." From time to time he would reinforce his commands with light taps of his whip. The oxen, which appeared to have no enthusiasm either for his singing or for the whip, continued to plod along at the same unhurried pace, raising little puffs of dust.

We arrived at the field around ten. The sun was already approaching its zenith and beating down mercilessly. The men had removed all their outer clothing and undershirts. The women were wearing only their brassieres and underpants. Using scythes, the men lazily started to mow the grain. Since I had never harvested and knew nothing about it, the foreman assigned me to stacking the cut sheaves in ricks. It was very hard work. Even those used to field labor could tolerate no more than half an hour of it. They poured cold water on themselves and crawled under the *arba* to dry off and cool down a bit. I did the same with even more pleasure.

In a spot where the rye had already been cleared, a fire burned in a pit with a huge kettle suspended over it on two iron beams. The kettle contained our midday meal. Next to it stood two old women stirring its contents with paddles. The meal began at one. People got in a line to the kettle and with a large ladle served themselves using whatever containers they had brought with them. Elizaveta Ivanovna, who was already familiar with the ineptness of her new lodger, had an extra bowl into which she put a portion for me. She brought it to me, and after tearing off a sizable hunk of bread for me from her loaf, she said, "Here, eat this! And don't be fussy about it, or else . . . Well, you know what. Tomorrow you'll go over to the kettle yourself. If it isn't enough, get some more."

The bowl contained a thick cabbage soup with beans, peas, millet, and pieces of some kind of meat. The laborers around me ate with gusto. A few accompanied the soup with pork rinds they had brought from home and then went back to the kettle for seconds. I, however, had trouble eating even half a bowl with the bread. It was all I could manage. It made me nauseous. Elizaveta Ivanovna, who had evidently been keeping an eye on me, came over, handed me a cup of *kvass*, and said sympathetically, "It's all right. You'll get over it, sweetie."[5] After we had eaten, the foreman announced a two-hour break. Everyone crawled under the *arba* and quickly fell asleep. But I could not. My nausea was worse. With the help of two boys, I got over to the place where even tsars go by themselves. At a distance of no more than a hundred meters on either side of the field extended two pits, one for the men and the other for the women, with boards laid over them. And there you did whatever it was you needed to do.

The break lasted not two but three hours. Only when the sun had started to go down and the heat to abate did we return to where we had been working. After another two or three hours of harvesting, we climbed into the *arba* and returned home to the driver's now familiar song. It was already dark when we entered the house.

Elizaveta Ivanovna, after fussing about in the kitchen, silently brought me a glass of milk and a piece of bread. She looked sympathetically at me for a long time, not knowing where to begin. First she got up and then silently came back. Finally she asked, "Well, then. Did you get enough to eat? If not, just say so, and I bring some more. Today you're eating your own food, what you earned. So don't be shy, or else . . ." She wiped her face with her apron without finishing. After a few appreciative words from me, she said, "So now you know how we live. That's the way it is. It's nothing. You'll get used to it."

I slept badly that night. I was tormented by terrifying dreams. Either my weeping mama appeared, or else Grandfather would be standing next to the bed, or Libche and Rozochka would be quarreling about something. I woke up frequently from a pain in my back or a rumbling in my stomach. Elizaveta Ivanovna got up at first light. She busied herself in the kitchen and periodically came to the door of the room where I was sleeping. She would stand there a while with her arms folded under her apron and loudly sigh and then go away. Finally, she started to call to me from the other room. "Get up, sonny, get up! The *arba* will be here soon."

Soon afterward the *arba* and oxen did arrive, and everything continued just as it had the day before.

After the midday meal my nausea returned and by the fifth day constipation had appeared along with stabbing stomach pains that, despite Elizaveta Ivanovna's maternal concern and the folk remedies she suggested, failed to go away. The next day she took me to the collective farm dispensary. An old man, a medical assistant respected on the farm, listened with an ancient stethoscope, palpated my stomach, and whistled. "You aren't doing so well, sonny. You'll have to go to the hospital in Dubovka."

The next day, July 20 or 21, I was taken there in a truck, the collective farm's only motor vehicle. After examining me, the doctor on duty said to the nurse,

"He has an obstructed bowel." For treatment he ordered "a warm enema and a hot-water bottle. Keep changing the bottle during the night. If there's no improvement by morning, prep him and call the surgeon." With that the examination ended and the doctor moved on to the next patient.

The nurse came to see me several times to check my pulse, take my temperature, and ask how I felt. Fortunately, I did feel a little better around midnight and fell into a deep sleep. In the morning I was examined by the ward chief, a woman of around fifty who resembled a Jewish mama, with dark, melancholy eyes, a penetrating but compassionate gaze, carelessly arranged gray hair, and a characteristic lilting accent. After greeting me, she gazed sympathetically at me and asked, "Well, how are we doing?" And without waiting for an answer, she pulled back the blanket and while intently watching my face felt my abdomen, first gently and superficially, then harder and deeper. She then ordered me to stick out my tongue, listened to my lungs and heart with a wooden stethoscope, and asked me to stand and walk back and forth with my eyes closed. Finally, she asked me to lie back down on the bed so she could feel my stomach again.

"It's resolved itself, thank goodness! At least for the time being. Stay in bed another day or two at the most, and then you can return to work. Only not at the collective farm but here in Dubovka. You'll need periodic observation and a special diet. After I've made my rounds, I'll call the regional committee and tell them what I think." And after a reserved, bittersweet, but captivating smile, she proceeded to her next patient.

The next morning the ward chief returned (to my everlasting shame, I am unable to recall either her first or her last name), accompanied by a limping young man with a white coat over his military tunic. Greeting me again with her gentle voice and lilting accent, she asked, "Well, then? Still alive? This is a representative from the regional committee," she added with a simple gesture as she introduced me to the limping veteran accompanying her. He nodded, remained silent for a moment, and then announced, "We've already talked everything over here. I'll inform those in charge and I think they'll agree with me. After you're released, you'll come to see me and we'll put you to work in a local enterprise."

The enterprise turned out to be the Lenin Weaving and Textile Factory. Without a single question, its manager handed me a piece of paper and said, "Fill out this application. My secretary will show you how. Then wait here."

With the secretary's help I entered all the required information. She disappeared into the manager's office and after coming back out said, "As of today, July 23, 1941, by order of the manager, you are hired as a probationary timekeeper. The shop foreman will come get you and explain your duties."

The shop foreman was a stout, vivacious woman of about forty with smallpox scars on her chubby face and penciled eyebrows and bright lipstick. She gently took my arm and escorted me to the shop floor and her office. She asked me how I had come to Dubovka. When I began to explain in my broken, barely intelligible Russian, she audibly exhaled in mild exasperation, then guffawed, and then after a few more incomprehensible sentences from me grabbed her head in her plump little hands and cried, "I'll go crazy!" In the end she asked, "Where do you live, sweetie?" Upon learning that I had just been discharged from the hospital and still had no place to go, she jumped up from her chair and ran off somewhere. She returned a few minutes later pulling a fellow a couple of years older than me by the arm, and then said in a commanding voice without any introductions, "Izya! This little guy is alone and a refugee just like you. Today after work take him home to the dormitory with you. I'll call ahead. Look after him. Make sure he gets something to eat tonight. Tomorrow he'll receive a worker's ration card and coupons for the cafeteria." And turning to me, she said, "Don't lose heart! I won't let you perish! Now let's go to the shop and I'll show you your duties."

In the entrance booth was a blackboard with the names of all the shop's workers. In boxes under the corresponding headings, I was to enter in chalk the time of each worker's arrival and departure. At the end of the shift, I was also supposed to get information about each worker's production from his supervisor and record it in a special ledger. I was accountable by law for the accuracy of everything I wrote, a matter of real importance, since according to a proclamation regarding the criminal penalties for malingering from the chairman of the NKVD, or People's Commissariat for Internal Affairs, arriving more than twenty minutes late could be punishable by up to a year in prison.

Izya came for me after work and took me to the factory dormitory. The woman in charge brought a cot to his room, along with a straw mattress, sheets, and a pillow. He and I became friends at once. And he really did look after me and help me to acquaint myself with the particulars of the local Soviet reality and learn how to handle the basics of my new existence.

Before the German invasion, Izya had been a third-year student at the Lvov Engineering Institute, and like me had survived by sheer luck. His parents, who had lived their whole lives in the city of Brest, had failed to get out before its capture in the first hours of the war.[6] He could explain himself reasonably well in Russian and was much better adapted to practical life than I was. He had taken his textbooks with him when he fled and was now studying for admission to a similar Stalingrad institute. He scolded me for not having brought any medical textbooks with me and promised to get some from a doctor he knew. He was counting the days until he could return to Stalingrad, where a friend had promised to help him get into the Tractor Institute. He advised me to return to Stalingrad a week or so before the beginning of the term to acquaint myself with the situation at the medical school and talk to the dean of instruction. He promised to help with that in any way he could. And so he did. I spent my first night back in Stalingrad in his little room, since he had left Dubovka before me, on August 15.

Meanwhile, I had been getting a better sense of my duties at the factory. I am not sure why all those working in the shop treated me with such kindness, but it was probably the shop foreman's doing. She was the only one who called me by my Russian diminutives *Mosya* and *Moska* rather than by the more formal *Moisey*. All the same, I still had not gotten over my depression; on the contrary, after Izya's departure it grew worse. I gave little thought to myself, nor indeed to much else. My thoughts were all back with my family. My pangs of conscience had reached the point where every night I would make new plans for returning home, for crossing the front lines, and, if the Germans did not kill me first, for making my way back to Manevichi and Kovel to look for my family, or at least to find out what had happened to them.

On August 24, however, I submitted a request for a work discharge in order to take up my studies again at the Stalingrad Medical Institute (students were entitled to a release from work and, after the draft age of nineteen, to a military deferment), and on August 25, 1941, I left Dubovka for Stalingrad by steamboat.

Stalingrad. Medical School. Work as a Loader. Trenches. Bombardment and the Front.

♪♪♪

As it turned out, I would remain in Stalingrad a long time—almost two years. Izya, who had a room in the Peschanka district, greeted me warmly but without superfluous sentiment. He invited me to stay with him until I got a dormitory assignment ("if they admit you"). The next morning he took me to the medical institute, where he interpreted for me, since my Russian had gotten no better. It was possible to understand me, but only if you had a genuine desire to do so and made an exceptional effort. But in that anxious time of economic disarray and alarming rumors, people in the city were brusque, impatient, and always hurrying somewhere. Could they really have been expected to listen to and try to make sense of my Polish-Ukrainian-Russian mishmash? Good Izya understood all that long before I did. In half an hour I was standing in the main administrative office. The secretary stared at me in amazement and then told me to wait while she ran to the office of the dean of instruction. Coming back into the room, she said with barely a glance, "Go. The assistant dean, Toviy Davidovich Epstein, will see you."[1] I knocked on his door. A kind, gentle voice replied, "Come in, come in."

As I did so, a tall man of forty-five or fifty stood up and stepped from behind his desk. He had a clean-shaven face and warm eyes with a pince-nez on his thick nose and was dressed in a well-starched white coat. He offered me his broad, warm hand, held my cold one in it, and gazed at me sympathetically, which surprised me. Only now in feeble old age have I come to realize, much more keenly than I ever did before, that good deeds are truly good only when they are warmed with love; otherwise, they become a burden or an occasion for resentment, as Grandmother Rivka would have said. From the beginning, I intuitively sensed in Toviy Davidovich Epstein a truly righteous man who was ready to help anyone in need. Shyly, with tears in my eyes, I blurted out my double given name, my last name, and my patronymic. He asked me to sit down and at once proceeded to put me at ease.

"Why make it so hard? Calm down and tell me about yourself. Everything will be fine."

In a trembling voice and in broken Russian I tried to give him a brief account of the hardships I had experienced from the day of my arrival in Stalingrad, of myself, of what I had gone through before arriving, of my medical studies at University of Lvov, and of the fact that I was all alone in Stalingrad, without family. Toviy Davidovich gazed at a book lying open in front of him and remained silent for a long time. Then with a deep sigh he looked up at me and said, "I won't pretend otherwise, your situation is complicated. But with our combined efforts we can deal with it." Opening the University of Lvov course record book I had brought with me, he wrote "Confirmed" in it without looking at it and then signed it with a flourish. "Now we'll go see Ezer Israilevich, the dean of instruction. He'll enroll you as a third-year student and assign you to a study group."

The dean was sitting at the desk in his office, dressed in a military-style blouse and polished high-top boots. He gazed at me with a skeptical frown and then looked at Toviy Davidovich. The latter briefly explained the gist of the matter, after which the dean said, "I think the best thing will be to put him in the eighth group with the student union organizer, Fedotov. I'll tell him to take the new fellow under his wing." And turning to me, he added in a gruff, soldierly way, "It's not going to be easy for you. You should know that as of this semester the program has changed. An accelerated course of study has been introduced in all the medical institutes—instead of the usual five years, three years, after which you'll receive a certificate instead of a diploma. You have only one year left. There will be no vacations. During that one year you'll cover the program's third, fourth, and fifth years, but without the comprehensive state examinations at the end. They will come when the war's over."

Toviy Davidovich silently took me by the arm and led me back to his office. "You'll stay with us tonight. Elizaveta Elefterievna and I live off the institute courtyard. I'll send for Comrade Fedotov tomorrow and he'll find lodging for you. The dormitory's now being used as a hospital for the seriously wounded. The students have been assigned housing in private apartments instead. Fedotov has all the information. He'll give you my vouchers for three days in the faculty cafeteria, and then on September 1, when the term officially begins, you'll get a student ration card. After that we'll see. Keep your chin up."

Flushed from excitement and with tears in my eyes, I started to express my gratitude. "Stop that right now. These days each of us has to do whatever he can. Without unnecessary words. Elizaveta Elefterievna and I will expect you for supper at five."

After I left his office I thought, "The sacred souls of my grandfathers, Grandmother Rivka, and my parents are looking after me. It is in answer to their prayers and tears that God has sent me a guardian angel." As it turned out, Toviy Davidovich was indeed that angel, along with his wonderful wife, Elizaveta Elefterievna, a Greek by nationality.

I knocked on their door promptly at five. It was opened by a well-proportioned, slightly plump woman of no more than thirty who looked like Catherine the Great but with a broad, warm smile on her lips. She said that she knew all about me. She took me to the bathroom and gave me two towels and some clean underwear. Remembering that now brings tears to my eyes. I was so filthy, and the two of them were so clean and holy! Not only then but later in my life God and my ancestors have sent me, along with much else, many kind strangers who have rescued me from hunger and death. And I shall speak of them all without fail in what follows.

Clean and ruddy after a shower, I sat down for supper with the wonderful Epstein couple. Our heartfelt conversation begun during the meal continued long after it. Subtly so as not to embarrass me, they probed my knowledge of world history, literature, and art. Elizaveta Elefterievna had herself been trained as a singer. Toviy Davidovich was surprised by my knowledge of religion and languages—of Latin and especially Hebrew, that is. He was not a believer himself, but in his heart, as it seemed to me then and still does today, he was a true Jew, who had inherited from his father, a Jewish writer, the ethical norms of Jewish morality. It was in the company of those two angels that I felt human for the first time in the whole period of my separation from my family and my subsequent wanderings. It is hard to convey just how they made me feel that way, but every word and action of theirs was filled with warmth and genuine kindness. That kindness was unremitting to the last day of my time in Stalingrad and then afterward in Kazan.

When I presented myself at Professor Epstein's office the next morning, there was a man already waiting for me there dressed in an officer's tunic without insignia and holding a cane and a cap of the *budyonovka* type with ear flaps.[2] It was the union organizer and perpetual student, Comrade Fedotov (to my enormous regret, I cannot remember his first name).

He appeared to be a strong, well-built person but in fact was a lame invalid and someone who in any event deserves to be remembered and to have a few warm words written about him. He was born and grew up in the ancient Russian city of Voronezh, northwest of Stalingrad near the Ukrainian border. When he was ten his mother and father were shot by the Bolsheviks as "enemies of the people." He was sent to an orphanage but escaped to engage in petty black-market trading along the railroad system, eventually reaching Stalingrad. There he was caught and put in a reformatory, where he displayed great industry and a genuine desire to learn. After graduating from high school in 1938, he was sent to work on the construction of a building for the Stalingrad Medical Institute. In recognition of his "Communist attitude toward labor," he was enrolled without examinations as a student at the institute and appointed head of its trade-union committee. It was there that his distinctive human qualities—a fondness for the downtrodden and concern for the poor—revealed themselves. He was a mediocre student, but he categorically refused special treatment and had repeated every year of the institute's curriculum. Everyone respected him for that, and at institute and regional committee meetings he invariably sat on the dais with the presiding officers, which in the Soviet understanding of things was a conspicuous honor.

"Greetings!" Fedotov said in his Volgan accent, which even I with my poor Russian could recognize, and held out his hand to me as if to an old friend. And then without further ado, he said, "Let's go!"

He took me to his office where he resumed our interrupted conversation. "So you've decided to study in our city. That's both good and bad. Good, because we have fine people here and they will all try to help you. Bad, because it could very soon all come to an end. The war could reach us before . . . ," and without finishing he changed the subject. "So don't put off things until tomorrow. Here are two notes for you. One's for the manager of the grain elevator. He has a small dormitory for loaders. There are lots of people there, of course, but that won't make any difference, since they all work at night while you'll be asleep. And they'll share a piece of bread with you, and when things get tight, you'll help them load the grain. For which they'll pay you . . . Here's the other note," but before giving it to me he hesitated for a moment and read it over, and then he added, "It's a message for the student Korol. He's an important, a very important person in our institute and on the local union committee. He's a refugee, from Kharkov, if I'm not mistaken, and a fantastic operator, if you can imagine that. He feeds the professors, and they grade him without exams. He gets work for all the students who want it. All the city's food-enterprise directors know him and carry out his requests. Everybody calls him 'Papa.' The only person he reports to is me. So go see him. He lives by himself in the office of the chairman of the Department of Marxism-Leninism. The chairman, Professor Sverdlin, has been working for the regional committee the past six months and temporarily gave Papa his office. Papa reports to me and only listens to me. So go see him."

Sitting in the office at the departed professor's polished desk was a sleek young man dressed in a well-pressed black worsted suit from whose sleeves protruded starched white cuffs. Every two or three minutes the telephone would ring, or he himself, dialing a number, would call someone else. The conversations were striking for the brevity of their replies and questions: "Yes," "No," "Tomorrow," "Twenty," "The same," etc. Or, "Hello!" "Where are you?" "How much?" "Are you sure?" "When?" "Well, go ahead, go ahead, only be careful!" Each time before picking up the phone and after each conversation, he would automatically apologize, adding, "They won't leave me alone," or "Damn them," and so on.

Finally, he looked at Fedotov's note and then gave me a brief order. "You'll work this afternoon at the wharf. Here's a work card. Show it to the foreman. He'll have a band on his right sleeve with two letters in white, *M. I.*, for Medical Institute. He'll explain it all to you. Off you go, then!"

The foreman took the work card while running back and forth and then yelled to one of the men, "Here's a helper for you!" before running off again. After giving me a once-over, the man said, not in the least shy about it, "Well, well, they've even found me a helper! It's pretty clear from your ragged gymnasium overcoat what kind of help that is. Let's saw some firewood."

After the first movements of the saw he spat and started to curse the foreman in the vilest language. But then he noticed my embarrassed, sweating face and abruptly changed his tone. "What's the matter with you? Don't start whimpering, now! I was just like you once. Today you'll suffer a little, but tomorrow you'll be an expert." And after an hour or two as I applied the suggestions of my boss and partner, the saw really did begin to move with much greater rhythm and speed.

I was starting to get hungry. I wanted something to eat and drink. My boss could see it all at a glance. "Looks like we have a hungry boy here!" Taking a hunk of bread out of a pocket of his wide pants, he tore off a piece and handed it to me. When instead of *spasibo*, the Russian word for "thank you," I automatically replied with the Polish *dziękuję*, he whistled in surprise and said, "It turns out you can't speak Russian either, poor devil! Where on earth did you come from?" I gobbled down the bread. He started to question me about who I was and how I had come to Stalingrad. After I anwered his questions in my broken Russian, he indicated a water pump, handed me a bottle, and sent me over to fill it. We drank and parted amiably. "Come back again tomorrow! With a coat like that, you'll be a marshal yet! Well, off you go, then!"

Toviy Davidovich tracked me down after work and invited me home for supper. And Elizaveta Elefterievna greeted me just as warmly as she had the day before. Over supper I told them about the day's encounters and events, and Toviy Davidovich informed me that classes at the institute would probably start two weeks late on September 15, since the students had all been ordered to help dig fortifications outside the city. He and the dean of instruction, Ezer Israilevich, would be going there too.

The next morning I went back to the wharf. We had just started sawing firewood again when my partner suddenly said in a low voice, "Have you got your documents with you? It looks like a round-up has begun." I didn't immediately understand, since the term "round-up" was new to me. He explained and could tell from my sudden pallor that I had no documents at all. Taking his head in his hands, he moaned, "I knew it! You're about to get a cartload of trouble!" A policeman came over to us with a soldier carrying a rifle. When he heard that I had no documents, the policeman gave my worn-out Polish overcoat a closer look and said, "Come with me." I was taken to the wharf commandant's office, where a strenuous interrogation began. I told them everything exactly as it was, and said that they could confirm it with the assistant dean of instruction at the medical institute or with the chairman of the union committee. The duty officer made a call somewhere, and judging by the fact that the severe expression on his face was soon replaced by a smile, he had gotten through to Toviy Davidovich or Fedotov. He hung up and turned to me.

"What a strange little bird you are. I'll inform headquarters just what kind of 'spy' we've caught," and with a laugh he made the necessary call and then laughed again. "A strange little bird! Listen, get yourself a student card at the institute office and don't go out or show your face in any public place again without it! It's wartime and we don't have time to fool around with snotnoses like you. Hear me? Now march!"

But even after I got the student card, those escorted visits to the commandant's office would be repeated because of my suspicious appearance and miserable Russian, which continued to resist any improvement. The instruction staff was getting tired of the calls. After the third or fourth time, Toviy Davidovich sent for me and explained the situation in a paternal way. "You need to understand us. I certified your student record book. I'll take your first examination in social hygiene in German, but the other professors won't. I've spoken about your situation with the institute director, Eduard Bernstein. He'll probably call you in too, although he did tell me that you must learn Russian in three months, since you'll have to take your end-of-semester examinations in it. As for your appearance, Fedotov and I will figure out something."

On September 1, 1941, as anticipated, the students of all five Stalingrad institutes were taken to dig fortifications fifty kilometers west of the city. It was an arduous task for all of us, but especially for me and the few others like me.

The fortifications were dug in the open steppe. There were no residences nearby, nor any tents, nor a proper field kitchen either. Large haystacks stood on the bare ground. Each of us was supposed to hollow out a burrow in them to make a sleeping place for himself. The kitchen, as at the collective farm near Dubovka, consisted of pits dug in the earth with huge kettles suspended over them containing the same sort of gruel. In addition to that fare, we got 400 grams of bread per day and one packet of tea for the entire period of our stay. The local students, who had come straight from their homes, had brought additional supplies with them. Several of them were even visited by their parents, who had found a village a few kilometers from the encampment where they could purchase milk and other provisions. Most of the students eventually took advantage of that resource. My own less than meager funds, however, were used up within a couple of days. I lost a lot of weight as a result. Toviy Davidovich and Fedotov could not, in front of everyone, share with me or give me special treatment. They had no time to, anyway. They were occupied all day long on their two-way radio arranging the delivery of additional food for everyone, along with a few more blankets, at least, since it was getting colder every day, with dangerously low temperatures at night, especially after our return to Stalingrad was postponed. Instead of two weeks, the digging lasted a month, until October 1.

I was half starved and frozen when I got back to Stalingrad and my grain-elevator burrow. My bunkmates gasped when they saw me. They gave me 100 grams of vodka (the first time it touched my lips), fed me some bread, and said they would complain to the Party regional committee. "People in your condition shouldn't be out digging fortifications." Shortly after that Fedotov called me in and, as usual without wasting any words, handed me a set of keys and said, "I've made you the manager of a sports equipment storeroom. You'll live there. Change your clothes! You'll find lots of woolen ski suits, long underwear, and especially warm boots there. You'll get a little salary to go with your university stipend of 130 rubles a month and a worker's ration card entitling you to 600 grams of bread a day and 300 grams of sugar, 1,200 grams of cereal grain, and 1,200 grams of meat a month, which should be enough for you to live on. If it isn't, you can always load grain on the freight trolleybus at the wharf and take it to the elevator. Keep your eyes open and you'll always be able to find something. Just remember one thing: give nobody anything from the storeroom without a chit from me—nobody, nobody, nobody! And hold on to the chits! Got it? Well, off with you, then!"

Fedotov was another one of those righteous people sent by God in answer to my family's prayers. He had saved me once again.

Finally classes began.

The first day I was summoned by the institute director, who praised me for helping with the fortifications but immediately warned me to devote myself to the diligent study of Russian and advised me to work in the library, since textbooks could not be taken home. After the first day of lectures, I went down to the library and asked for a volume on introductory therapeutics. I sat down at a desk and started to read, but either because I could not understand a word of it, or because there was no one else in the reading room, I felt so forlorn and helpless that tears began to fall from my eyes onto the book lying open before me. The librarian, a gray-haired woman of about fifty with deep creases on her forehead and around her drooping lips, and melancholy eyes gazing through the thick lenses of her glasses, came over to me and sat down and gently stroked my hair. "What's the matter? Why are you crying?" she asked. She had never seen a reader cry in her library before. It is hard for me to explain even now why her gentle way of speaking made me cry even harder. I covered my face with my hands and, stifling my tears, asked in a mumble for a glass of water. She brought it and remained beside me waiting for my answer. Upon hearing the reason for my tears, she sighed (it seemed to me that there were tears in her eyes too), put her hand on my shoulder, and said in a maternal way, "My name is Elena Elistratovna. I've worked here many years and helped many people in that time. Don't cry. I'll help you too. In half an hour I'll close the library, we'll take all the textbooks you need to my home, and every day—you hear, *every day*—I'll teach you the language and at the same time help you prepare for the winter examinations. You'll pass with distinction."

Her one-room apartment was near the institute at No. 8 Voroshilov Street. She opened the door and turned on the light, revealing walls glistening with frost, two stools, a table knocked together from boards, and a tiny kitchen.

"Don't be surprised! I'll explain everything to you in due course. But right now we'll have a glass of tea and work on your Russian." She lit an alcohol burner, put a kettle on, and in five minutes a strong glass of tea was standing before me. She got a lump of sugar from a drawer, broke it in two and gave a piece to me. After she had drunk her tea, she suddenly pointed to a picture on the wall of a gently smiling man pressing a kitten to his face.

"Do you recognize him? Do you know who that is?" When I said that the face was unknown to me, she quietly explained. "Well, true, why should you know? He's a famous Russian poet, Vladimir Mayakovsky, whose 'love boat was smashed against everyday life' and who committed suicide.[3] We'll start our study of Russian with him." She began to recite:

> Taking its mass of duties
>   and swirl of events,
> the day has departed,
>   gradually darkening.
> There are two of us in the room.
>   I
>   and Lenin—
> he as a photograph
>   on the white wall.[4]

After reciting the poem to the end, she asked, "Did you understand any of it?" I nodded that I had. "Then repeat it after me, word for word," and she began to recite, while I did as she asked.

"Well, that's all for now. Take the book and learn the poem by heart. I'll ask you about it tomorrow and then we'll continue. Recite it to youself at home. Until tomorrow!" And just think, that evening I memorized not only the poem she recited, "A Conversation with Comrade Lenin," but also Mayakovsky's "Lines about My Soviet Passport"![5] When the next day I recited to my wonderful teacher that poem too, she was very pleased and hugged and kissed me.

My repertoire eventually moved beyond Mayakovsky, making the transition to Turgenev and his poems in prose, several of which Elena Elistratovna had me learn by heart and a few of which I can still remember.[6] After two or three weeks, my Russian had improved enough for me to read my textbooks with my teacher's help and to start preparing for the winter examinations. If I happened to miss an evening, she would get very angry. I had to explain why I had failed to come.

"After all, I promised that you would pass your examinations with distinction. Are you trying to make a liar out of me? That's very bad of you!" Our sessions continued in that way until the last day of the winter examinations in December. Thanks to Elena Elistratovna, I did in fact pass them all with distinction and have kept that page from my student record book to this day. For all my success, however, the other students teased me for a long time about my translation of the Latin anatomical term *crista galli*; instead of the correct "cock's crest," I had answered "Crester's cock." I was therefore often mockingly referred to as "Crester's cock."

Elena Elistratovna and I became fast friends. Gradually she told me about her bitter lot. Like Toviy Davidovich's wife, she was a Greek by nationality. Although she was older than Elizaveta Elefterievna, they had both come to Stalingrad at the same time. There Elena Elistratovna had married an architect well known in the city. In 1937 he had been arrested and sent into permanent internal exile in the far north.[7] She received "joyful" letters from him twice a year. She had asked permission to visit him many times but it had always been denied: "For security reasons a meeting is not possible at this time." Finally, in 1947, she was allowed to join him. On the way to his place of exile she stopped over in Moscow for two days with my wife and me, sharing her plans with us and recalling my first Stalingrad success.

After that success, I got ready for the next semester's examinations on my own. My situation was complicated by the fact that I had a second, night job—unloading grain at the wharf and transporting it to the elevator—which left only a few hours every day for sleep and class preparation. My good memory and ability to listen while dozing saved me more than once. I remember one amusing instance. During a lecture on infectious encephalitis, the professor asked if we knew what that disease had been called before its etiology was discovered. "Who knows the answer?" A long silence followed. Finally the professor, who had apparently noticed that I was nodding off, said, "Perhaps you, student Wolf, can tell us?" I jumped up from my place and without even opening my eyes replied, "Sleeping sickness!" The lecture hall erupted in laughter. But to the astonishment of all, the merciful professor replied, "Correct, my friend! Correct! Now get on with your nap!"

In the meantime, the military situation had been getting worse. Despite severe frosts, the enemy had enjoyed one victory after another, and the radio bulletins were growing ever more disturbing. On November 21, 1941, it was announced that the Germans had taken Rostov-on-Don, four hundred and ninety kilometers to the southwest, that the city had passed back and forth in bloody battles several times before the Germans finally captured it, and that their army was now moving toward Stalingrad. People became increasingly worried and started to dig trenches in their building courtyards. Many abandoned the city and headed east. Panic mounted in February 1942 when German planes attacked the town of Serafimovich, just two hundred kilometers northwest of Stalingrad, and bombed a nursery school. Rumors were rife that the institute would be evacuated eight hundred and twenty-five kilometers north to the Volga city of Ulyanovsk. The director dismissed them and ordered the digging of trenches in the institute courtyard and the construction of a large bunker where the professors and their families could take refuge in the event of an air raid. On August 15, 1942, we had our last examinations. All of us were given certificates stating that we had completed the five-year course of study at the Stalingrad State Medical Institute and could be employed as doctors in wartime. Inscribed in large letters at the bottom of each certificate was the addendum, "This certificate is not in lieu of a diploma." And further, "To receive a diploma, the holder of this document must pass the comprehensive licensing examinations at a state medical institute."

The war continued its stride toward Stalingrad in seven-league boots. Finally, the institute received an order from the People's Commissariat of Health to prepare to evacuate one thousand and ninety kilometers north to another Volga city, Kazan, since Ulyanovsk had rejected our request. The institute director appealed to the Stalingrad military medical command to postpone for a week the call to the front of forty male graduates, since they were needed to pack up the institute's equipment and load both it and the baggage of the faculty and instructors onto steamboats scheduled to depart from the main Stalingrad wharf on August 23.

From early morning until late at night, the instructors, laboratory staff, service personnel, and former students packed and loaded the institute's inventory and transported it to the wharf. Several graduates were assigned to help the professors, since their baggage was to go first. The most essential items and documents were put in suitcases, which the professors would carry with them when it was time to board the steamboats.

Everything was loaded and ready for departure at five in the afternoon on August 23. Meanwhile, the engine of war had been drawing nearer with each passing day. Fifth-column saboteurs, traitors to the motherland infiltrated by the Germans, had begun to take action. On August 17 the post office was burned. On August 18, a water main was damaged. On August 19 the bread plant was shut down. Crowds of people, including us, ran there and to the bakeries and took away as much as we could carry. The same day a number of electrical lines were cut, bringing the trolleys to a halt and depriving many parts of the city of power. People had begun by every available means to cross over to the east bank of the Volga away from the approaching German army. On August 22, the airbase was bombed. Soviet fighters returning from sorties had nowhere to land and were forced to go to airfields far away from Stalingrad, leaving the city without air cover.

The professors and staff anxiously awaited their departure the next day.

And that day came. The morning was silent, the sun shone as hot as ever, and the sky was blue, without a wisp of cloud. Trucks arrived at the apartment buildings of the professors, who were waiting by the entrances with their families. In front of one of the buildings stood a piano that had been too large or heavy to load, with Professor Deladier, the chair of the Department of Hygiene, weeping beside it, for her son was a talented pianist and the piano and the life it represented had been precious. Several children were gathered around her, while silent old men and women lay nearby on cots. And then all of a sudden, there was a terrific roar! The radio managed to broadcast that there were several hundred German warplanes overhead and that they were dropping incendiary bombs.[8]

Except for the apartment houses by the river reserved for distinguished experts, institute professors, and high-ranking officials; the concrete and steel grain elevator; the buildings of the medical and other institutes; a few hospitals and clinics; and the train station, five-story state department store, and a handful of other structures, the city was built entirely of wood. It was therefore quickly engulfed in flames, and after three days of continuous bombing, nothing remained but charred rubble. People sought refuge in the bunkers and trenches they had prepared. And then the bloodthirsty enemy began to drop on those pitiful human remnants high-explosive bombs that, for the most part, fortunately failed to hit their targets.

Around three o'clock on August 23, two hours before the steamboats were scheduled to depart, the German vultures began to bomb the wharf. The already loaded ships caught fire in front of the assembled passengers. Their own and the institute's property was rapidly reduced to cinders. Thanks to the efforts of the institute director, Eduard Bernstein, and his close ties to the military medical command and the head of the army hospital that had occupied the institute dormitory from the first days of the war, several trucks had been requisitioned. They were used to transport the now homeless passengers, as well as those of us having no other residence or affiliation, either as former students or newly fledged doctors, to the large bunker in the institute courtyard, since no one dared take refuge in the still intact but empty building of the institute itself. Professor Bernstein and Dean Ezer Izrailevich both made a tremendous effort under extraordinarily difficult circumstances and proved to be amazingly resourceful, arranging twice daily meals, obtaining drinking water for everyone, and even finding mattresses and pillows for the women. Professor Sergey Nikolaevich Kasatkin, the chair of the Department of Anatomy, and his daughter, the poet Irina Kasatkina, were responsible for maintaining order and discipline in the bunker.

Eventually, the military medical command provided launches three times a day to evacuate the medical institute staff to the other side of the Volga, and then an armored steamboat to take everyone one hundred and ninety-five kilometers upriver to the city of Kamyshin, after which they went by regular steamboat the rest of the way to Kazan. The director of the Kazan Medical Institute had agreed not only to accept the faculty and staff of the now defunct Stalingrad Medical Institute but to ensure proper employment for every one of its former members.

During the last boarding of the professors and their families for the exposed river crossing an extraordinary event occurred. The captain of the launch was in a great hurry and kept urging the passengers to move "faster, faster," since the German air raids were repeated every twenty to thirty minutes. The previous one had ended while the launch was still moored. After it had cast off and was starting to pull away, Professor Delaroux suddenly realized that her son had been left behind, and began to shout, tear her hair, and plead with the captain to stop. Her son leapt for the launch but misjudged the distance and fell into the narrow space between the launch and the dock and started to sink. The captain pulled him from the water barely alive and immediately administered artificial respiration. What the distraught mother and the others in the launch were going through is beyond description. Fortunately, the boy survived, but because of what had happened, the captain announced that the crossing would have to wait until after the next raid. And in fact enemy planes soon appeared, but after circling the dock, they for some reason flew away without dropping any more bombs. The launch immediately set off for the other side of the river, leaving the rest of us behind on the dock.

Now on our own, we young doctors were by a special order of the medical command given the rank of lieutenant of the medical service, issued appropriate uniforms, and assigned to various military hospitals. Another new lieutenant of the medical service and I were sent to Military Hospital No. 1,584 to be used in whatever capacity its commandant deemed appropriate.

I will never forget the tragicomic events of my first day at that hospital. The commandant was not in his office, so we introduced ourselves to his adjutant, the head of the medical unit, whose name I have forgotten. He greeted us coldly, with no particular interest, as it seemed to me. He said that that we would have to report directly to the commandant and that he was in the courtyard.

We found him there, a colonel of the medical service in an unbuttoned tunic running around giving orders to a group of soldiers who were unloading crates of medical equipment. As they moved the crates, they talked among themselves, occasionally turning to look in the commandant's direction and loudly laughing. He scurried among the crates, holding a small piece of plywood over his head and moving it first to the right and then to the left. We later learned that he had sustained a mild concussion and had since that time carried the board to protect himself from potential shrapnel wounds.

We went over to him and started to report. But instead of waiting till we finished, he glared at us and shouted, "W-what?! About f-face! M-march! G-get out of here! W-wait inside!" It turned out that after his concussion he had also begun to stutter. Startled and trying not to laugh, we ran back into the hospital building. After a long interval, the commandant, his tunic still unbuttoned, returned to his office. We did not dare go in without being called. Seeing us, the head of the medical unit asked why we were sitting there. We described our encounter with the commandant in the courtyard. He went into the latter's office, and when he came out he said with a shrug, "The commandant ordered me to assign you to triage the wounded, and to find places for you in the barracks." After another shrug, he left. I cannot say how my colleague fared, since he was assigned to triage at a different entrance, but the following is what happened to me.

Tarpaulin-covered trucks pulled up at the entrance. Two orderlies then took the wounded, who were on stretchers, from the back of each truck and placed them on the ground around the entrance. The entire area was littered with wounded men, many of whom quietly moaned or else were completely silent, while a few wept, swore loudly, or shouted for immediate attention. My task was to identify the most gravely wounded—the ones who needed immediate surgical intervention. Having no experience whatever, and being all of twenty years old, I ran to those who shouted, attaching a little red flag to their stretchers as a sign to the orderlies to take them at once to the operating room. But in fact I should have done exactly the opposite: those who were silent or quietly moaning were the ones who were most seriously wounded and were perhaps already losing consciousness and thus needed to be sent to the operating room first. But of course I did not realize that.

After about fifteen minutes the commandant ran out, followed by the ward head in a bloody surgical gown. Clutching his holster in a fury, the commandant rushed at me shouting, "I'll sh-shoot you d-down on the s-spot, you s-s-son of a b-b-bitch! What the hell are you d-doing?! Are you t-trying to s-s-sabotage us?! P-people are d-dying r-right under your n-nose, and you're s-sending healthy f-fighters to the operating r-r-room?! I'll c-c-court-m-martial you!"

Frozen in fear, I started to open my mouth but had no idea what to say or how to respond. I was rescued by the officer who had come out after the enraged commandant. He stood between us facing the commandant and tried to calm him. "How could someone still wet behind the ears who's never even had a whiff of gunpowder be assigned to triage? It's my fault. I should have come out at once myself to see who was behind this mess. But I went to tell you. All right, then. Calm down, now. I'll immediately replace this character with the surgeon Davidov. He'll get it straightened out soon enough."

The commander, gasping with rage, turned around and went back to his office muttering to himself. My rescuer then addressed me. "And you, young man, don't let it bother you! He's not going to do anything. Captain Davidov will be here in a moment. I advise you to pay close attention to what he does. Learn from him. It will stand you in good stead!"

The next morning the head of the transportation unit called me in and said, "I'm reassigning you as a river escort for those needing additional treatment at hospitals in the rear. Here's a first-aid kit, if you need it. Provide whatever assistance you have to."

"Yes, sir!" I loudly replied and after an about-face set off for the door.

"Wait a minute. Straighten your blouse and belt. Don't give anybody an excuse to make fun of you or . . . us! Is that clear, Lt. Moishe Shloymovich? That's all. Dismissed."

Escorting the wounded to the other side of the Volga was a dangerous business too. As I have mentioned, the German vultures would return every twenty to thirty minutes and attack anything on the water. And that included any wounded being taken across.

Once just before my return to the hospital from across the river, a German plane dropped a high-explosive bomb near where I was standing with an empty stretcher, waiting to board a launch. According to the launch captain, the concussion lifted me two or three meters off the ground. By some miracle the explosion itself had not hurt me, but falling back to the ground I struck the lower part of my face against some hard object. The blow knocked out three of my front teeth and part of my lower gum. The captain administered first aid, packing the wound with gauze and cotton wool and making the bandage so tight that I couldn't move my jaw. Back at the hospital a surgeon in the orofacial department removed another loose tooth and put a clean dressing on the wound. After that, the department head examined me every day for two weeks and predicted that I would have complications and need the help of dentists more than once. And so it proved to be. My remaining teeth got progressively looser, and in 1954 while I was living in the far north on the White Sea, they finally started to fall out. I had to replace them with a denture, which, because of my injured gum, I was never really able to use.

The military situation continued to worsen. Despite the truly heroic resistance of Soviet troops, the German hordes got ever closer to the city. Only the arrival of severe frosts slowed their advance. In November it was announced that their easterly movement had been stopped at the Dzerzhinsky Tractor Factory fifteen kilometers from the city center. In late November, despite artillery shelling and periodic bombing of the city, the movement of the German forces from the south was halted as well, just a few kilometers from Peschanka. The stream of wounded to the hospital slowed. The river froze and the evacuation of the wounded over it to the town of Krasnoslobodsk was first done by sleigh and then by truck. The need for escorts was also reduced. As a result, several of the new people, including me, were transferred to various wards to work as senior medical assistants. Only with the accumulation of a certain number of wounded needing treatment at hospitals in the rear were we used as escorts too.

Around the middle of December Soviet fighters and bombers reappeared overhead. It was announced that Hitler's forces had been repulsed in every direction, suffering massive losses in men and materiel. Even so, the Soviet counterattack bogged down, and it was only in January 1943 that the reports of bloody battles were accompanied by the news that Soviet troops had surrounded the enemy. The encirclement and destruction of the main German force were completed on January 30. The next day the German commander, Field Marshal Friedrich Paulus, announced the surrender of his entire army group.[9] Those of us working in the hospitals were given the opportunity to line up opposite the state department store where Field Marshal Paulus had made his headquarters in the basement. At exactly three o'clock in the afternoon we had the pleasure of seeing one of the most important German commanders emerge from the basement in his German tunic without a belt or holster and with his hands raised. After him came a number of other generals and officers of high rank. I am unable to recall if it was the next day or several days later that we were assembled to watch a column of German officers and soldiers who had been taken prisoner in the tens of thousands. They were a pitiful sight. Many wore stolen women's coats and furs over their greatcoats. Their heads were covered with women's kerchiefs or with blankets, and their boots were bound with rags. As they shuffled along, they hardly looked like fighting men. They were a horde of marauders who had been cornered and then reduced to barely human form.

Although the Bible forbids us to rejoice "when thine enemy falleth," each of us was glad to see the physical and moral devastation of those barbarians who had destroyed so many millions of innocent lives.[10] But it was a joy greatly tempered by the memory of the innocent victims. No victory could bring back my family. The pain and grief at their loss that had been dulled in the times of struggle surged to life again and became even stronger and more unbearable. Again I was unable to sleep. I was woken by terrible nightmares that continued to torment me even in the daytime.

But life went on, even so. The first fragrance of spring was in the air. In mid March an order came from the Supreme Commander of the Soviet Army, Josef Stalin, regarding the immediate transfer of "doctors who have not received their diplomas" to the military departments of the medical institutes for the completion of their studies and awarding of their degrees. I, like the professors and staff of the Stalingrad Medical Institute, was sent to Kazan on the Upper Volga in the Tatar Autonomous Soviet Socialist Republic. Fate had smiled on me once again, and at the end of March 1943 I left Stalingrad for good.

Kazan. The Magarils. The Military Commissariat. The Naval Medical Academy. Septic Angina. The Mogilevskys and Epsteins.

♪♪♪

In Kazan I would after a long interval again see my Stalingrad saviors, Toviy Davidovich Epstein and his wife, Elizaveta Elefterievna, as well as Dean Ezer Izrailevich, Professor Kasatkin and his daughter, Irina, and Professor Mogilevsky, the former chair of the Department of Clinical Medicine, who in Stalingrad had provided me with textbooks, and who in Kazan would introduce me to his son, Ruvim, a second-year student at the medical institute there. Before Professor Mogilevsky went back to Stalingrad in June 1944 to resume control of his department in the reconstituted Stalingrad Medical Institute, he would give me a room in his large, well-furnished apartment in Kazan ("It will be good for you and less boring for Ruva"), where I would remain until my transfer the following September to the 2nd Moscow Medical Institute to complete my studies and receive my medical degree—but more about that later.

Lest I give the unjust and sinful impression that the medical school professors were the only ones who took an interest in me, let me now speak of the other, "simple" people who befriended me during that Kazan period of my life. It would be an exaggeration of my importance and an inexcusable oversight to forget the good done by those who shared the "bread and salt" they received during the wartime rationing—who shared with others not even close to them but simply with *kol dichfin*—all who were hungry.[1]

It is impossible in this short account to describe everyone who helped me, but I am obliged to say a few words about one family that became very dear to me and, I would say, even like my own. They were the Magarils from Leningrad (St. Petersburg, today), with their father and grandfather, Judah, at their head. As the Germans approached Leningrad, the Magarils had, with thousands of other people from the city, been evacuated to Kazan, where after a great effort Judah had managed to find a basement apartment with windows looking out onto the street.

The family had six members: Judah himself, in his fifties; his wife, Feiga; their elder son, Mikhail, a student at the Kazan Medical Institute and a disabled veteran who had lost his right arm at the front; their only daughter, the beautiful

Moisey and Zhenya Magaril

Raya, whose husband had been at the front since the beginning of the war; her two-year-old son, Zhenya; and Judah and Feiga's younger son, also named Zhenya and sixteen.

The only one in the family who worked was the fifty-year-old Judah, and they were all very different not only in age but also physically and psychologically. A master portrait photographer, Judah was short, lean, energetic, loud-voiced, short-tempered, and fiercely intransigent in his judgments. Bent under the load of his old view camera, boxes of photographic paper, and bottles of chemicals, he would go early every morning to the Kazan marketplace, in the center of which was his "darkroom," a crude booth with a tiny window. From early morning until late at night he would take pictures, develop the negatives, and make prints. His customers had to be happy. At the least sign of dissatisfaction, Judah would turn red, tear up the picture, and yell, "Don't blame the mirror if the face is ugly!" and sarcastically advise, "Next time you want a picture taken, go see a make-up artist at the theater first!" Carrying a rucksack crammed with scarce groceries picked up over the course of the day, he would come back at night even more loaded down than he had left in the morning. He was met by the entire household, led by the grumbling Feiga, who was never satisfied. His first action was to take his little grandson in his arms, give him a piece of candy, and whisper something in his ear. The smiling Raya would then serve her father supper with half a glass of vodka, which he drank before eating his food with zest. After supper he would share the latest news of the Kazan marketplace in his characteristically sardonic way.

Judah was a kind man who helped the poor and especially his hard-up relatives. One of them ate regularly in the Magaril home—an orphan with criminal tendencies. Because of his crimes, his other relatives had all rejected him. Judah found him on the street. He was able to exercise a sort of temporary influence over him and was indeed the only person who could. The relative would periodically vanish and then come back filthy, with his clothes torn, and, more often than not, a swollen face. Judah never rebuked him, never questioned him, but took him straight to the bathhouse, put his clothes in order, and silently fed him. When the Magarils finally went back to Leningrad, they took the relative with them.

Judah had another quality. He loved to sing. He had a pleasant baritone and even though he was not religious himself, he liked to sing synagogue prayers, imitating the great cantor Gershon Sirota.[2]

Let me add a few words about my own relationship with Judah.

To say that he liked me would be both insufficient and not quite right. He was glad when I dropped by and would invite me to stay for supper. He would often ask my opinion in family disputes and, amazingly, would listen to me even if I took the opposite side. Thus, when his sons needed money for their personal affairs, he would often wait for my opinion, and if my "judgment went against" him, he would mutter, *"Meyle zol zayn azoy"* ("Let it be so, if it must be so"). There was an occasion several years after their return to Leningrad when his grandson Zhenya, by then a highly skilled engineer, already married, and living in cramped conditions with his wife's parents, asked Judah how he could be so indifferent to the fact that his only grandson, whom he loved very much, still did not have his own home.

The exasperated Judah angrily asked me, "What does that have to do with me? Let his wife's parents take care of it!"

Feigning irritation, I replied, "Shame on you for haggling! Can you afford to buy your grandson an apartment, or not?"

"Are you joking? Of course I can. I could do a lot for him!" he answered, softening.

"Well, since you can," I answered more boldly, "then the first thing you're obliged to do is go out tomorrow and buy the young couple an apartment!"

He frowned, bent his head, and as usual muttered, "I'm obliged to! I'm obliged to! It's my duty to them!" And the next day he went out somewhere and bought them a beautiful apartment in the center of the city.

Nevertheless, I always sensed a certain aloofness in his dealings with me in Kazan. He suspected that my relationship with Raya, whose husband was still at the front, as I mentioned, was less than innocent. He was particularly displeased whenever she and I would go out for a walk or to the movies. "Only not for long, otherwise little Zhenya will wake up and start crying," he would say in an irritated voice as we left.

I should emphasize that Raya—Raisa—occupied a special place both in my life and that of her family. She had just recovered from typhoid and was very lonely and always under the vigilant eye not only of her father but also of her brother, Mikhail. He was a student at the same medical institute to which I had initially been assigned, and it was he who had introduced me to their family. Raya, being of a passionate nature, naturally suffered from her loneliness. I sensed that and sympathized with her. It took a great effort on my part to keep from crossing the line of legitimate friendly relations and betraying the trust of her family. I was also attached to little Zhenya, who was drawn to me too.

I enjoyed friendly relations with Judah and his sickly wife, Feiga, until the end of their days, and, before I emigrated, with Raya and her husband, who had returned from the front unhurt, and with Mikhail. Judah's grandson, Zhenya—may he live to be 120!—and his wife, Ada, and their talented daughter, Yana, a poet who writes in both Russian and English, have remained dear friends to this day. They live in New Jersey, and from time to time we call each other or exchange e-mail messages.

Let the gentle reader forgive me for dwelling so long on the Magarils. It could not have been otherwise. They occupied an important place in my life and still do.

Time had not stood still after my transfer to Kazan, and it was not long before I met new difficulties. As it turned out, there was no fifth-year course at the Kazan Medical Institute, nor was there a department of military medicine either. The institute had already graduated its accelerated fifth-year class, awarding its members medical degrees, while the accelerated fourth-year class had not been promoted, since the same order that had sent inadequately trained students like myself to Kazan had in the next paragraph cancelled the program of accelerated study altogether. The fourth-year curriculum had thus been re-established on its normal footing, but no concurrent normal fifth-year had been organized. The question then was what to do with those of us who had been sent to Kazan from other medical institutes.

In my case, the Kazan Military Registration and Enlistment Office made a Solomonic decision. In mid-April 1943, a few weeks after my arrival from

Stalingrad, it assigned me to Evacuation Hospital No. 2,775, where "until further notice" I was appointed a medical assistant with a monthly salary of 435 rubles (at the time the price of two loaves of bread) and the right to a civilian ration card. I was saved from starvation by the daily bowl of soup I got from the hospital cafeteria, along with whatever I could scrounge from patient leftovers. I was ashamed to take the latter at first, but then I got used to it, just like all the other assistants, duty nurses, and orderlies. The hospital's chief of administration, Colonel Aron Lvovich Lifschitz, also gave me a place in the hospital dormitory, where I remained until late the following spring.

Moisey, 1944

At the end of May 1944, I received a summons from the Military Commissariat and was given orders reassigning me to the Academy of Naval Medicine, which had earlier been relocated from Leningrad to the city of Kirov, just west of the Urals on the Vyatka River. The document stated that "by Command of the Main Military Medical Administration of the Commissariat of Defense, Lieutenant of the Medical Service Avrom-Moishe Shloymovich Wolf, currently on extended leave, is sent to take his state comprehensive medical examinations and receive his degree." I was accordingly released from duty at the evacuation hospital and given three days of rations and a ticket on the steamboat *Uralets*, which would take me to my new destination.

Upon my arrival in Kirov I was assigned a place in the institute barracks and given a standard mess allowance. It turned out that I was not the only one who had been sent there. In the barracks and later in the mess hall and the dean's office, I met a number of people who like myself had been on extended furlough and reassigned to the Academy of Naval Medicine for the same purpose. Over the next three days we were called in one after another and asked the same questions. On the fourth day, June 5, the head of the administrative section gathered us together and announced that "in view of the fact you have received no military training at all, let alone in naval hygiene and naval surgery, the Academy of Naval Medicine cannot register you as students or allow you to sit for the state examinations, which include questions about naval medicine."

In the face of that disappointing decision, each of us was forced to return to his former place of residence. My own, as it happened, had already been reassigned. I went to the evacuation hospital chief, told him about the bureaucratic confusion at the Academy of Naval Medicine, and asked him to give me back my place in the dormitory. He replied, "You'll spend the night in my office and tomorrow go to the Military Registration and Enlistment Office. If they renew your assignment here, there will be no problem. But heaven only knows what their decision will be."

The military commissar was no happier to see me. He was already aware of the rejection and the reasons for it. He had been informed through the chain of command that in issuing the Military Medical Administration order, he had acted improperly from the start. His order did not have the consent of the navy's main medical administration. "All right," sighed the military commissar, an old warrior with white hair, "tomorrow I'll get in touch with my superiors. There is an urgent need for civilian doctors here. The Commissariat of Health of the Tatar Autonomous Republic has come to me with a request for help. My clerk will prepare an order reassigning you to Evacuation Hospital No. 2,775 for the time being, and I'll sign it."

Cheered by that development, I went back to the hospital chief. In a bold hand he added a corresponding instruction to the quartermaster and then signed the document in an illegible scrawl. Returning the order to me, he said with a heavy sigh, "I've signed it and they'll give you a place in the dormitory, but I can't enroll you as a member of the staff. Your position has already been taken by someone else. So, brother, you now have another problem to deal with. Go talk to the Tatar Commissariat of Health tomorrow. Maybe they really will have something for you."

The next day I waited at the Commissariat of Health for over an hour to see the head of the personnel department. When I finally entered his reception room, his secretary looked in her notebook and gruffly informed me I was not on his list of appointments and even more gruffly asked me when I had signed up to see him. My mouth went dry. Noticing my confusion, she added, "He only sees visitors once a week. You have to sign up ahead. I'll need to provide a brief summary of your question at least two days before your appointment. What's your question? I can put you down right now for next week."

And then another miracle occurred. The head of personnel came in, accompanied by my Stalingrad guardian angel, Toviy Davidovich Epstein. By the deference with which the other man treated him and the way the secretary jumped up from her seat, I could see that Toviy Davidovich was held in high regard by the local bureaucracy. He stopped in front of me, extended his hand, and asked with an astonished expression, "Where did you come from? Where have you been? What have you been doing all this time?"

The secretary turned red and began to justify herself in embarrassment. "I put the comrade down for an appointment next week, since I didn't know . . ."

In his relaxed way Toviy Davidovich asked her to sit down, took me by the arm, and said, "It's all right. Don't worry about it. I'll deal with it myself." He led me to an office across the hall. It was only when we got to it that I noticed its doorplate, which to my delighted surprise read, "Deputy Director T. D. Epstein."

Almost sixty years have passed since that time. I can no longer describe all the thoughts and feelings I experienced as Toviy Davidovich sat me down in the soft armchair next to his enormous desk. I remember only that I blushed from embarrassment and was overcome with a feeling of shame like that of an ungrateful, wayward puppy.

I sat there with my head bowed until Toviy Davidovich gently broke the silence. "What's the matter with you? Why don't you say anything? Tell me what you've been up to all this time. Elizaveta Elefterievna wondered about you a number of times, but the demands of my position kept me from trying to track you down."

I told him everything as it had happened and about my currently ill-defined position and the fact that I had no idea what would happen next. I also told him about my talk the day before with the military commissar and the request for help he had received from the Commissariat of Health of the Tatar Autonomous Republic.

"Quite so," Toviy Davidovich calmly replied. "There has been a rare, but very serious outbreak in the Kalinin district of septic angina from grain mold. Dozens have died from it.[3] We're quickly putting together a team of doctors to send to the source. The team will be led by the chair of the Department of Clinical Medicine of the Kazan Institute for Advanced Medical Studies, Professor Emil Ruvimovich Mogilevsky, whom you'll remember from Stalingrad. During the next week he'll acquaint the doctors with the appropriate clinical procedures, preventive measures, and treatment protocols. I'll send you to him. I think he'll be glad to include you on his team." And Toviy Davidovich at once called Professor Mogilevsky, told him about what and whom he was speaking, and asked him to include me on the team and to look after me.

"There, you see, it's all taken care of! Here are Professor Mogilevsky's address and phone number. He remembered you, of course, and asks that you come by this evening. You'll decide everything then." Accompanying me to the door, he added, "Only don't disappear again for so long. Elizaveta Elefterievna and I will be glad to see you too."

When I arrived at the Mogilevskys' apartment, Emil Ruvimovich, his wife, a teacher of Marxist-Leninism, and their son, Ruva, had already started supper. They immediately invited me to join them. Ruva was, as I have mentioned, in his second year at the Kazan State Medical Institute. As a child he had lost his right eye in an automobile accident, although his glasses and a remarkably well-matched artificial eye almost completely concealed his disability. Over supper, a friendly conversation started in which we recalled various episodes of the Stalingrad epic. Emil Ruvimovich said that he would be glad to add me to his team, which after the completion of preparatory lectures would proceed to the Kalinin district to treat the outbreak. He regretted not being able to join us to conduct on-site instruction, since both he and his wife would after the lectures have to return to Stalingrad to resume their work at the reorganized medical institute, although their son would stay behind in the Kazan apartment. "It would please us if you'd agree to move in with him."

It was all I could do to keep from leaping to my feet in joy. I could never have imagined living in the Mogilevskys' spacious apartment, even in a dream. I gratefully accepted their offer and said that I was confident that Ruvim Emilievich (who had been silent the whole evening) and I would be able to help each other. Ruva smiled with an affirmative nod. His mother, the head of the family, judging by her imperious tone and gestures, said, "I doubt that you have many things, so don't put it off, move in tomorrow." And I did, remaining there until my transfer to the 2nd Moscow Medical Institute in September.

The next day Toviy Davidovich called me in. He already knew about my move to the Mogilevskys' apartment, which was close to his own modest residence. Without wasting words or questions, he handed me a warrant for travel on official business and a letter to the secretary of the local Communist Party committee and the chairman of the Kalinin District Council. The letter stated that I had been appointed chief physician of a temporary hospital for combating the epidemic in two villages, Tat Mushuga and Rus Mushuga, with, as it turned out, Tatar Moslems in one and Tatar Christians in the other, and neither group able to speak Russian. The letter also indicated that in keeping with a resolution of the Supreme Soviet and the Party Regional Committee, I was authorized to set up the hospital in the Tat Mushuga school during the school break and to undertake all the prophylactic measures specified in the corresponding wartime regulations, and it asked on behalf of the Commissariat of Health of the Tatar Autonomous Soviet Socialist Republic that I be given any assistance that might be required. After asking me to report once a week by phone about the medical situation and wishing me luck, Toviy Davidovich sent me on my way.

On June 14 I proceeded by steamboat to the regional center of Menzelinsk.[4] Its district council and local Party committee were in the same building. I went there directly after docking. The Party and district authorities both received me warmly and promised to do everything they could. But both emphasized that much would depend on the quality of my relationship with the chairman of the Tat Mushuga collective farm, since the outfitting and supply of the temporary hospital would ultimately depend on him.

Thirty minutes later the district council's jeep had already taken me to the Tat Mushuga school. I was met there by a one-armed veteran, the school's principal, Abdul Irkimovich, who had in his time at the front learned to pronounce some Russian phrases and understand the language. All the classrooms were empty and without beds. The school principal told me that a meeting of all the residents of Tat Mushuga was scheduled for the next morning and that I would have to speak to them and explain what kind of disease it was and what needed to be done so that people would stop getting sick and dying. But the main thing was to establish a bond with the chairman. "You and I will go there now. He'll receive you as guest and you and I will eat. You do whatever I do."

We were met at the door by a broad-shouldered, mustached sixty- to sixty-five-year-old Tatar of medium height. Continuing to chew the tobacco he had raised in his garden, he made a deep bow and then turned to bark something to one of the women busy inside. She instantly disappeared, returning with towels and two wooden basins. My guide whispered that we would now remove our footwear. Following his lead, I took off my Stalingrad boots and socks, and like him lowered my feet into one of the basins. Without a word, the woman poured cold water over our feet and handed us towels. Noticing that my socks were not woolen, she went into the next room and came back with a pair of hand-knit white socks, which she silently offered me. Leaving our footwear in the entry room, we sat down in the dining room. And there began my baptism by fire. Our host filled our glasses with a murky liquid of some sort, said "*Allahu Akbar,*" ("God is great!"), lifted his glass, drank everything in it without a wince, sniffed some bread lying on the table, and then looked at me. My guide whispered with a wink, "We must drink." And following our host's example, he emptied his own glass. Then it was my turn. Overcoming my revulsion and fear, I swallowed the vile stuff. And then everything in the room started to spin. The host's homebrew caught in my throat and burned my insides. I began to cough and for a long time was unable to stop. The host sat me down on a cushion and kept repeating, "Gowon, gowon," while Abdul Irkimovich made a clucking sound and repeated over and over, "Oustanning! Oustanning! Gud! Gud! Oustanning! You lissen me!" He carried me back to the school on his back.

The next morning, June 16, the schoolyard was filled with residents from both villages. I addressed them, and, as Professor Mogilevsky had instructed, explained that the source of the illness was the rye they had left unharvested the year before. Because of the mild winter and absence of severe frosts, it was covered with a fungus that produced toxins unaffected by milling or baking. Therefore, the first task was to burn all the flour and unmilled rye harvested that spring from last year's crop. I told them that the state was ready to provide good-quality flour to replace whatever was burned. I also told them that starting the next day we would open a field hospital with fifty beds, which the collective farmers from both villages would have to create themselves by bringing cots and bedding to the school that afternoon without delay. The next day at noon the hospital would start to accept anyone who was sick with a sore throat, swollen tonsils, or pharyngeal bleeding, or was otherwise believed to have ingested the toxin. The hospital staff (its nurses and orderlies) would help to organize the village committees, and after that a clinic would be set up for anyone still in need of outpatient treatment.

After I had finished and provided further explanation for him, the school principal translated my words into Tatar. The chairmen of the collective farm and the village councils also spoke. The principal briefly translated their remarks for me and assured me that everything would be "gud" and that both villages would help with whatever the hospital needed.

By evening, there were fifty beds with clean sheets and blankets in all ten rooms of the school. The next day the patients began to arrive. Dealing with them was hard. The overwhelming majority did not speak Russian. I called the Menzelinsk regional health department with a request for six nurses who could speak both Tatar and Russian. The department promised to send them the next day, although it was only three days later that four actually arrived: Maria, the most knowledgeable, with ten years' experience, and Tanya, Olga, and Ekaterina, young women who had completed a Red Cross medical course just two weeks before. All the same, their arrival made things a little easier. Under Maria's guidance, they all worked hard, putting in as many hours as needed.

To describe all that we experienced and accomplished in the six weeks the hospital was in operation would be impossible. A separate article could be written about that time and its importance for my subsequent professional life. Nevertheless, there are a few important facts and circumstances that should be singled out.

During the time of my work in that unique hospital, I felt myself to be a necessary and useful person for the first time in my life. One hundred and twenty-four patients were treated, and only three died, all of them elderly people who had reached the final stage of the illness: necrosis of the tonsils with hemorrhaging. All the others recovered. Thanks to the joint efforts of the representatives of the Party district committee, the district council, and the regional department of health, a great deal of prophylactic work was done. All the grain harvested in the spring was destroyed and replaced with good-quality substitutes. The residents of both villages had come to our aid at once after the first appeal. The Tatar Commissariat of Health regularly supplied the hospital with medications, vitamins, and dressings, and promptly responded to my weekly reports.

I was treated with great respect. The first secretary of the Party district committee and the chairman of the district administrative council expressed their gratitude and gave me a flattering reference letter in the Tatar language. (Since a copy had been sent to the Commissariat of Health, Toviy Davidovich was able to tell me what it said after I got back to Kazan.) All the same, I cannot pass over an instance of anti-Semitism in the person of the head nurse with whom I had had more than cordial relations.

One evening toward the end of our stay at the hospital, while discussing the question of "love and friendship," she announced that she "could love a man of any nationality, except a Jew."[5]

I was taken aback.

"But why not? What don't you like about Jews?" I asked.

"What? Don't you know any?"

"I do, I do know a few. How many do you know?"

"None. But when I was a little girl and didn't want to go to sleep, my grandmother would always scare me by saying, 'Quiet now! Go to sleep at once, or else a kike will come for you with a bag and take you far, far away!'"

"In that case, you already know someone of Jewish nationality."

"Who?"

"Me!" I exclaimed. "I'm the real thing. I can even show you my identity papers."

"But that can't be!" she replied. "Everyone says you're a Pole. You yourself told me that you escaped from Poland," and she started to cry bitterly. I soothed her and said that it wasn't her fault, that her grandmother had given her a false idea. But inside it was as if something had been ruptured in me.

We never saw each other again after my departure from Menzelinsk, which was surely a timely one and for the best.

I mention that episode not only because it has stuck like a sharp thorn in my memory. I can say with satisfaction that neither in Stalingrad nor in Kazan did I ever suffer from anti-Semitism. Even those people who were startled by my double Jewish name never openly expressed any hostility toward Jews or me personally. I mention the unhappy incident because it is evidence of a deep, I would almost say congenital, antipathy among some Christians and Moslems for the Jewish people. Children and youths and even adults who have never seen and never known a single Jew in their lives have been infected with that terrible racist disease by their grandmothers and grandfathers.

I returned to the Mogilevskys' apartment on August 1, 1944, laden with two boxes filled with cookies, pies, fruits, and other gifts. Ruva, who had been alerted I was coming by Toviy Davidovich, met me when I arrived and was very glad of my return. Seeing the contents of the boxes, he gasped with delight and said, "We'll have a feast!" He and I quickly became close friends, and until my transfer to Moscow we shared everything half and half, like brothers. He told me that he had a fiancée, Tatyana Afinogenova, the daughter of the chair of the Department of Epidemiology at the Kazan Medical Institute, a third-year student who "took charge of everyone" and whom he had known since they were little children in the same class, and intended to marry before they moved to Stalingrad to live with his parents. He called her at once and she promised to come the next day with some other friends to prepare a delicious supper.

The next morning I called Toviy Davidovich from Ruva's and told him that I would be glad to present a report on the work that had been done. We made an appointment for me to come to his office. He listened attentively with genuine interest and expressed in writing his gratitude for what I had accomplished. (I kept a copy of that document for many years but apparently burned it along with a pile of other things in my personal archive before I left for the United States.) He then asked me what plans I had for the future. Seeing that I was disconcerted by the question, he said that he had a few ideas for the completion of my education. He would know more by the end of the week and invited me in any case to come for supper the following Sunday.

But as before, those few happy hours alternated with many sad days and weeks. Before I left for Menzelinsk, the radio announced that Soviet troops had liberated Kovel and Manevichi. The same day I sent special-delivery letters to the local administrations of both towns asking them to reply to me in care of Ruva with any information they might have about my mother and sisters and brother in Manevichi, and the family of Ronya and Avrom-Osher Zeltzer in Kovel. I got no answer from Kovel. But from Manevichi, a Jew who had been assigned the task informed me on the letterhead of the administrative council that my mother and brother and sisters had all been murdered by the German fascists and buried in a common grave. Like the other refugees from such places, I had already learned from Soviet newspapers and the radio about the tragic fate of those who had been left behind. And like all the other refugees, I too had nursed the hope that perhaps my relatives had somehow survived, had somehow been rescued. Now after reading the letter from Manevichi, that last hope was gone. If not quite so raw, the old wound was opened once more. Gnawing thoughts of self-reproach and condemnation returned with even greater force. As before, the Epsteins provided moral support during those difficult days, as did Ruva and his future wife, Tanya.

When, after sitting *shiv'ah* for the prescribed seven days, I presented myself at Toviy Davidovich's, he realized from my haggard, expressionless face that something terrible had happened. He looked searchingly at me, silently waiting for me to explain. "Well, what happened?" he finally asked in a low, sympathetic voice.

It was difficult to speak but finally I did so. "Everything! My last hope is gone!" In the end, in response to his gentle questioning, I told him of the bitter news from Manevichi.

Toviy Davidovich removed his pince-nez and began to wipe it. It seemed to me that there were tears on it. After a long pause he said, "There is nothing you can do. Hitler's thugs killed millions of innocent people, including millions of Jews. That doesn't make it any easier for you, I know, but you must live your own life. Who knows what other trials we may yet have to face? Gather your strength and finish the institute and earn your degree. My commissariat will do whatever it can to help you." And he invited me to come by his office again a few days later.

When I did, he greeted me with a reserved smile.

"Sit down, please. Your case is moving along. Yesterday I spoke with Academician Orbeli,[6] the vice president of the Academy of Medical Sciences" (as Hitler's hordes neared Leningrad in the first weeks of the war, the Academy of Sciences had been evacuated to Kazan, where it remained until the end of 1944). "He promised to write to the head of the Central Administration for Medical Institutes, Professor Shabanov, a former student of his, to ask for his help in transferring you to one of the Moscow medical institutes to obtain your degree."

A week later, a letter from Professor Shabanov arrived at the Commissariat of Health of the Tatar Autonomous Republic, authorizing my transfer to the 2nd Moscow Medical Institute. He sent a letter as well to the 2nd Moscow Medical Institute regarding my enrollment in the fifth-year course and preparation for the comprehensive state medical examinations. And, finally, he enlisted the daughter of the renowned Professor Alexander Romanovich Luria,[7] who lived in Moscow, to obtain lodging for the days between my arrival in Moscow and the assignment to me of a place in the medical institute dormitory.

Toviy Davidovich and Elizaveta Elefterievna organized a farewell party for me at their home. Ruva and his future bride saw me off at the station. Just before the train left, they invited me to their wedding, which would take place a month later in Stalingrad.

The 2nd Moscow Medical Institute. The Kozlovsky Family. Marriage. Our Daughter Noemi (Nadezhda).

$$\int \int \int$$

I arrived in Moscow on October 3, 1944. Lydia Alexandrovna Luria had arranged for me to stay with her elderly aunt, Tsilya Mironovna, who lived by herself in a small ten-square-meter room in the center of Moscow by the Revolution Square metro station. Aunt Tsilya, a kindly old woman, greeted me warmly, made up a bed for me on an old chest of drawers, and said that if I liked the accommodations, I could stay until I graduated from the institute or found something more comfortable. "I'm all by myself and it's a good place. And with you here it will be cheerier." I remained with her for the rest of the month.

Shortly after my arrival, the 2nd Moscow Medical Institute dean, Professor Mikhail Abramovich Averbakh, called me in for a chat. When he learned exactly how I had been transferred to the institute, he warmed up a little. "I'll assign you to the strongest group. I hope you'll be able to keep up with them. But I can't provide you with dormitory space, since all the places are taken," and extending his hand, he added, "Good luck to you!"

It took two days to obtain a residence permit[1] and it was not until October 6 that I was able to join the group I had been assigned to. I was greeted by the most beautiful young woman in it. She introduced herself as the group leader, gave her name as Susanna Kozlovskaya, and immediately lodged a complaint: "Why did you miss two days? I was told by the dean's office three days ago that you had been assigned to our group. Keep in mind that I'm responsible for attendance and that I submit daily progress reports. Mine is a group of honor students. Where would you like to sit?"

"In the back row," I said.

"Why so far away?" she asked in surprise. "There are plenty of empty seats in front."

"Oh, no! I like to gaze at beautiful young women from a distance!" And so we parted, already dissatisfied with each other. At least until the first break.

During the break we "accidentally" ran into each other again. She unwrapped a small packet—a piece of strudel. "Help yourself! My mother made it. You see, the day after tomorrow is a major feast day, *Simchat Torah*. Do you know what that is?"[2]

Moisey and Susanna

I heartily thanked her and said that along with the rest of my family I had observed all the Jewish holidays for many years and knew all the Hebrew traditions and prayers very well. Susanna gave me a sympathetic look and then disappeared. The next day during the break she came over to me with a note. "It's from my mother. When she was a girl she studied Hebrew with the poet Chaim Bialik and—can you imagine?—remembers it to this day."[3] In the note my new acquaintance's mother informed me in good Hebrew that in keeping with the feast day there would be a celebratory supper at their home the following evening, and that their whole family would like me to join them.

The invitation was obviously not one that I could refuse. It was my first chance during the whole time of my wanderings since 1941 to meet with a family that, in spite of the war and the anti-religious conditions of Soviet life, still observed Jewish traditions. Moreover, the invitation had come at the initiative of a young woman who had understood what kind of person I was, and whom I had liked at once.

When I arrived at their home, the entire Kozlovsky family and their closest relatives were already seated at the table: the hostess, Tsilya Shmuelevna, and her brother and his wife and their two daughters, and the host, Moishe-Boaz, and his sister and aunt and uncle. There was an empty chair for me next to Susanna, their daughter, who had so captivated me. The only family members absent from the table were Susanna's two brothers, Yury, the elder, who would die in Moscow at the age of eighty-one, and Semyon, the younger, who now lives in New York with his wife, Klara, and their daughter and granddaughter. At the time, however, both men were at the front. The supper was a typically Jewish one, and the evening passed in a cordial atmosphere with conversation about my life in Poland and the loss of my family and the events following my escape from Poland and then from northwestern Ukraine.

After that memorable evening, the relationship between the group leader and honor student, Susanna, and me grew closer and closer. By the end of October, I had asked her to marry me. She accepted and her parents gave us their blessing.

My appearance was far from suitable for a groom intending to marry according to the Jewish rite. I had nothing but my uniform. My bride's parents bought me a black worsted suit and a wedding ring, which I had to place on the index finger of my bride under the *chuppah.*

On November 6, 1944, in the presence of my bride's parents and all her relatives, the marriage ceremony and prayers of blessing took place under the direction of Sh. M. Shlifer, the rabbi of the Moscow Choral Synagogue on Arkhipov Lane (now Bolshoy Spasoglinishchevsky).[4] The happiness that every bridegroom experiences at his first family wedding supper was diminished in my case by a sense of loss. I could not suppress the thought that none, not one, of my unforgettable, beloved family had survived to see my wedding, which would change my lonely life for the better in the most fundamental way. I found solace in the kindness, generosity, and warmth that my bride's mother and father constantly showed me.

Until 1930 the Kozlovsky family had lived in the Ukrainian city of Konotop[5] and before the revolution had been very prosperous. Moishe-Boaz's father, Iosif, had been a merchant and grain exporter and had owned a vegetable oil factory and other real estate in the city. Even though Moishe-Boaz himself had turned everything over to the Bolsheviks in a timely fashion and had subsequently been appointed chairman of one of the area's first collective farms, the security apparatus began to hound him, and he and his family were compelled to hide out for long periods, changing their residences frequently and finally moving to Moscow. There Moishe-Boaz found work as a laborer in a tannery. When the war started, he volunteered for the home guard and frontline defense of the city. After he was wounded in 1942, he was discharged and given a small pension as a disabled veteran.

Moishe-Boaz's wife, Tsilya Shmuelevna, was born in the same region to a well-educated but poor family with many children. She had become a beauty and a talented student at a Jewish school where Hebrew was taught by the great Hebrew poet Chaim Bialik, as mentioned earlier. Her parents objected to her "unequal" marriage, but, after she had joined the Kozlovsky family, they were forced to accept it. During much of the wandering from city to city of Moishe-

Boaz, Tsilya Shmuelevna, and their children both before and during the war, she had been the only provider and in Moscow was employed as a custodian in a workers' cafeteria.

When I joined the family, they were all living in a one-room apartment in a little stucco house on a hill at No. 1 Hospital Lane across from the German cemetery on one side and the Main Military Hospital on the other. The apartment needed major repairs. There was a gaping hole in the wall separating the single room from the kitchen, but because of the straitened wartime conditions, the property manager had been unable to fix it. After I moved in, I got hold of some plaster and closed up the hole myself. Living wasn't easy in those crowded circumstances, but Susanna soon got pregnant anyway. Collecting the last of their money and borrowing the rest from relatives, her parents bought us a small room in the center of the city at 15 Kirov (now Myasnitskaya) Street, across from the Main Post Office and near the Kirovskaya (now Chistye prudy) metro station. It took several years of petitioning the corrupt housing administration to register the room as my permanent place of residence. We lived in that tiny space for thirteen years.

It might be wondered why we married so quickly. After all, we both had places to live and stipends, and the local administrative council had found work for me so I would not have to live hand to mouth. And less than eight months remained before our graduation from the institute. Why not wait at least until then? There were several reasons, but the principal one was the war and the inevitable order for me to return to the army, which was still engaged in bloody battles against stubborn German resistance. There was no guarantee that I would survive the last stages of the war. If I didn't, my own family line would disappear from the face of the earth. I very much wanted to avoid that—wanted in the event of my death to leave at least one survivor of our once large and splendid family.

Susanna and I graduated together on July 23, 1945. The war with Germany had ended, with the whole country, but Moscow especially, celebrating May 9 as Victory Day. At last we could breathe easy. It seemed that the danger had truly passed and that everyone would be demobilized. But as the Yiddish proverb says, "Man plans and God laughs." The war was over only for the wounded and for officers and soldiers past a certain age.

Right after I graduated from the institute, another important event occurred in my life. I made another effort to find out if any of my family had survived. I appealed through various channels but got nowhere. Then it occurred to me to direct my inquiries to the country's most prominent Jew, the director of the Moscow State Yiddish Theater and chairman of the Jewish Anti-Fascist Committee, Solomon Mikhailovich Mikhoels.[6] I decided that no one could be better informed about those who had survived the vast genocide of the Jewish people perpetrated by Hitler—curse his name and memory!—and his criminal hordes. I wrote numerous letters to Mikhoels and finally his secretary called to say that he would see me. Our conversation was conducted in literary Yiddish. Mikhoels was pleasantly surprised by my knowledge of Yiddish literature and the history of Yiddish theater. He responded sympathetically to my story and my hope that he could help me in my search for any relatives who might not have perished. At the end of our meeting, he stood up, took my arm, and said, "*Kum, lomir geyn!*" ("Come, let's go!")

We proceeded to the Yiddish theater school, where he told the staff to summon a student who would be able to look up the names of any who had survived in Kovel. A few minutes later into the room walked—my goodness!— Shmuelik Samet, a schoolmate of my first love, Chaya, and her sister, Polina. He recognized me too. We embraced, and then he yelled, "Polina's alive! She's in Kiev!" A few minutes later he had given me her address and phone number. I talked to her that evening and the next morning was already speeding to her by train. I learned from her about my mother's search for me, about the last hours of her parents, her brother Dodik, and our grandfather Yeruchim, who had spent the last days with them, and about how both she and Chaya had been rescued by a Jewish partisan, whom Polina had married. He was supposed to be demobilized soon. She also told me about Chaya's tragic death. A partisan traitor had come to Kiev, called her down to the courtyard, and shot her. The subsequent fate of Polina herself, her husband, Mikhail Krell, and their son is a story for later.

Upon their notification of my graduation from the 2nd Moscow Medical Institute, the Main Medical Administration of the Commissariat of Defense summoned me to report without fail on August 10 for active duty in the just-declared war on Japan.[7] That meant that I would not see my first child, whose birth was expected any day. But in that situation too God and kind people helped. The assembly-point commander listened sympathetically to my request and agreed to defer my departure for thirty days, that is, until September 10.

On August 15 Susanna gave birth to a girl and returned home with her a week later. From the baby's very first days she looked just like my father, and that was yet another reason for my joy in and love for that tiny continuation of the Wolf family. We gave her my mother's name, Noemi, although when she started school, Susanna changed it to something more euphonious, at least to Russian ears: Nadezhda, Nadya, Nadyenka, which means "hope" in Russian.

The thirty-day deferral I had received was soon over, but the short Soviet war with Japan had ended in the meantime. Japan surrendered unconditionally to the Allies in August, and there was no longer any reason to send troops and officers to the Far East. I was assigned instead to Filtration Camp No. 309 of the Ministry of Internal Affairs (MVD) for Soviet citizens repatriated from enemy territory after the war.[8] And although service with the MVD troops was a moral torment to me, in that camp I once again had the

Moisey at MVD camp, 1946

sense of being useful and worthwhile. With the internees' help we managed in the shortest possible time to construct in an empty field five so-called Quonset huts to house a medical office, a temporary hospital, and an outpatient clinic. The commandant, General Gromov, gave me a positive evaluation for that work, as did the other supervising bodies. I was promoted to senior-lieutenant of the medical service, with a corresponding increase in my salary and living allowance, which proved to be more than ample to feed my family. Three civilian physicians were also assigned to help me.

Despite the strictness of our instructions with regard to the internees, I tried to provide my patients with whatever help was within my power, along with every possible mitigation of the oppressive camp regime.

Two circumstances complicated that effort, however.

The first was the great distance of the camp from my home. On the days when the camp driver did not pick me up, I had to use three different modes of transportation to get there and then walk another two kilometers. Susanna, at her father's urging, had gone to work as a community physician. When she was gone, her mother took care of the baby. Susanna's work was very demanding. On coming home, I would often find notes on the table: "Mozinka, I didn't have a chance to visit patient X at such and such an address. Please see him for me and make a note in his chart." When I got home I would often have to bathe the baby and change her diapers.

The second circumstance was the proximity of the camp's interrogation or SMERSH unit (the acronym comes from the Russian for "Death to Spies"), which had a powerfully adverse effect on me. The unit occupied half of the hut in which the outpatient clinic and my office were located. It had been arranged that way on purpose, so observers would be unable to tell where the internees were going—to the clinic or to "them" for questioning.

The head of the interrogation unit would often engage me in soulful conversation, trying to persuade me to work for them. After each encounter, I was required to sign a statement agreeing not to disclose the content of the conversation or even that it had taken place.

The number of internees gradually dwindled. After a "prophylactic" interrogation, they were all charged with "betrayal of the motherland" and condemned to long sentences, ten years or more, in the "corrective" forced-labor camps of the Gulag. In March 1946, Filtration Camp No. 309 was closed and a Ministry of Internal Affairs scientific research facility was set up in its place. But since the responsible bodies had not cleared me for the facility's top-secret work, I was released from duty and automatically discharged from the Soviet army.

After my discharge, I began a postgraduate internship at the Serbsky Institute of Forensic Psychiatry.[9] The institute's director at the time was T. M. Feinberg, an old Chekist (NKVD officer) and a quarrelsome sow. She had introduced into forensic psychiatry draconian standards and dictatorial discipline, for the violation of which she would without any discussion relieve people from duty and expel them from the institute with a black mark on their records. After completing my internship and without asking the old sow's permission (which would have provoked her furious indignation), I resigned from the institute at the end of 1947 and was assigned by the chief psychiatrist of Moscow, I. K. Yanushevsky, to the October Psychoneurological Clinic as a psychiatrist for the Timiryazev municipal district in the northern part of the city.

My years at the clinic were the most useful and instructive of my psychiatric career. The clinic was headed by one of the most experienced psychiatrists in Russia, Andrei Mikhailovich Barkov, a former *zemstvo* doctor and a veteran of the 1905 Russo-Japanese War.[10] His elderly wife, Anna Gavrilovna, worked in the clinic as a treatment nurse. They had no children or any other relatives. They were both the kindest of people and had devoted their entire lives, not to mention a significant part of their income, to their patients. Andrei Mikhailovich was soft spoken, never lost his temper, never even raised his voice, and never refused his patients' requests. He was a true defender of their interests. He taught us by his whole demeanor and sage advice to "hasten to do good." The most senior psychiatrists in the clinic emulated him in that, especially the eighty-year-old Lev Davidovich Pevzner and Alexander Andreyevich Zurmüller, a German and former student of Emil Kraepelin, the founder of modern psychiatry, and my mentor in mastering the fundamentals of civilian psychiatry.[11] Zurmüller was the only German expert and consultant of standing who had not been expelled by Soviet authorities from Moscow during the war.

After I had assimilated with time the basic principles of the clinic's work, I became more and more popular with the patients. Once my skeptical father-in-law dropped by the clinic incognito and asked the patients in the reception area which doctor would listen to him most carefully and help him. He later admitted the ruse to me and said that when he had asked for the patients' advice about whom he should see, they had all answered that there was a young army fellow there and that he should make an appointment with him.

It should be noted that it took the "young army fellow" a while to master the lessons in "goodness" taught to him by his teachers at that clinic pleasing to God.

I remember one especially instructive lesson. Once an old man of about seventy, a cooper who worked in a tire factory, came to me. He told me that during the war his home had been destroyed by a bomb and that he had found work in a military factory that needed coopers, a skill that had become scarce in the years before the war. Along with work he was given a room on the factory premises. But now instead of military goods the factory, having become a civilian enterprise again, was making tires for cars and no longer needed coopers, who were thus to be evicted from their quarters. Only second-class invalids would be spared.[12] The old man had therefore come to me to obtain a certificate stating that he was ill, unable to work, and in essence a second-class invalid. I started by asking him what his complaints were, expecting him to identify a goodly number of them, but to my surprise he stated that he had none, that he was perfectly healthy, and that his memory was excellent, which he demonstrated by recalling a number of events and dates that many patients his age had long forgotten.

Noting my perplexity and the awkwardness of my situation, the old man said, "Doctor, I see that it will be hard for you to carry out my request. Don't worry about it. If you can't give me a certificate, that's all right. I'll find another way to deal with my situation." He then got up, apologized for taking up my time, and left.

The next day Andrei Mikhailovich called me into his office just before it was time to start receiving patients. "Sit down, my friend. Tell me how your work is going. Are you happy with it?" he gently asked. I thanked him for his interest and added that I was satisfied with everything and very grateful to him for his readiness to answer all my questions, and for the very interesting consultations he had provided, and that it was getting easier with each passing day to work in a treatment facility whose principles and methods were so utterly opposed to what I had been taught at the Serbsky Institute of Forensic Psychiatry.

The wise Andrei Mikhailovich, a smile spreading beneath his thick white mustache, paused for a moment and then replied, "It's true, the principles and methods here are different, but then the Serbsky is in fact a forensic institute. We, however, aren't in the business of judging people. Our task is to treat our patients by word and deed. And by the way, my friend, tell me what happened yesterday with the old patient you saw. Why did you refuse to help him?"

Blushing but failing to see the mistake I had made the day before, I started to explain that I had examined the patient very carefully and asked him many times how he felt and if he had any complaints. He had stubbornly denied having any. I had thus been unable to give him a certificate for second-class invalid status.

"That was a mistake, my friend, a mistake! He had a serious illness, a very serious one." Stammering and blushing even more, I quietly reiterated my assessment and asked him what the patient's illness had been. "Old age, my friend, old age, and the complete absence of a critical awareness of his condition. It never even occurred to him that he could have deceived you, that to attain his goal he could have made up any complaint he wanted. Please, give him the certificate, give it to him, my friend! I'll cosign it."

I have in my subsequent work and in my lectures on psychotherapy spoken to my colleagues and audiences about that lesson taught to me by my truly humane teacher, and about his perceptive understanding of the psychological state of our patients.

It was my good fortune as well to make the acquaintance at the psycho-neurological clinic of two other psychiatrists and scientists who would play a large part in the growth of my psychiatric knowledge and in the shaping of my understanding of the psychological condition of my patients and their treatment. The two were the celebrated, indeed world-famous psychotherapist

Professor Semyon Isidorovich Konstorum, and the founder of the Soviet school of psychological fitness testing and an innovator in the rehabilitation of the mentally ill, Dmitry Evgenievich Melekhov.[13] Both men had been pupils of Professor Pyotr Borisovich Gannushkin, and after Professor Gannushkin's death, assistants of his colleague Professor Tikhon Alexandrovich Geyer.[14]

I once happened to take part in a consultation with Professor Geyer. It concerned a young district doctor whom the department of health had sent to me for an evaluation of her work fitness. The report accompanying the referral contained an account of her strange behavior during house calls. She would write down the details of the anamnesis, or patient's case history, and carefully reflect on them, but when it was time to prescribe medications and other treatments, she would open a therapy manual, retrieve her student notes from her briefcase, look at the manual and notes for a long time, begin to write down her prescriptions and recommendations, but then immediately tear them up and start to cry. She would apologize and say that she had just graduated from medical school and would have to consult with a senior doctor at the clinic and drop off the prescription the next day, along with the medication from the pharmacy. The young doctor's behavior was not only met with astonishment but had even led to complaints about her and requests that she stop making house calls.

Before me sat a young woman with a narrow forehead and long hair combed straight back, bright lipstick, and a childlike face. During our interview she answered all my questions in a formally correct way and then showed me the transcript attached to her diploma in which "good" and "excellent" marks had been entered. In matters pertaining to professional competence, the examining doctor's opinion, diagnosis, if appropriate, and judgment in regard to the subject's fitness had to be submitted to the Medical Review Board for a final decision. On this occasion, the board's representative was Dmitry Evgenievich Melekhov. He interviewed the young doctor in his turn, and sympathizing with my inability to give a clear assessment of her condition, he acknowledged that it was "a very complicated case," that he "was unable to reach a definite conclusion" either, and that "the subject would thus have to be examined by Professor T. A. Geyer and a committee at the Central Institute for Fitness Standards." A week later it fell to me to introduce the young doctor to Professor Geyer and the committee, including Professor Melekhov.

Professor Geyer, a tall old man with a drooping white mustache, asked the young doctor to leave the room after directing two or three questions to her. He then invited each of us to share his opinion. Silence followed. No one dared to start the discussion.

"I don't understand you! Why don't you say anything? I see nothing complicated about this case at all. It's an ordinary instance of oligophrenia or mental retardation. The signs of it are her infantile features, primitive replies, and lack of critical awareness of her condition and the situation in which she finds herself. In reply to my question about how her work was going, she said that it was going well; to the one about whether her patients were satisfied with her, she said that they were; and to the last about what her plans for the future were, she said that she would continue "to work with the same collective." It's clear that she belongs to the category of superficially functional oligophrenics and is unfit for work. Go ahead and write it up."

In response to a committee member's question as to how we were in that case to explain her good and even excellent marks during several years of study at her institute, Tikhon Alexandrovich said, "Even a cow can get good or excellent marks. But to be a good doctor, you have to have a strong intellect, the ability to differentiate between black and white, and a capacity for self-criticism. The person presented to the committee has neither the one, nor the other, nor the third. There's no point in inflicting more torment on her and any patients she might come into contact with. Any further work by her as a doctor could expose her patients to the risk of a misdiagnosis or, Heaven forbid, harmful treatment."

I cite this episode to illustrate not only the brilliant ability of that patriarch of Russian psychiatry, Tikhon Alexandrovich Geyer, to teach with a few well-chosen words the differential diagnosis of disease, but also his humane regard for patient welfare, a regard given primary expression in the ancient maxim, *primum non nocere*—first, do no harm.

The progressive principles of Professor Geyer also guided the most talented of his pupils, but especially his former assistants, Dmitry Evgenievich Melekhov and Semyon Isidorovich Konstorum. The latter was an assimilated Jew whose roots reached back to Holland, although his parents had lived in St. Petersburg. During the First World War, he had served with officer's rank as a military doctor on a hospital train that brought the wounded from the front to hospitals in the rear. After the end of the Civil War in 1921, he was invited to work as a psychotherapist in a private psychiatric clinic run by the husband and wife team of Yu. V. Kannabikh and S. A. Liozner.[15] Soon after the Soviet authorities nationalized all of the country's private medical facilities, the Kannabikh-Liozner clinic was reorganized as Moscow Psychiatric Hospital No. 13 for patients with "borderline" conditions. Semyon Isidorovich was eventually assigned to the Clinic for Work-Fitness Assessment of the Gannushkin Neuropsychiatric Institute. At the same time, Andrei Mikhailovich Barkov asked him to serve as a consultant at the psychoneurological clinic he himself had set up. It was my good luck to meet Semyon Isidorovich there and to study clinical psychotherapy and, in particular, hypnotherapy, under his guidance.

Unlike a great many psychotherapists, Semyon Isidorovich not only protected his patients but also gave them a sense of security. Like a strict father, he taught them to take an active part in the therapeutic process. He never talked down to them, nor indulged in false compliments, nor patronized them, but instead raised them up to his level. Every Sunday he would invite them over for dinner (he invited me too once, and I witnessed what took place). Sitting around the table, they discussed on an equal footing various topics of art and literature. They could speak and ask about anything they wished except their illnesses. Semyon Isidorovich himself had a fine knowledge of painting and encouraged his patients to take up various forms of art. The patients brought examples of their own creative work with them. Sometimes the discussions turned into a showing of pictures and a discussion of their quality and other features. Semyon Isidorovich also organized regular "literary soirées" at the clinic, during which the patients, and sometimes the nurses and other doctors, would read their own work. The organizer of the soirées set the tone and character for the following discussion. Any criticism the discussion might produce always consisted of good-natured advice and calls to continue to create, whatever the artist's mood or state of mind.

Over the many decades since, I have often observed to my colleagues and students that Semyon Isidorovich was not only the teacher but the mentor of an entire cohort of Soviet psychotherapists in the pre-psychopharmacological era when the only medications and therapies in the psychiatric arsenal were bromides, barbiturates (Luminal), Ravkin and Bekhterev preparations, insulin, and electroshock.[16] I will till the end of my days bless the memory of my exacting teacher and mentor, Semyon Isidorovich Konstorum.

Dmitry Evgenievich Melekhov had an equally strong influence on several generations of psychiatrists, and on me especially. Both his grandfathers had been Orthodox priests, and his father had served as the senior priest of the Church of the Transfiguration (Savior on the Bank) in Riazan until the Bolsheviks closed it at the beginning of the 1920s, arrested him, and sent him into permanent exile in Siberia. It is no surprise that Dmitry Evgenievich himself was arrested too in 1923 and then again in 1933 on the charge of "anti-Soviet" religious activity. But he was lucky. Patients of his who occupied high positions in the NKVD interceded for him the second time, and after eight days in the Butyrka transit prison in Moscow he was released and his case dismissed—a great rarity in those years.

Outwardly Dmitry Evgenievich led a Soviet way of life and invariably gave his support to patriotic Soviet activities and events, did not go to church, and left religion out of his discussion of patients and their subsequent fates. Eventually, the authorities trusted him to diagnose the sanity of the imprisoned. His assessments on behalf of the latter were so objective and sound that even the forensic psychiatrists of the Serbsky Institute were compelled to agree with him.

For all that, however, he remained in his heart a believer till the last day of his life. A very limited circle knew about it. To this day I have been unable to determine the signs by which Dmitry Evgenievich guessed that I, like him, had a covert religious life. Once, just before *Yom Kippur* (the Day of Atonement), he called me into his office, switched on the radio, turned on the faucet in his office sink full force, and asked me in a low voice if I happened to know the melody of the *Kol Nidrey* and could find the musical notation for that sacred prayer.[17] After I had sung the prayer against the background of the running water and the voice of the radio announcer, he embraced me. When several days later I told him that, along with the musical notes, there was in the *Jewish Encyclopedia* published at the turn of the century an article by the violinist and composer Mikhail Erdenko on the subject he had asked about, tears welled in his eyes and he whispered, "Never perform services like that for anyone again." It turned out later that he had long had the music and text of the *Kol Nidrey,* and that asking about them had merely been a way of confirming his conjecture about my worldview and trustworthiness. He was never disappointed in regard to the latter, nor did he ever disappoint me. I remained faithful to him till the end of his life, as he did to me. Whenever I needed his support and advice, he always gave them unstintingly. But more about that in due course.

The friendly atmosphere that prevailed in the October Psychoneurological Clinic and the opportunity at any time to obtain expert advice from and consultations with experienced senior doctors nurtured the growth both of my qualifications as a psychiatrist, and my standing among my colleagues and patients and within the local public health organizations. In January 1949 the head of the Timiryazev district department of health, Lyudmila Manosyan, gave me additional employment as the chief doctor of the House of Medical Education. My responsibilities were to provide the area's residents with lectures and colloquia on preventive medicine and the treatment of infectious and other communicable diseases, and to supply the doctors of the district clinics with essential popular literature and offer medodological assistance in the preparation of their own presentations and lectures. I received in that, for me, new and not uncomplicated endeavor a great deal of help from the methodology section of the Institute for Medical Education of the Ministry of Health of the USSR, on whose recommendation I had been assigned the work in the first place. I could have limited myself to carrying out the responsibilities listed above, but as in other instances I wanted to introduce into that sphere of my activities a certain new current or stream. It seemed to me that it would be interesting for the doctors and area residents to see how the work of medicine was reflected in literature and art. I organized a series of lectures by well-known writers, who readily responded to my initiative. I even managed to enlist such celebrated figures as Konstantin Simonov and Ilya Ehrenburg.[18] Thanks to timely announcements and other publicity, those lectures enjoyed great success among the area's residents and attracted a large audience from the Moscow intelligentsia, as well.

All those activities improved the material situation of my family. As a mark of gratitude, former patients employed in the food-distribution networks issued us scarce goods against our ration cards without our having to wait, and provided us with groceries at reduced cost. The Timiryazev Agricultural Academy, several of whose students and instructors were patients of mine, helped me to acquire the land for our out-of-town *dacha* in the village of Kratovo, where thirty apple and other fruit-tree saplings were eventually planted. The academy's deputy director for science also gave me and my family at a discount two vouchers for the academy's spa in the Crimea. It was during that time too that I accepted my first private patients, who paid as much as they were able, although it was often necessary to give them material help, too. Our only daughter was growing and developing well. We could even permit outselves to hire a maid. It seemed that our trials and tribulations had at last come to an end. In any case, there was nothing to suggest that new ordeals might be in the offing. But that prankster Fate would mock me yet again.

A Bureaucratic Odyssey. Khabarovsk. Vladivostok. Korsakov. Yuzhno-Sakhalinsk.

♪♪♪

At the end of November 1949, Susanna and I returned to Moscow after a vacation in the Caucasus and Kislovodsk. Coming home from work a week later I found a letter ordering me to report at once to the local Military Registration and Enlistment Office "with internal passport, service record book, and citations in hand." I reported to the head of the Third Section, a cutthroat named Major Bormotov, who casually tossed my documents into his desk drawer without explanation. I was taken aback. He looked at me with cold, watery gray eyes and intoned in the voice of a judge pronouncing sentence, "By order of the Ministry of Defense of the USSR, you are called back into the Soviet Army. Here are your transit orders. You will proceed to Khabarovsk. There you will present yourself to the headquarters of the Northern Pacific District, where you will be given a uniform and a remittance order for your family and assigned to one of the combat units being formed to assist the fraternal republic of North Korea in its struggle with the southern half. You will receive food vouchers for eight days and a train ticket to Khabarovsk from the military command at Yaroslavsky Station. You have forty-eight hours to settle your affairs. The station commander will inform you of your departure time. Questions? Dismissed."

A black cloud descended over our family. The frantic efforts of my father-in-law and his friends and my friends to put off my departure for a couple of weeks were unsuccessful. On December 8 the Moscow-Khabarovsk train carried me off to my new assignment. I arrived in Khabarovsk on December 15. The duty officer at the station gave me directions to army headquarters. There another officer explained without hesitating that I had been "poorly informed," that the headquarters of the "new army group" was farther on—in Vladivostok. He gave me a rail voucher and I set off again that same evening. Twelve hours later the duty officer on the platform at Vladivostok Station told me the address of the headquarters of the new group, and with a significant little smile wished me luck.

I was received by a navy captain, junior grade. After examining my documents and taking a quick look at my travel orders, he sighed and quietly explained the situation. "I'm afraid I'll have to disappoint you again. I can't execute your orders here in Vladivostok. You'll have to go by ship to Yuzhno-Sakhalinsk" (the regional center of the southern half of Sakhalin Island, which until the end of the war had belonged to Japan).[1] "There you'll report to the commandant of the military hospital, who'll make the final decision about your posting. You'll have to spend a couple of days here at the Chyornaya rechka (Black Creek) assembly point until your ship arrives."

There were many people at the assembly point, including officers who were returning to their duty assignments from leave. I tried to learn what they could tell me about Yuzhno-Sakhalinsk. "It's the capital of Sakhalin," but beyond that they had no interest in continuing the conversation. "Why are you bothering me? You'll go and then you'll see for yourself."

The assembly point was the only structure on the banks of Chyornaya rechka. Despite a severe frost, the creek was rapid and turbulent, although the surrounding terrain was barren. For two weeks we lay on our bunks in idleness and tedium, waiting for the happy day of our departure. Finally, it came—December 31, 1949—and we boarded a Liberty ship obtained by the navy from the United States through Lend-Lease in 1942.[2] Filled with passengers, it set off for South Sakhalin.

No sooner had the ship entered the open sea than it was struck by a powerful gale and started to pitch and roll, tossing us from side to side like matches in a half-empty box. It was impossible to stand or walk. The passenger hammocks in which we took refuge in the absence of bunks swung back and forth with violent force, quickly producing nausea, and many people started to vomit and exhibit other symptoms of severe sea sickness. The ship's captain requested by loudspeaker that any medical personnel on board come to his cabin at once. There were three of us—two nurses and me. Alluding to the Hippocratic oath, the captain observed that we were obliged under the circumstances to provide the passengers with whatever assistance we could. He gave us each a quarter-liter bottle of vodka. "This will help you move around," he said and asked us not to be shy about it but to take a few swigs in his presence. "You'll see. It really will help." He gave me a first-aid kit with tablets for nausea and vomiting, along with special plastic bags to fasten around the neck of each passenger to catch the ejecta. He asked us to distribute the tablets every eight hours and to make the rounds of the passengers every three or four hours and record their condition in a special log. We carried out all the captain's instructions and requests. I am not sure our care helped everyone who was sick, but many did show some improvement.

Finally, after six days of tossing about, our greatly martyred Liberty ship put in late at night at Korsakov, the closest South Sakhalin port. Each of us was then faced with trying to find lodging in one of the city's hotels. The night was very dark. The streets were covered with snowdrifts as tall as a man. The local residents, used to the treacheries of their fierce climate, had adapted to it and wore high, warm, waterproof felt boots. They came out of their one-story dwellings through attic doors and descended to the street by means of specially constructed stairways. Down the center of the snow-clogged streets, narrow passages had been cut along which you could walk. I was still wearing light shoes, which were supposed to have been replaced with boots by the Khabarovsk quartermaster. Naturally, the shoes were soaked. The first three hotels I managed to find had no vacancies. At the last one, the desk clerk advised me "confidentially" to try one nearby called the *Yuzhsakhugol,* an acronym derived from the city name and the Russian word for coal. "They always have bunks," he said with a significant wink.

It took me an hour to reach that "nearby" hotel. Exhausted people were asleep on the lobby floor. I squeezed my way through to the registration window in expectation of some sort of accommodation. Glimmering in me was the hope that since as I was an officer on official Defense Ministry business, there might be a reserved bunk I could use. In front of the window, however, was a piece of cardboard with the words *NO VACANT BUNKS* inscribed in emphatic capitals.

I was so worn out that I decided I could go no farther, whatever the consequences. I propped myself against a wall and was about to fall asleep when I suddenly felt someone tugging on my sleeve. Opening my eyes with effort, I saw a middle-aged woman standing in front of me in a long burgundy velvet robe and a hairnet over her curlers. She was avidly puffing on a cigarette and exhaling clouds of smoke in my direction while staring at me with an astonished smile. "Doctor! What are you doing here?" she asked in a raspy voice. Rubbing my sleep-filled eyes, I replied, "I'm doing what everybody else is doing. But how did you know I was a doctor?"

"How did I know?!" she rasped, exhaling another stream of smoke. "Why, you saved my life on the ship. You gave me medicine and came by several times to see how I was. Without you I'd have given up my soul to God!" And then she turned away and started to rap on the window next to the piece of cardboard with its dispiriting words. The window abruptly opened, revealing the angry, sleepy face of the night clerk.

"Damn it, again?! What a . . ." she started to snarl, but then on seeing who had dared to violate her sweet slumber, she asked a bit more calmly, "Well, what's happened?"

"What's happened? What's happened? Why hasn't the doctor been given a bunk?" the woman in the robe said, pointing her half-smoked cigarette in my direction.

"What are you talking about? Are you crazy? Didn't you see that there aren't any?"

"What do you mean, there aren't any? In our room, only four have been taken. The fifth one's empty. Register him at once or I'll write up a complaint against the crowd of you!"

"All right, but that bunk's for a woman!"

"Well, so what if it is? He's not going to impregnate the bunk!" the stranger replied, puffing away.

"All right! Bring me a note that your roommates have no objection and then leave me alone!" the clerk said and slammed the window shut.

Five minutes later the woman came back with a note in her hand and rapped on the window again. It opened and my savior handed over the note, along with ten rubles—payment for three nights. After obtaining a receipt, she turned to me with a look of triumph and said, "Grab your suitcase and come with me!"

When we entered the room, three women dressed in velvet robes just like their leader's were sitting round a table playing cards. Stopping their game, they turned to look at me with frank curiosity, as if wondering what new adventure she had gotten them into. They proved to be a team of purchasing agents for the commercial department of the South Sakhalinsk coal combine, which owned the hotel.

"All right, then," their "commander" said as she entered the room, "don't just sit there. Can't you see that the man, our doctor, is barely alive and soaked through? Get his shoes and socks off at once!" she said, motioning with her head to one of the woman sitting at the table; and then to another, "Get a basin of hot water. Hopefully, he'll be all right by morning." She herself got busy with the table. She gathered up the cards, tossed them on the couch, and covered the table with a white cloth.

I warmed my feet and then dried them with the towel I had been given. Next to me lay long white woolen socks and warm fleece-lined slippers, probably from the supplies the women had procured for their bosses, I could not help but think. I put the slippers on with a feeling of tremendous gratitude.

"My name's Varvara Koptyaeva. Just call me Varya, for short," their leader said, and then pointing to each of the others, she added, "This is Polina, this is Tanya, and this one who brought you everything is Dusya and a sweetheart. Now sit down at the table and we'll have some tea."

"No, no, Doctor, don't believe her! It's our boss who's the sweetheart. She just seems gruff. She takes in all the stray cats. As you yourself may already have noticed."

Warmed with a couple of shots of cognac, something to eat, and the kindness of those four women, I gave them a brief account over tea of who I was and how and why I had turned up there. And they, in general terms, told me about themselves. None of them had come to Sakhalin from a good, easy life. No one had forced them to change their warm places of permanent residence in European Russia, but each of them had experienced some misfortune or bitter event from which she had fled wherever her eyes had taken her in order to change her woman's lot and forget.

"And now to bed!" their boss ordered. "Don't be shy!" she said to me. "We'll go out in the hallway for a few minutes. Get in bed. The sheets are clean and . . . Good night!"

When I awoke the next morning, the four of them had already left. After a hot shower, I sat down at the table before a steaming samovar and various things to eat covered with a paper napkin. Written on the napkin was a note: "Doctor! Have breakfast and don't be shy about it. It's all paid for with state funds. Our combine is rich. Don't go anywhere. We're out on business and will be back soon."

They returned toward evening, their cheeks rosy from the cold, and like old friends asked me how my day had gone and shared with me their own interesting news. "The snow will be removed in a few days. Tractors and a grader will be out on the streets tomorrow. They'll clear a wide path and automobile traffic will resume. We called the hospital—forgive us, since it was without your permission. They know us there. A car will come for you tomorrow."

The next morning the driver sent by the hospital knocked on the door and came into the room. He had breakfast with us. The women and I parted warmly. A few hours later I was standing in the office of the hospital commandant, a Colonel Koshik of the medical service, although I don't remember his first name. He gazed searchingly at me with a sharp-eyed squint over glasses resting on a long, broad nose. After looking me over from head to toe, he said in a friendly voice, "Well, sit down, sit down! What have you got to say for yourself?" And looking at my assignment order, he continued, "Well, what have you got to say for yourself, Avrom . . . and . . . Moishe Shloymovich? Ho-ho!" Colonel Koshik added with an amused smile, before continuing our chat. I briefly told him the story of my assignment to his command for the continuation of my military service and asked him what I should expect. "Well, as for the 'newly formed army group' and North Korea, we'll have to wait and see—until May," he grinned. "Until then, you'll have to serve here with us, since navigation has ended for the season. I'll see you again tomorrow and then we'll make a decision."

On the transfer order lying in front of him he wrote in a bold hand, "To quartermaster: a dormitory billet, an allowance, and uniforms. Rank: senior-lieutenant," signing it "Koshik" in a scrawl. And then he returned the order to me and said, "Well, good luck! If there's anything, let me know. I'll help in any way I can."

I thanked him and went to look for the quartermaster. It took about an hour to obtain everything that Colonel Koshik had written on the transfer order. Well fed and dressed in an appropriate uniform, Senior-Lieutenant A.-M. Shloymovich went to find his dormitory billet. It was in the semi-basement of the hospital, the only one in Yuzhno-Sakhalinsk and a five-story brick structure solidly built by the Japanese. There were, in addition to me, nineteen other doctors in the dormitory, all of them Jews. I tried to find out from them what fate had brought us all to the same place, but it was not a topic they were inclined to dwell on. All the same, they briefly shared what they knew about the main point.

"Another hundred and fifty like ourselves have passed through this hospital. All have been assigned to various medical units on Sakhalin. Stay here a while and you'll hear about the rest of it . . . from others."

The next morning I was called in by the hospital commandant. Since I was in uniform, I addressed him in the prescribed way: "I report as ordered."

"My goodness, why so formal? How did you sleep? Are you settled in? Sit down," he said. Receiving positive answers to all his questions, he returned to our previous conversation. "Your affairs are coming together very nicely. The head of the medical department of the Northeastern Military District agrees with me that you should be assigned to our hospital as a psychiatrist. The psychiatric ward is run by Major Vladimir Viktorovich Morozov of the medical service, a very kind but unfortunate man. We put in a request to the Main Military Medical Administration for another psychiatrist some time ago. So you'll be assigned to work here," Colonel Koshik concluded, rubbing his hands together. "Don't disappoint me!" he said as he picked up the phone.

"Vladimir Viktorovich! It's all been taken care of! I've made the arrangements. I'm giving you an excellent psychiatrist. Send a sleigh for him every day, here and back. Good, then!" And with that brief instruction, he hung up and wrote down on a slip of paper the Yiddish phrase *zay gezunt* ("be healthy" or "farewell") and handed it to me. "Read it and give it back!" Then, lighting a match, he burned the paper and said in a loud voice, "Carry out your orders! Dismissed!"

The next morning a rickety one-horse sleigh took me in thirty minutes to the derelict village of Vladimirovka and its two or three buildings belonging to the municipal health department. The driver, a patient with an expressionless face and squinty eyes with frozen pupils who had apparently been released for outpatient treatment but was homeless, told me with relish the story of how the "military ward" had turned up in the village "loony bin." After ill soldiers had set fire to the wooden building in which the hospital's psychiatric ward had originally been housed, the regional public health department had provided a floor and fifty beds in one of its own buildings for servicemen with mental disorders. "The locals are on the first floor, and the military people are on the second. They're all treated by a military doctor and a young woman. The doctor's wife and three of his children died in the 1948 earthquake in Ashkhabad.[3] His youngest daughter survived, but she has a defect—a harelip," he said, finishing his account.

Dr. Morozov greeted me guardedly, even warily, with feigned indifference, as it seemed to me. But after we had made his rounds together and he had listened to my comments regarding the psychological state of the servicemen being evaluated, he nodded in agreement and warmed up a bit. In the evening we returned to the city in the same sleigh and exchanged a few words about the peculiarities of the Sakhalin climate, the weather, and the frequent fires to which the city's wooden houses were susceptible. "That never happened under the Japanese." Noticing my surprise, he briefly explained. "Japanese women don't work in the winter. They stay home and keep a sharp eye on their little iron stoves, the only source of heat in their homes. Except for invalids and nursing mothers, our women rush off to work and forget about the stoves, which overheat and start fires. Stay here a while and you'll see what I mean."

The sleigh stopped in front of his house. He invited me to come in for a home-cooked supper. I didn't dare refuse. We were met by three representatives of the female sex. The youngest was a girl of eight or nine waiting by the door with a face just like her father's. As soon as she saw Dr. Morozov, she jumped up like a little puppy, grabbing his neck with her little arms and hiding her face in his unbuttoned quarter-length fur coat. He kissed her, smoothed her long, silken hair, and patiently, without moving, stood in the doorway while she slowly lowered herself onto the carpet covering the wooden floor.

Next a smiling older woman came over to us—a typical "good-hearted nanny" between sixty and sixty-five. "This is our guardian angel, Anastasia Leonidovna, who was the senior nurse in our ward. After she retired, she came to live with us to help out, look after the house, and help raise Nadyenka," he said with a heavy sigh.

The last to be introduced was a young woman of about twenty-five who stood next to a chair shifting her weight from one foot to the other with an anxious smile on her lightly daubed lips. Her simple dress emphasized the sleek lines of her well-proportioned figure. She gripped the back of the chair with one hand and was clearly torn between coming over to us and waiting for us to come over to her. "And this," my host said, indicating her with his hand, "is our intern, Dr. Borisova" (I've forgotten her first name). "She'll return to the ward in a week after her vacation. You can be a great help to her. You can share your experience and teach her clinical psychiatry," my host added, finishing the introductions.

Dr. Borisova held out her hand in a welcoming gesture and invited us to take our seats at the table, which was already set, and then poured a glass of red wine for everyone and proposed a toast in honor of "new acquaintances and friendship." Refusing to sit down, the former senior nurse, Anastasia Leonidovna, instead served us a delicious first course of Siberian *pelmeni* and other examples of her culinary skill.[4] Nadyenka ate several *pelmeni* but remained silent the whole time and didn't look at us, and then, apparently offended by something, got up and went out to the kitchen. An awkward silence followed. Vladimir Viktorovich tried to tell a story about something, but the conversation never recovered. After supper he walked me to the hospital dormitory, which was nearby. We walked slowly without saying anything. Finally, he broke the silence. He apologized for not telling me earlier about his "family situation." "I think you've already guessed that it's complicated," he said before continuing.

"Perhaps I shouldn't be telling you this, but since I hope you won't mind continuing our friendship, I think it will be good for you to know . . . a few things about my relationship with the . . . young woman," he said haltingly, choosing his words with care. He told me that after graduating from the Khabarovsk Medical Institute, Dr. Borisova had been assigned to the Sakhalin Ministry of Health. Afraid that she might be sent to the interior, she had asked the hospital commandant to hire her in any capacity he wished and promised to "serve faithfully and to be useful." Colonel Koshik, having no right to hire civilians without an official transfer from the local department of health, called the appropriate office and suggested that she be assigned to the civilian psychiatric ward that, as mentioned above, was located in the same building as the military one. Having no experience at all, Dr. Borisova turned to Vladimir Viktorovich for help several times a day. After a month, she announced that she had fallen in love with him and proposed that they get married. Lonely and depressed as he was, he agreed but suggested that she move in with him without formalizing the marriage in order to be sure they were "compatible in every way." She moved in at once, sharing his bed from the first night and calling him by his pet name, "Volodya," in front of everybody. Nadyenka and Anastasia Leonidovna, who had become like a mother to the girl, not only did not accept the newcomer but openly expressed their dislike. As a result, the atmosphere in the family had became more and more strained, and it was for that reason that Vladimir Viktorovich had asked me not to deny him the "courtesy" of visiting their home frequently. I was thus in spite of myself drawn into all the difficulties faced by that unhappy family. In the ward, Dr. Borisova began to accompany me on my daily rounds, asking for instruction on how to prepare an anamnesis, precisely describe a psychiatric condition, do a differential diagnosis, and so on. She would demand an elaborate reply to every question, express her gratitude in the most effusive way, and complain about her fate.

After I had spent fifteen or twenty evenings in the company of Dr. Morozov's family, Dr. Borisova asked "Volodya," who had had a tiring day, to lie down and rest and let her escort me back to the dormitory instead. We walked silently for several minutes and then she said, "Why are you so indifferent to me? Don't you want to know why I married a man thirty years older than I am and have moreover taken on the responsibility of his deformed daughter?"

And without waiting for a reply, she started to complain about her hard life, about Dr. Morozov's weakness and passivity, and about the fact that he did not satisfy her "in any way." Might I advise her what to do? I replied that I was a very poor counselor and that she would, as a fully rational person, have to solve her unofficial family problems on her own. We parted coldly. For a long time afterward I wondered about what had prompted her to embark on the adventure she had, and then to be so frank about herself without any inhibition. If she had supposed that I would report the substance of her confession to her spouse, she was deeply mistaken, for it was and is against my rule to pass on anything that might inflict additional trauma on an unhappy person. It would unexpectedly become clear a year later just how sinister a role the intern Borisova had been playing in the life of the unfortunate Major Vladimir Viktorovich Morozov on behalf of "competent authorities."

In order to spend less time in that unhappy home, I suggested to Dr. Morozov that I start making official trips to the field units in his place, since the trips were physically and mentally exhausting for him. He readily agreed and I started to acquaint myself with the severe conditions of the North Sakhalin climate and its psychological affect on the officers and men. But, astonishingly enough, those trips were not tiring for me. I always returned refreshed and enriched with vital new experience. It is impossible, however, to give a full account here of Sakhalin, of my service in the hospital's psychiatric ward, and of my various experiences in the region, so I will instead limit myself to two clinical episodes of a kind that I had seen neither before Yuzhno-Sakhalinsk, nor after in my long experience as a psychiatrist. As I mentioned, one hundred and fifty Jewish doctors had passed through the semi-basement of the hospital dormitory. Because of the severe winter conditions, another twenty had, like me, gotten stuck there. Obviously, none of us was eager to serve even in nearby military units, let alone in more remote areas. But realizing that protesting or refusing to follow the orders of the Defence Ministry could have grave consequences, including a long prison term, we were all prepared to serve wherever we might be posted.

There was, however, one defiant exception among us, an Odessan with the queer last name of Tsenopay, a decorated veteran who had even marched into Berlin with the Soviet army. From the very beginning of his new "folktale existence," as he called his life in the hospital dormitory, he engaged almost daily in extravagant behavior (and especially for a doctor) that filled everyone around with dismay. The dormitory doctors called him a *tsedreyter* ("crackpot" in Yiddish). Either he would come into the treatment room in the middle of the night in only his underpants and a shirt and demand that all the nurses and orderlies come "at once" to give him a glass of wine, or, on the contrary, he would himself bring a bottle of vodka and order them all to drink it. His nocturnal escapades would always end in rows with several orderlies forcibly returning him to his bed. After each incident, the hospital commandant would call him on the carpet and try to persuade him to put an end to the rowdy scenes and histrionics "for his own good." But none of kind Colonel Koshik's remonstrations had the least effect, and Tsenopay would frankly declare, "I'll drive them to the point where they'll send me back to dear old Odessa," ending that bit of bravado with a few lines of the sailor's heroic ditty, "You're an Odessan, Mishka."

Once after a local medical conference, the major general (I've forgotten his name) in charge of military medical administration for the region summoned Major Morozov and me to the commandant's office. The general had heard about the Odessan's antics at the conference and wanted to ask us if we knew "the military doctor Tsenopay" and what our assessment of him was. Vladimir Viktorovich answered that he had heard about him but had never seen him. I added that I saw him in the evenings but only found out about the rows the next morning and of course had never witnessed one. The general gave orders for the Odessan to be brought to him. Shortly thereafter the latter burst into the room with his tunic unbuttoned and no cap and yelled, "By your most exalted order, Mishka Yaponets reports."[5]

Astounded by those completely unexpected words, the general leapt to his feet, his eyes bulging and mouth agape, and for several seconds stood speechless. Colonel Koshik sprang to his feet too, pressed the button for the guard, and started to shout, "How dare you! Hooligan! Hooligan! Enough clowning! Kindness you don't appreciate! To the guardhouse then. You'll . . . come to your senses soon enough there!"

The guards came running, reported, and awaited further orders. The general had recovered in the meantime, and turning to the commandant he said, "Let the guards wait outside while we have a talk with this hool . . . We'll figure out just what sort of bird has flown into our nest." And he ordered the Odessan to sit. The latter moved a chair over to the general, flopped down on it, and asked for a cigarette. "What's your last name?" the general asked him.

"Yaponets," the Odessan calmly replied.

"What? What? Comrade Colonel, you told me his name was Tsenopay!"

"Quite right, Comrade General! That's what it says in his documents."

"But it's the same thing!" the Odessan interrupted in complete seriousness. With a roguish grin, he took a pencil and paper from his pocket and in capitals wrote the word *TSENOPAY*. Handing the piece of paper to the general he said, "Now, Comrade General, read it Yiddish-style from right to left. What do you get? Yaponets! See? It wasn't me. It wasn't me! Yaponets-Tsenopay was the work of my grandfather, my grandfather! During my circumcision! He was afraid of what would happen if I got called up into the service. He knew what to do.

My grandfather knew what to do," the grandson said, chortling in delight as he explained the transformation of his awkward last name.

"Why as an adult do you now wish to disgrace your grandfather?"

"Disgrace him? Not at all! It's you who are disgracing his heroic grandson! If you don't believe me, I can prove it to you right now." And jumping up from his chair, he started to unbutton his fly.

The general's reaction was instantaneous and together with the colonel he started to shout, "Guards! Guards! Report at once!" The guards ran into the room. "To the guardhouse with him! To the garrison guardhouse with him, the scoundrel! Until further notice from me!" the general ordered.

Yaponets was led away. A moment of silence followed. We all sat there looking at the floor. I was ashamed that within our brotherhood of Jews and doctors there could be such rogues, whom neither Sholem Aleichem nor any contemporary satirist could have invented. For there was something oddly calculated about his behavior. The general and Colonel Koshik, agitated and embarrassed, finally turned to Major Morozov and me. "He should be sent to you, Comrade Major, for a forensic psychiatric evaluation, and then it will be clear how we ought to proceed," the general testily observed.

"A ruling by a military prosecutor or magistrate would be required for such an evaluation. The only thing within your and our competence would be a military medical evaluation to determine his fitness for duty," my immediate superior quietly noted, while trying not to look the general in the eye. I nodded in agreement.

"What would be needed for that?" Colonel Koshik asked. "An order sending him to you, Vladimir Viktorovich? If so, I'm ready to sign it at once. Your psychiatric opinions?"

My superior gently prodded me with his elbow, as if to say, "Your turn."

"Allow me to express my own view. I think that to transfer the doctor for a military medical examination is the correct decision. But, for many reasons, not to us. Whether we like it or not, he's our colleague. He and I share the same lodging. We run into each other at meetings. He'll be within his rights to claim that any evaluation we produce was not objective but made under pressure from our superiors. I therefore suggest that it would make more sense to transfer him to the central military hospital in Vladivostok or Khabarovsk, including with the transfer the required documents and recommendations."

Colonel Koshik agreed, and the general said, "So be it! I'll transmit the order tomorrow!" And touching his hand to his general's Astrakhan hat, he said goodbye and left.

Information later reached us that the Khabarovsk military medical board had determined that Tsenopay was a sociopath "fit for service in war but not in peacetime." What his subsequent fate was, I am unable to say.

The other clinical observation that bears telling is even more interesting in its essence and for the results of the military assessment carried out in our psychiatric ward.

Around the beginning of March 1950, a certain Major Danilenko (I have forgotten his first name) was sent to us for a psychiatric evaluation on the orders of the commander of a combat unit stationed in the South Sakhalin town of Kholmsk. An addendum to the transfer order stated that Major Danilenko, born in 1918, was a disciplined, highly qualified officer who had received many military honors and who enjoyed the respect of his superiors, comrades, and subordinates. "He is devoted to the cause of Marx, Engels, Lenin, and Stalin. There are no demerits or reprimands in his service record."

Our evaluation determined that Major Danilenko was physically fit, had not in the past sought the help of a neuropathologist or psychiatrist, had no history of mental illness in his family, and had no particular complaints. He had, however, been sent to the hospital under military escort on the orders of his regimental commander for an assessment of his psychological state, since he had recently grown very suspicious, claiming that his wife had been unfaithful to him and tried to poison him, and that she was having an affair with the regimental deputy commander of the political section, whom she wished to marry.

During the initial interview and every subsequent one, Major Danilenko remained calm, without extraneous affects, and confirmed everything that had been set down in his medical evaluation, even adding that he had further proof of the malicious intentions of his wife and her lover and was willing to submit to "any examination or other test. That's necessary first of all for me personally. The fate of both my marriage and my military career depend on it." With regard to the events that were the basis of his commander's suspicions about his mental health, Major Danilenko had this to say.

He had been married five years. For undetermined reasons there had been no pregnancy. His wife had insisted that he continue his military service on Sakhalin Island, claiming that the climate there was very good for conception and a full-term pregnancy. (There really was such an idea, and many infertile young women moved there as a result.) From their very first days on Sakhalin his wife had frequently gone out in the evening on various pretexts. Soon afterward he had noticed that the beverages he drank tasted bitter. In response to his questions about it, his wife replied, "I have no idea. Perhaps it's just your imagination." The laboratory to which he had turned refused to test the beverages, since it was not authorized to do so. Meanwhile, rumors had begun to circulate in his unit that he had lost his mind and was planning to kill his wife and his rival.

In order to find out the truth, he started to examine his wife's mail and to look for evidence in the places where she kept important documents. He found a note that said, "Tomorrow at 10:00 a.m. at your place." He left for work in the morning as he always did. At 10:20 he returned home and looked in the window. After assuring himself that a rival was indeed in the house, he quietly opened the door and caught them in bed together. It was the deputy commander of the political section. Wishing to avoid a row, he suggested that the latter leave the apartment at once. But his wife started to scream and called the regimental commander, asking him to send a soldier right away, since she was afraid that her husband was going to kill her. The deputy commander of the political section had already reported that Major Danilenko often beat his wife, since he was convinced that she was unfaithful to him. The commander sent two officers with the transfer order in hand, and they brought Major Danilenko directly to the military hospital for an assessment of "his fitness for military service."

Careful observation of Major Danilenko's behavior in the psychiatric ward and in daily conversation with him disclosed no pathologies or impairment in his thinking, critical faculties, or awareness. He behaved modestly. Unlike the majority of our patients he carefully observed all the rules of hygiene. He regularly read newspapers and books. He could sensibly discuss their content. He went to bed and got up on time. He slept well.

In order to obtain objective information from Kholmsk, his wife was called in. She turned out to be primitive, fearful, and poorly educated. She gave confused answers to all our questions. When Dr. Morozov said to her, "Tell the truth. When did your romance with the deputy commander of the political section begin?" she started to cry, fell on her knees, and implored us, "Only don't tell him or he'll leave me." She confirmed everything that we had been told by her unfortunate husband. We accordingly declared him "sound and fit for military service with no limitations whatsoever" and he returned to duty.

The time in South Sakhalin passed quickly. Spring arrived. The snow melted. Impassable puddles appeared on the streets. It rained hard and dense gray clouds covered the sky, bringing with them a melancholy mood.

In the meantime, however, my family had not been sitting quietly on their hands. Susanna and her relatives and friends had been doing everything possible to bring me back to Moscow. During one of our phone conversations, she passed on encouraging news. She had met with the head of the Main Military Medical Administration, and he had promised that at the first opportunity, namely, the appearance of a vacancy corresponding to my medical specialty, he would transfer me from the Northern Pacific Military District back to his own command. Soon after that, toward the end of May, Colonel Koshik, that kindest of men, called me in and with unfeigned sadness informed me that he had received a telegram transferring me to the Main Military Medical Administration. "It's a shame, of course. My superiors and I had been planning to retire Major Morozov and appoint you in his place. But in the army, the orders of a superior may not be questioned. I wish you good luck. You'll get your documents from the quartermaster." Embracing me in farewell, he asked me if I remembered the note he had handed to me on our first acquaintance. I thanked him and repeated the words he had written in it. It was the last I saw of him.

I arrived in Moscow on May 30, 1950, to be reunited with my beloved family. But alas it would not be for long.

A Bright Beam of Light in the Kingdom of Darkness

♪♪♪

I reported the next day to the Main Military Medical Admistration for further orders. The duty officer informed his superior of my arrival. The latter appeared shortly afterward and informed me that I would be given a month's leave, at the end of which I would be required to report for a new assignment. I returned home with mixed feelings. On the one hand, I would have a break. After Sakhalin and the daily shuttle by sleigh from Yuzhno-Sakhalinsk to Vladimirovka and back, the evenings with Vladimir Viktorovich's troubled family, the official trips to the North Sakhalin interior, and the gloom of the frequent burning of the city's wooden houses (there were rumors that the residents set the fires themselves to obtain better and safer lodging)—after all that I had experienced on Sakhalin, the prospect of spending a month with my family was unquestionably an occasion for joy, a bright beam of light in my life as it was then. But on the other hand, the uncertainty about what would follow, about where at the end of my leave I would be sent to "serve my homeland," filled me and my family with unease. All our attempts to clarify the situation were unavailing. The general anxiety even infected our five-year-old daughter, who with tears in her eyes pleaded with me not to go away again for so long.

During that interval a sad event occurred. My beloved teacher Semyon Isidorovich Konstorum suddenly passed away. There was an enormous crowd of mourners at the cemetery—his relatives, dozens of former students, and numerous grateful and now orphaned patients for whom he had become, as I indicated earlier, a dear family member. Many wept. I, along with my former colleagues and friends at the clinic, stood for a long time by his coffin in silence. Forgetting our own adversities, we sadly contemplated the impermanence of life and its glories.

My leave slipped by imperceptibly, as if the Main Military Medical Administration had forgotten about me. Nevertheless, at the end of June I was ordered to present myself again for my new assignment. I was received by the deputy commander, Colonel Valery Yurievich Novak. After a few perfunctory questions, he informed me that "in view of the poor health of your daughter and the persistent entreaties of your wife, the command has decided to send you to the headquarters of the Don Military District in Rostov for a dual assignment as the chief specialist in military flight evaluation and head district psychiatrist. They're expecting you. The first duty opened up a month ago. A selection of candidates will be presented to the district flight schools. You'll show there what you're capable of. Here are your orders and a rail voucher. You must report in Rostov by June 4. I advise you to take your family with you."

Giving advice is fine, but as Grandfather Yeruchim liked to say, "*Oyf a fremd toches iz gut tsu tantsn*" ("It's easy to dance on somebody else's bottom"). There were many serious objections to my following Colonel Novak's advice, but the main one was stated by my father-in-law, Moishe-Boaz: "Rostov-on-Don isn't Sakhalin, of course. You're one day away by train. But who can guarantee that they won't send for you tomorrow and bring you back again? The army isn't your *tachles* (goal). You need to get your discharge. If Susanna moves to Rostov, you never will. But do as you think best." There was a good deal of truth in what he said, except for one thing: separation is never good. But Susanna herself had no desire to leave the city in which she had spent most of her adult life.

And so I set off alone.

I arrived in Rostov early the next morning. Illuminated by the still merciful early morning sun, everything gleamed, and with a fresh summertime fragrance, too. The city had started to recover from its war wounds and become healthier and more vigorous.

The chairman of the military medical board for the Don Military District, Colonel Shcherbina, was an older man with a perpetual smile and a fondness for cards. Like his three adjutants, all of them colonels too, he had served in his post for twenty-five years and was now dreaming of retiring to his comfortable Rostov apartment for a well-deserved rest with a full pension and all the perquisites enjoyed by former officers. The four colonels greeted me skeptically. My low rank of senior-lieutenant, my young age (twenty-eight versus their sixty to sixty-five), my insignificant experience in the areas of military flight evaluation and especially in general civilian and military psychiatry—all that provoked not merely surprise but even undisguised resentment.

The vice-chairman of the board, a certain Yakov Zakharevich Kipperstein, was particularly indignant. Every day under the guise of instruction, he would stress that the district military medical board was the supreme arbiter of the correctness of any judgments about the health and fitness of those drafted into military service or about to be discharged. He warned me several times that the task of the evaluator was a highly responsible one and was to be based on two decrees of the Ministry of Defense with an appended list of defects. The list had to be memorized by every evaluator. Especially important was the decree regarding the fitness of aviation candidates in the various branches of the service. Moreover, that decree was secret and it was necessary to know how to apply it. Our discussions ended with my being given three weeks to absorb the wisdom of the medical and air force testing protocols. The other members of the district board treated me coldly and said nothing.

Three weeks later I was examined in the presence of the full membership of the military medical board of the Don Military District and a representative of the regional department of health. The results weren't disclosed, but after it was over, Colonel Shcherbina, who chaired the examination, said with the smile that never left his face, "A fine job! Next week you'll take an extended trip to a camp for flight-school candidates."

"Yes, sir!" I replied, touching my right hand to the bill of my cap. Judging by his ever-widening smile, he was satisfied. From that time on, the attitude of the board's other old warriors grew more tolerant too.

The usual lodging problem had also been solved. It was particularly hard then to find a place in Rostov, which, having changed hands at least three times during the war, had been largely destroyed, and even in 1950 was still under reconstruction. But I was lucky. Learning that I was looking for a apartment, the same Colonel Kipperstein said after one of our "amiable" chats that a widowed relative of his had a large room for rent next door to the board on Nakhichevansky Lane. He gave me a brief letter of introduction and urged me to go see her. As a result I acquired not only a large, elegant, well-furnished room, but also many wonderful Armenian and Russian friends who lived in the building in two-room apartments of the same kind. The whole time I lived there, they looked after me, vying to see who would be first to offer various kinds of help. I continued to correspond with some of them long after I left. They all deserve individual description, but that would add appreciably to what has already become a large manuscript.

I gradually entered the round of military medical and especially flight evaluation and the various problems it presented. My first test, passed with distinction, was an assessment of aviators who were to be launched from a device that imitated the acceleration of a jet plane. The assessment was carried out in field conditions near the town of Bataisk. The flight-school commander conveyed his appreciation to me and to my immediate superiors, as well.

Soon afterward, around the beginning of August, I was sent to another flight school to chair a special board for examining conscripts who wanted to become military aviators. The board consisted of five civilian doctors of different specializations. The conclusions of each were turned over to me, and after summarizing them I issued the final determination regarding the fitness (or lack thereof) for flight school of each examinee, utilizing the special secret decree and appended list of defects. That work was carried out in field conditions too in a restricted zone in the steppe not very far from Stalingrad. Each doctor and the nurse assisting him lived and worked in a separate tent. I had a slightly smaller one to myself.

That work lasted a month.

I recall that period of my service with pleasure and have come to realize that it had an important meaning for me. I felt myself needed again and was able to show my organizational skills, since I directed a diverse group of doctors and nurses that month and was able without any misunderstandings to manage the complex practical and other issues faced by the medical staff and by me. For that work I received a commendation from the commander of the Don Military District.

The biggest test for me, however, was an official vist to the Stalingrad Military Registration and Enlistment Office to examine the medical records of the next class of Soviet army conscripts. The difficulty lay in the fact that I, a mere senior-lieutenant, was obliged to review the work of the Volga Military District commissar, the distinguished Major General Anatoly Vasilievich Stavenkov, an old warrior and defender of Stalingrad.[1] The disparity in rank resulted in complications that I was unable to resolve on my own, forcing me to call my superior in Rostov and ask for his assistance and advice. But the trip also brought much joy unconnected to my military duties.

Stalingrad had been completely rebuilt after the war, becoming vastly richer and more beautiful. The old wooden structures had been replaced with large multi-story brick buildings. The streets had been decorated with landscaped medians, and boulevards and parks had been added, along with magnificent sculptures and other monuments honoring the heroes of the great battle that had taken place in the city.

I had the pleasure in Stalingrad of visiting both the Mogilevskys and the Kasatkins, whom I had not seen since Kazan. After helping to reorganize the Stalingrad Medical Institute, Emil Ruvimovich Mogilevsky was again head of its Department of Clinical Medicine and also the chief of therapy for the regional department of health. Sergey Nikolaevich Kasatkin was head of the Department of Anatomy, just as before. The fates of their children were various. Irina Kasatkina had married and moved to Moscow. Emil Ruvimovich's son Ruva, with whom I had shared the Kazan apartment before leaving for Moscow, had graduated from the Kazan State Medical Institute and was now working in Stalingrad as an instructor in the Department of Introductory Diagnostics. He had, as planned, married his childhood sweetheart, Tatyana Afinogenova, and moved into his parents' luxurious apartment. There a son was born.

During her pregnancy, Tanya's relationship with her mother-in-law had grown increasingly rancorous, with the result that after the baby was born her breast milk dried up and she fell into a reactive depression. My visit coincided with the apogee of that conflict and Tanya's illness. She and Ruva were very glad to see me. They told me all about the oppressive atmosphere that had emerged in the family and blamed the petty despotism of Ruva's mother, from which the oldest family member, Emil Ruvimovich, also suffered in silence. By chance I happened to hear of a small one-family dwelling being rented for a pittance. Ruva was very glad to hear about it, and together we went for a look. He liked it and so did Tanya. The next day the young couple and their baby moved to the new residence with my help in transporting their belongings. When Ruva's mother discovered that I had been behind the move, she got terribly angry and declared that she did not want to know me anymore or see me in her home again.

Although I received no commendation from General Stavenkov on that visit to the Stalingrad Military Registration and Enlistment Office, the commander of the Don Military District and Colonel Shcherbina approved my report on the reorganization of the activities of the municipal military board and the other boards in the Stalingrad region.

My successes were regarded with some ambivalence by the other officers, the old warriors of the district military medical board. On the one hand, they were happy to be relieved of the burden of those official trips, of which they had long since grown tired, but on the other hand, the fact that I had become a prominent figure on the board, and that Colonel Shcherbina had been giving me more and more of the assignments he had once given them, inclined them to take a suspicious view of my activities and perhaps even to regard them with envy. More problematic, however, was my relationship with the head of the Department of

Neurology of the Rostov military hospital, Vitaly Alexeyevich Kulashkin, a gray-haired intellectual colonel who, like me, was serving out his military obligation. Before my arrival, the duties of regional psychiatrist had fallen to him; after it, they fell to me, in accordance with the order of the Main Military Medical Administration. I was required once a week to visit the borderline psycho-neurological patients subject to evaluation or treatment in his department, and to verify the quality of the treatment and its documentation (the patients' charts and the certification of any disorders that might affect decisions about their continued military service). Despite all my efforts to respect the authority of both the department head and the staff physician, Major Dolunyan, their attitude toward me remained one of indifference, if not ill-concealed disdain.

And then an extraordinary thing happened. A certain Captain Mayorchik had been undergoing treatment in their department for more than a month. Professor Karganov, the head of the Department of Psychiatry of the Rostov Medical Institute, had been asked to assist with the diagnosis. He concluded that Captain Mayorchik was suffering from mild depression and did not need to be transferred to a psychiatric hospital. And, in fact, toward the end of his stay at the military hospital, the patient did seem to be making significant progress. The department head was thus ready to discharge him and grant him medical leave, although a final consultation with another psychiatrist would be needed first. The head of the local psychiatric clinic, with whom I had an excellent relationship, just as I did with the rest his colleagues, was away from the city on vacation. My chief therefore sent me to do the consultation instead. When I arrived at the hospital neither the department head nor the staff physician was there. A senior nurse brought the patient to me in the staff room. It became clear after a long interview that he was dissembling—skillfully concealing his chronic depression in an attempt to show that he was healthy. I therefore entered in his chart that he was still suffering from severe depression and only feigning improvement, and that he required strict supervision and for his own safety should be transferred to a psychiatric hospital.

The department head disregarded my conclusion and decided to wait for the head of the local psychiatric clinic, who was expected back from vacation shortly.

Two days after my consultation, however, the patient quietly sneaked away while the staff was taking him and other patients to the lavatory for their morning wash-up, and dove head first into a tall barrel filled with water. His absence remained undetected until breakfast, so that he was dead when they found him.

A terrible scandal ensued. The board that conducted the inquest did not find me culpable in any way; instead, it blamed the department head and the staff physician, and each of them was given a severe reprimand, which seemed to bring the matter to a close. By no means. The department head accused me of negligence for not calling him that morning about my conclusions, and insisted that I receive the same reprimand. He got partial satisfaction: I received an admonishment, although without its being entered in my service record.

Despite that protracted scandal, the attitude of my superiors did not change— externally, at least. So I could celebrate the 1951 New Year with my family, Colonel Shcherbina even gave me a week's leave. And he sent me a New Year's card, too!

My father-in-law came to a visit for the following May holidays. On some pretext or other, he introduced himself to Colonel Shcherbina and got on friendly terms with him. He asked him and his wife out to a restaurant several times and even invited them to visit him in Moscow. While saying good-bye just before his return to Moscow, he asked his new "friend" if he could demobilize me. Colonel Shcherbina explained that military discharges lay outside his competence. Only the Minister of Defense had that right. Nevertheless, he promised that if he should hear of any staff vacancies in Moscow, he would certainly offer me as a candidate. Soon afterward such an opportunity did indeed present itself and Colonel Shcherbina kept his word, as a result of which, although unintentionally, he in fact did me more harm than good.

In July 1951 I successfully passed the final examinations and received a diploma from the so-called National University of Marxism and Leninism, in which I had enrolled while still in Yuzhno-Sakhalinsk.[2] Studying with me at the university's Rostov branch was a certain captain, an officer in the regional Special Department, or MGB (Ministry for State Security), the successor of the NKVD. He behaved superciliously and during breaks would remain in his seat looking through his notebook, as if unaware of what was going on around him. Of course, the other students were not especially interested in talking to him either. Without identifying him by name, they discreetly bandied the phrase, "he who sees and hears all."

During the graduation party, the officer sidled up to me, and without looking at me muttered between his teeth, "Wolf, come and see me after work tomorrow. I need to talk to you," and handed me a piece of paper with an address on it.

Naturally, I accepted his "invitation." Sitting me down across from him, he went without any preliminaries directly to the matter of his concern. "You're probably aware that we know everything about you, but in the present instance we're interested in what you can tell us about your former Yuzhno-Sakhalinsk superior officer, Vladimir Viktorovich Morozov."

"I can say that he suffered a great personal tragedy—he lost almost his entire family in the Ashkhabad earthquake. He's a qualified psychiatrist and lives very simply."

"That's all true. What can you tell us about his second wife?"

"It's difficult for me to judge her as a person. As a psychiatrist, so far she's . . . just a tyro. He's teaching her. But her appearance in his family hasn't brought him much joy."

"Why is that?"

I told him what I knew from Morozov's words and those of his so-called second wife.

"Tell me, what kind of anti-Soviet literature did he show you?"

The unexpected question startled me. I leaned back in my chair, rubbed my eyes, and after a short pause in which I focused my mind I answered, "I can swear that he didn't show me any anti-Soviet literature. I used his library more than once. There was nothing illegal in it. And all our conversations took place in the presence of the young doctor, his so-called wife, whom he hadn't trusted for some time and with whom his relationship was strained."

"Just so! She in fact stated during her interrogation that you were present during his anti-Soviet conversations and said nothing."

That remark indicated to me that Vladimir Viktorovich was either already in prison or under surveillance instigated by that viper whom he had once warmed at his breast. "That isn't true!" I exclaimed. "It couldn't be. I don't believe that even an unscrupulous young woman like her, who exploited the weakness of her temporary husband, would be capable of such lies! What need would she have for them?"

"Comrade Wolf, we're the ones who ask the questions here! You're required to answer them candidly. We have here in Major Morozov's file a copy of her statement to the Yuzhno-Sakhalinsk investigator. Would you like to see it?"

"No, I have no wish to!" I replied, although my head was spinning.

"That being the case, there's nothing more to say," he replied with a smile. "If necessary, we'll call you back in. I hope you realize that this conversation is strictly confidential."

I was outraged. I wanted to write or call Major Morozov's daughter at once, or Anastasia Leonidovna, the former nurse who looked after her, in order to find out what had happened to them. I was kept from that step by the certainty that all my mail was being examined and my telephone conversations listened to. I could not help them, and any attempt to do so would only make matters worse.

The thought that my Sakhalin friend was in peril, and that I was unable to help him, tormented me for a long time.

Everything became clear a few months later. Around the end of September there was an army-wide scientific conference on issues of military medical testing for young members of regional military medical boards. Naturally, I was sent to attend. I learned from the chairman of the Far Eastern board that Major Morozov had been removed from his post and had vanished from sight. "The acting head of psychiatry at the Yuzhno-Sakhalinsk hospital is his former wife, Dr. Borisova," he concluded with a significant smile. When I asked him what had happened to Dr. Morozov, my interlocutor brusquely replied, "If you're so interested, why don't you ask Dr. Borisova? She'll explain it all to you in very clear terms," and then he disappeared, evidently wishing to avoid further contact. As it would turn out, there was no need to ask Dr. Borisova. Toward the end of 1953, after the death of Stalin, I got a letter from Vladimir Viktorovich in which he said that he had been released from the Vorkuta forced-labor camp and been fully rehabilitated.[3] He had returned to Central Asia with his daughter and Anastasia Leonidovna and was employed as a physician in a Tashkent psychiatric hospital and clinic. Of Dr. Borisova, there was no mention at all.

After meeting a number of other young military doctors at the conference who seemed quite happy with their lives in the various capitals of the republics of my "broad native land," I was filled with envy and wanted to remain behind in Moscow, despite or perhaps even because of the anti-Semitic clouds that had been gathering in the Soviet Union for some time. After the campaign against the so-called "rootless cosmopolitans," which had disrupted the careers of many famous writers, artists, scholars, and other cultural figures, the Party Central Committee and "Comrade Stalin personally" had ordered a joint plenary session of two major national institutions, the Academy of Sciences and the Academy of Agricultural Sciences, to address the issue of "anti-materialist theories in Soviet biology." The most celebrated Jewish geneticists, biologists, and other experts were expelled from both institutions, and obscure, poorly trained biologists and agronomists—all of them students of Academician Trofim Lysenko—were appointed in their place.[4]

Immediately after the joint session, the Academy of Medical Sciences also met to address "anti-Pavlovian and anti-materialist tendencies in medical science." The result of that second session was the same: the most reputable scientists—and Jewish physiologists and psychiatrists, above all—were purged from the Academy of Medical Sciences, the medical schools, the research institutes, and even the central hospitals. A storm was gathering.

When I got back to Rostov after the September conference the trees had already turned autumn gold. I plunged into my routine, which gradually dispelled my feeling of homesickness. With the retirement of Colonel Kipperstein, the vice-chairman of the district military medical board, the atmosphere in the group grew warmer. My landlady and colleagues began to ask me why my family had never joined me. I was forced to invent various excuses. And then in mid October Colonel Shcherbina suddenly (it was always "suddenly") called me in and, averting his gaze, informed me that an order had come from Moscow transferring me to the command of the Main Military Medical Administration. It seemed to me that he stated the news drily, without any sympathy and perhaps even with a certain Schadenfreude. For that reason, the news gave me no pleasure. I also had a premonition that no good could be expected from the sudden change of place.

The premonition proved to be correct. Judging from the bilious mood of my father-in-law and the sad expression in the eyes of Susanna when I got back to Moscow, they were already aware that the Main Military Medical Administration had in response to their persistent requests played a malicious joke on me and on them too.

The Main Military Medical Adminstration had during my sojourn in Rostov been completely restaffed. The officers with whom I and my friends had been acquainted were all gone, including the chief of personnel. I was seen by the duty officer, who asked me to take a seat while he went off somewhere. He returned a few minutes later and silently handed me a travel warrant and transfer orders to the city of Arkhangelsk and the medical department of the White Sea Military District, where I had been assigned the same duties I had performed in Rostov: chief of flight evaluation and head psychiatrist of the district military medical board. This time I was given only a week before I had to report for duty.

I won't attempt to describe my family's and my own mood and fears. There was nothing to be done. Very likely it was just my fate. "Perhaps," I thought, "it's a punishment for abandoning Mama and the rest of my kin to certain death and fleeing to save myself."

Before I left, my father-in-law remembered that a friend of his, a former Konotop rabbi, Reb Moishe Litunsky, was in permanent internal exile in Arkhangelsk after having served a five-year prison term. Moishe-Boaz didn't know his address, but sure that I would find him anyway, he gave me a letter in which he asked his old friend to look after me.

On October 20, 1951, I left for my new assignment.

Black Days and White Nights

♪♪♪

In no part of Russia equidistant from Moscow is the change in climate greater than in the far north. The city of Vologda, for example, is only some five hundred and twenty kilometers north-northeast, yet spring and summer are significantly shorter there, and fall quickly yields to a harsh winter in which frosts and snow are much more common than in Moscow and the rest of the central zone of European Russia. In Tsarist times, Vologda was a place of internal exile. Arkhangelsk, the capital of northern Russia, is another seven hundred and sixty kilometers beyond Vologda. As I sat in the warm train gazing through windows partly covered with hoarfrost, I watched the sun grow duller by the hour as it descended the dark-gray expanse of sky toward the languishing, barren, permanently frozen earth. The closer I got to Arkhangelsk, the scarcer the settlements and train stations became, although from time to time on both sides of the track I could make out tall fences topped with barbed wire and, staring back at me, spectral figures in sheepskin coats with rifles slung over their shoulders. By itself the landscape was enough to fill any first-time visitor with dread and inspire a urge to lie down and sleep. That may be why silence reigned in the coaches of the Moscow-Arkhangelsk line almost the entire way. People lay down to sleep much more often than they sat up or moved around.

It was six in the morning when the train finally arrived at the station across the Northern Dvina from Arkhangelsk. From the station's information kiosk I was able to get the address of the former rabbi, Moishe Litunsky, now employed as a barber. The Northern Dvina was covered with ice, although, since it was still October, not yet thickly enough to support even light vehicles. People therefore crossed over to the city on foot or used sleds onto which they loaded their suitcases, goods, children, and the infirm. I set out on foot, dragging my suitcase behind by its strap. Once across the river I hired a taxi, which took me to the building where, according to the address, I would find my father-in-law's friend, the barber and former rabbi Moishe, but now Modest, Litunsky. I don't know if he had somehow been warned by my father-in-law, or if he was just used to guests arriving in the morning before he left for work, but on answering my knock and finding me there in my uniform with a suitcase, he exclaimed, "Welcome!" and opened the door wide to let me in.

Before me stood a short, wiry, narrow-shouldered, yet energetic man of sixty-five or seventy who made a real effort to be hospitable, even helping me off with my coat and stowing my suitcase in a convenient place. After I had introduced myself and given him my father-in-law's letter, I asked him if he remembered the Kozlovskys from Konotop, whereupon tears began to roll down his broadly smiling face.

"How could it be otherwise?" Reb Modest from Konotop answered with a deep sigh, and after seating me in a chair beside him he explained. "I was bound to the Kozlovsky family for many years by the warmest of feelings. They gave me their support in good times, but even more so in bad. Your father-in-law, Moishe-Boaz, tried to shield me from the Bolsheviks and as a result got in their bad books too. But we'll talk about that later. I hope you'll stay here a while and not shun my humble abode."

After providing breakfast, Reb Modest called a Konotop friend of his who had also been sentenced in that unhappy time to permanent internal exile after five years in prison. Arriving in Arkhangelsk, the friend had turned himself from Mr. Ezekiel, a merchant of the first guild, into Khatskya, the coachman, the authorities having allowed him a horse and a sleigh and, in the summer, a buggy. Khatskya, a tall, strapping fellow in a long sheepskin coat with a whip in his hand, said to my host in Yiddish as he came through the door, "*Nu, vos vider?*" ("What, again?"), suggesting that the call had not been unusual. All that was left was to find out what had happened and where he needed to go.

My gracious host sat his friend down, gave him a shot of vodka along with a glass of tea and something to eat, told him how important the visitor sitting across from him was, and said that he needed to take him to the Red Building, the headquarters of the White Sea Military District.

The Red Building turned out to be on the other side of the city. Khatskya was silent the whole way, which gave me an opportunity to acquaint myself with the city's external view. The first thing to strike me was the wooden paving of the roads and sidewalks and the stunted little snow-covered trees next to the stone buildings, although there were few of those, at least along the route we took: a second train station, a three-story hotel, the central post office, the Gorky Drama Theater, a school, the city administrative center, the office of the Communist Party, and a fire department bell tower. The other buildings were mainly single-story houses made of heavy logs and, for the most part, roofed with wooden shakes. Above them smoked tall chimneys, and between them stood pumps surrounded by people with pails on yokes.

Thirty minutes later I was inside the Red Building in the office of the medical department. The department chief, Colonel Beryozkin, saw me himself. Our first talk was far from friendly. He explained with a sullen expression that my assignment had not had his approval, since the district military medical board was already fully staffed and headed by Colonel Nikolay S. Pereverzev, whom everyone respected. "And, in fact, anyone assigned to a district military medical board must have wide experience and at least the rank of lieutenant-colonel. But you, Avrom-Moishe Shloymovich, are still untested and no more than a senior-lieutenant, and yet you're about to assume the duties of a colonel! It's against regulations! It would be more fitting to send you to a field unit in Vorkuta or Pechora."[1]

At the end of our chat, Colonel Beryozkin gave me a hard look and promised to call the Main Military Medical Administration in Moscow about my assignment and to get to the bottom of "this sorry mess." Then he sent me off to Colonel Pereverzev with a notation on my transfer orders that said, "Temporary, available for any assignment."

My meeting with Colonel Pereverzev was the exact opposite of the one with Colonel Beryozkin. He treated me and the duty indicated in my transfer in a very friendly way, sharing in confidence that my assignment to the district military medical board had had his approval. With it, he had, as he put it, bagged three hares with one shot.

First, his friends in the Main Military Medical Administration had been looking for an assignment for him on the Central Military Medical Board. Second, his duties in Arkhangelsk would be taken over by his deputy, a tremendous fellow, Colonel Sokolov. And third, the duties of the latter as head of flight evaluation would be assumed by Senior-Lieutenant Wolf. And if that responsibility seemed insufficient to Senior-Lieutenant Wolf, then he would also be appointed chief district psychiatrist. "Don't worry, there's nothing that Beryozkin and his crowd can do. If he calls Moscow, they'll tell him that the orders of his superiors must be obeyed. As for rank, that depends not on you but on him. He'll have to promote you. We had a captain on the district military medical board, Avdeyev, who was promoted to major only a month ago."

And that in fact was how it played out. I had the pleasure of a month's association with the remarkably simple yet great Colonel Pereverzev, an open-hearted and, especially for those times, courageous man who was ready to come to the aid of any in need. The other members of his group proved to be no less well-intentioned or endowed with exemplary personal qualities.

I should stress that in addition to having an especially harsh climate, the territory of the White Sea Military District was very large. It embraced the entire Vologda region, the Komi Autonomous Soviet Socialist Republic, the Arkhangelsk region with its twelve cities, the Yamalo-Nenets autonomous region with its population centers of Mezen and Naryan-Mar, the islands of the Arctic Ocean, and the huge expanse of the island of Novaya Zemlya. I had occasion during my northern tour of duty to visit all those remote, largely uninhabited places, and to be astonished by the rich variety, so striking in its contrasts, that God gave them to them. It also fell to me to view scenes of terrible oppression and the extreme humilition of human dignity, and to take part in the certification for release from prison on the grounds of ill health of "goners," Gulag oldtimers who had become little more than living corpses. After each episode of my involvement in that "humane" mission, I would suffer for weeks and be unable to sleep or rest peacefully. In everything else, however, my service life passed successfully enough and, under the circumstances, even provided some satisfaction. I was also fortunate, in the fullest sense of the word, to find a good apartment and an even better landlady, who in the more than four years of my life in Arkhangelsk was to me both "a mother and a sister" (Chaim Bialik). It would be a sin not to speak of her, however briefly.

My new acquaintance, Reb Modest Litunsky, with whom I stayed the first several days after my arrival, did not want me to leave and assured me that I would be no trouble for him and his family, and that it would even be more fun with me there. Nevertheless, in view of the distance of my workplace from his home, he agreed that I should try to find more suitable lodging. His own attempts to help me were unsuccessful. There were too many other officers or merely new arrivals in Arkhangelsk looking for permanent housing, and all the conveniently located apartments had been taken. Moreover, it was important for me to find a place in a building near the main post office so I could use its public phone to call home to Moscow once a week, since my family and I had gotten used to regular conversations. I was advised that the best procedure, given that requirement, would be to go from building to building in the area and ask if there was an apartment or room for rent. After several failed attempts, I entered a newly constructed, or at least refurbished, building with two rows of doors extending down either side of a long hallway. I knocked at the first door. It was opened by a sailor already three sheets to the wind who, mistaking me for a long-lost friend, immediately sat me down in a chair and proposed a drink in honor of the festive occasion.

Upon learning that I was actually looking for an apartment, he grabbed me by the sleeve, pulled me out into the hallway, and led me unsteadily to a second door, while explaining in a slur, "Let's try here, brother. There's a grandma living here alone. She just came back to the apartment a week ago. She rented it to actors before that. Now there isn't anybody. Good luck!" he said, shoving me toward the door.

The shove sent me flying into the front room, where I found a woman bent over painting the floor. Without even looking up, she asked, "Well, what is it this time, you lush?" But on hearing an unfamiliar voice—my question as to whether she might have a room to let—she turned around and said, "Oh! I'm so sorry! That drunk is a former friend of my son's and won't leave me alone. He comes by every fifteen minutes for money for a small bottle or something to eat. I'm getting very tired of it." In answer to my question, she pointed to a freshly painted door and said with a modest smile, "Go on in. That's the bedroom. If you like it, it's yours!" After looking the room over, I sat down in it. It seemed like a dream to me. Next to the wall were a wide bed and mattress covered with a white down comforter and a heap of soft pillows. And in every corner there were house plants—a rubber plant, china grass, Jacob's ladder, aloe, and even a miniature lemon tree. What a miracle to find southern flowers in Arkhangelsk where the ground never completely thaws!

I returned to the landlady. She was waiting with her index finger pressed against her wrinkled cheek. I asked how much it would be by the month. "Two hundred rubles," she replied.[2] I offered her the sum at once, but she refused to accept it. "We'll take care of that after you've been here a while. Bring your things over and get settled. There's a wardrobe and also a dresser for your underwear. If you need anything, just let me know."

An hour or two later I had already put my things away. A woman of few words and little wasted sentiment, my landlady said without any preliminaries, "Sit down and we'll have some tea and get better acquainted. My name is Lyuba—Lyubov Evdokimovna. What's yours?" I introduced myself and explained who I was and how I had come to Arkhangelsk, and I told her about the family I had left behind in Moscow. She listened in silence.

"Don't take it to heart, son," she finally answered. "My own life is wormwood and gall too. I raised four children. My husband didn't come back from the front, and they," she pointed to some pictures on the wall, "they've all gone off to different places in the country and rarely remember their mother. So you'll take their place. Will you be here a long time?"

Lyubov Evdokimovna lavished her unspent mother's love on me all the years I lived with her. She prepared three meals a day for me as her sacred duty—breakfast, a three-course lunch, and supper; went to the station to pick up the food parcels Susanna regularly sent from Moscow; got everything ready for my regular visits to the bathhouse; washed my underwear; received and entertained my friends like a devoted mother or grandmother; took care of Susanna and Nadya when later they came to visit; and—the main thing—protected me from the "scheming floozies" who surrounded me at work. All the money I got I gave to her to put to various uses, and there was never a time, not even once, that she abused my trust. My returns from official trips were very touching. Dressed in a fur coat in both summer and winter, she would go outside the day I was supposed to come home and wait for me on the street. Then without a word she would take my little suitcase from my hand and accompany me to a cafeteria.

Her passion was cultivating indoor plants, indoor since the permanently frozen earth would not have given the outdoor variety the necessary affection and warmth. And having herself been raised in a southern Russian village until the age of eight, Lyubov Evdokimovna could not live without the fragrance and vivid colors the plants provided. Whenever her friends and relatives came to visit or to work in the area, they would bring seeds and bulbs and roots, along with bags of good-quality loam. She planted everything in various unused dishes, fertilizing it all with leftover soup or the horse manure she collected from the more trafficked parts of Arkhangelsk's wooden roads. I was surrounded by greenery, colorful flowers, and maternal care all the years I lived with that quiet, loving woman.

Inasmuch as my service on the White Sea Military District medical board was the longest of my assignments and left a large and lasting impression on my mind, I consider it necessary to dwell on several of the men with whom I was associated during that period, all the more since the overwhelming majority of them treated me well, sharing with me both the happy and the bitter times that fell to my lot in that harsh region.

Let me begin with the very good relationship I enjoyed with the chairman of the district military medical board, Colonel Sergey Nikolaevich Sokolov, and the rest of his family. He was a tall, athletically built, rather stout man with a bristly red mustache who had taken part in the war from beginning to end and gone all the way to Berlin. That service had been rewarded with several distinguished service medals, among them the very highest, the Order of Lenin.

By character, however, he was the kindest of men. He had complete confidence in me and fostered in every way the improvement of my standing among the senior personnel at district headquarters. Thanks to him, I became a "court physician" and treated the family members of many of the highest ranking officers.

Colonel Sokolov's one shortcoming was his psychological and physical addiction to alcohol. That bitter circumstance led him to frequent violations of military discipline and conflicts with his wife and son. But everyone around him overlooked that because of his many other positive qualities. He would arrive at work after having already drunk a quarter liter of vodka at home. And then he was easy-going and would entertain those around him with various stories and jokes. But if he failed to obtain his usual dose at home, he would be irritable and snappish. On those occasions he would send me out for a quarter liter, shut the door to his office, and drain the bottle on the spot. Then he would stretch out for a short nap after locking the door and installing me in the reception room. "Mosya," he would say, using my Russian diminutive, "if anyone asks for me, I'm at headquarters. Get the person's name and tell him I'll call back later." During the whole time of my service with him those naps were never disturbed or discovered.

Colonel Sokolov did another important thing for me. He persuaded the district headquarters commander to issue an order authorizing a series of seven daytime meetings of the draft-board doctors to improve their knowledge of medical flight testing with me as the instructor. That activity provided me with a respite and raised my standing with the district's civilian departments of health. The doctors too were happy to have the additional free time and the opportunity it gave them to acquire new knowledge.

Colonel Sokolov also gave me one day a week to consult at the Arkhangelsk psychiatric clinic, then headed by Professor Iosif Ilich Lukomsky, the "misguided" and accordingly punished "anti-Pavlovian" former Secretary for Science of the Academy of Medical Sciences.[3] My relationship with him was a good one based on mutual trust. He always included me in the deliberations of the forensic psychiatry commission. We would work together again in Moscow in 1961 at the Gannushkin Psychiatric Hospital (formerly Neuropsychiatric Institute), where he was in charge of the alcoholism clinic at the same time that I headed the epilepsy ward.

Another member of the district military medical board was the above-mentioned Major Avdeyev, a remarkable fellow. He had been a first-rate wrestler but in everyday life was a quiet, easy-going man. He never objected but just went ahead and did everything his own way. In Arkhangelsk and all the other places he visited on duty he had lovers ready to carry out his every whim. All the shopgirls in the grocery and dry-goods stores knew him and would sell him whatever was in short supply. The amazing part is that even though his wife was aware of his romantic adventures, she pretended not to be. He carried out his duties slowly and deliberately. He took the most active part in any drinking parties and could consume three times as much as Colonel Sokolov, but unlike him, he never got drunk and never developed any dependency. On the official trips we took together, he was responsible for our expenses and provided for our everyday needs, meals, and cultural and recreational activities. Relying on his charm, he was always able to get his comrades out of difficult scrapes.

A third member of the district military medical board was Colonel Pavel Aleksandrovich Maidanov, the good papa of our group. All the hired civilian staff went to him with their domestic and intimate problems. He would gasp and express indigation and promise to "do everything within his power," but as a rule power was something of which he had very little. All the same, people would unburden their souls to him as if to a priest. Whenever he took part in drinking bouts, he would sip his drink, and then with a frown and a mouthful of food dump the contents of his shot glass with remarkable nimbleness into a container concealed in his tunic. And then what a pleasure it was to see how masterfully he would pretend to be drunk. Everyone called him "Zharov" after the celebrated film actor who specialized in jolly boozers.[4]

In addition to my excellent colleagues, I was fortunate in another way. In 1953, Major General Stavenkov, the former commissar of the Volga Military District who is already known to the reader, was appointed chief of staff of the Arkhangelsk district. When I first learned of it, I was afraid of running into him, lest he remember my critical assessment of the 1950 Stalingrad call-up. It turned out, however, that the principled way in which I had acted was very much to his taste. When getting ready for a general inspection of the political and military preparedness of this or that center, he would insist that I be included on his team as the representative of the district military medical board. "He's just the cocky sort I need," he once replied to Colonel Sokolov, when the latter intimated that I might not be afraid of him. Afterward, he and I would became close friends, and whenever he or his wife was ill, he would call me first. When he retired and returned to Moscow, we would frequently visit each other to recall past times and events.

I had a chance during my service to acquaint myself with the various climates of the district's far-flung territories: with the bitter frosts and heavy snowfall of Vorkuta and Pechora; with the less severe winter and dense forests—the taiga—of the remoter parts of the Volodga region; with the tundra of the Nenets region and the lichens and moss that are the only fodder for its reindeer; with the usual change of seasons and the daily alternation of sun and moon, of day and night, in the southern part of the Vologda region; with the remarkable six-month or even longer winter and short summer of Arkhangelsk itself; and with the astonishing endless day, the never setting sun, of summer in Mezen and Naryan-Mar.

In Naryan-Mar I saw an extraordinary "miracle" that recalled the Jews' ancient crossing of the Red Sea on dry ground.[5] The town is on the banks of the Pechora River, which flows into an eastern extension of the Barents Sea and is subject near its mouth to violently abrupt tidal changes. Once around nine, after supper, the local military doctor invited me to go for a walk. As we approached the river, it suddenly began to flow rapidly toward the sea. In about twenty minutes all the water was gone, leaving the river bottom exposed and stranding boats, scows, turtles, crabs, lobsters, and every other kind of creature. If someone had told me about it, I would not have believed it. I was unable to go to sleep in the bright midnight sunshine, and it occurred to me for the first time that the parting of the Red Sea might not have been an invention. The six hundred thousand Jews who escaped the Egyptian Captivity had conceivably taken advantage of a violent ebb tide.

About six hours later, while still in bed, I heard a roaring noise and loud cries. I jumped out of bed and ran outside. The city's residents were sprinting past me toward the river with heavy ropes and boat hooks and shouting in their, to me, incomprehensible local language. I ran after them. And before my eyes another miracle occurred. The flood tide had begun. It was so powerful that the fishing boats that had left the day before were now being carried back on the influx so rapidly that it was impossible for them to moor without help from those on shore. For that purpose, the entire population of Naryan-Mar, and not only the fishermen's families, had come running to toss them long ropes and hooks to bring the boats to the docks along the river bank. And once again the idea occurred to me that the miracle of the drowning of the Egyptians in the Red Sea was the result of a sudden flood tide that had not been expected and against which they were helpless.

As for the domestic political situation in the Land of the Soviets during that late Stalinist period, anti-Semitic articles had begun to appear with ever greater frequency in the central press, troubling the minds of the entire Soviet population—blue- and white-collar workers and intelligentsia alike. There were rumors that Solomon Mikhoels, the world-famous actor and head of the Jewish Anti-Fascist Committee who had helped me find the survivors of my own family in 1945, and who had been murdered at Stalin's behest in 1948, had been a spy; and in August 1952 a group of prominent Jewish writers, poets, artists, musicians, and actors had been similarly "unmasked," tried, found guilty by a military tribunal, and executed the same day.[6] The atmosphere had as a result become tense even on the district military medical board, at the time still under the command of Colonel Sokolov. Although no one spoke of what was taking place and I continued to receive responsible assignments just as before, I still felt a certain estrangement and suspected that I was under surveillance.

On January 13, 1953, I was in a village deep in the Vologda countryside with a commission sent from district headquarters. One of my colleagues, the good-hearted Colonel Berkutov, came back unexpectedly from the local Military Registration and Enlistment Office and handed me the morning paper, *Vologda Pravda*. In bold capitals on the front page was the headline, *TASS REPORTS! ASSASSINS IN WHITE GOWNS.*

The report stated that officers of the MGB had unmasked a cabal of doctor-saboteurs who had been deliberately treating leaders of the government and the Central Committee of the Communist Party with toxic medications that had made them gravely ill.[7] The first and last names of the "assassins in white gowns" suggested that except for Professor Vladimir Vinogradov, Stalin's personal physician, all the accused were Jews. They had all been arrested and had allegedly confessed to their criminal activities. A "stern and righteous judgment" awaited them.

Colonel Berkutov stood expectantly across from me. Seeing my face suddenly turn pale, he snatched the newspaper from me, stuck it in the inside pocket of his overcoat, and said, "A new . . . deliri . . . It's obviously rubbish! Let's get supper!" The cafeteria was packed, with a thick tobacco haze and a noisy hubbub in which you could make out, "It's the Jews again," "Enemies of the people!" "Execute the lot of them!" Colonel Berkutov listened for a while and then he suddenly shouted, "Silence! Or I'll have you all shot!" The effect was instantaneous. The room fell silent, and those who had not eaten sat down, while the others quickly left.

We returned to our rooms. It was hard to concentrate, but I finished up a report on our work that needed to be signed by the local military commander. He did so without a word and then squeezed my hand hard as we parted.

Colonel Sokolov and our other colleagues in Arkhangelsk were waiting for us. He met me in silence with emphatically pursed lips. Only the sad look in his eyes revealed his true state. He shook my hand and held it for a long time. "Keep your head. God willing, the cat won't gobble you up. Go to your office and get to work on the files that have accumulated. Things will look better in the morning."

But it was difficult to work, since each tomorrow brought news that was gloomier than that of the day before. The situation was becoming more and more menacing. There were denunciatory rallies all over the country. Ethnic Russians refused to be treated by Jewish doctors, and threats against the latter were growing more common. Many Jewish doctors were fired from their positions. The same thing happened in the combat medical units and the military hospitals. All the Jewish doctors who were a month or more away from completing their service were immediately discharged, thus depriving them of full pensions. Young Jewish military doctors serving in hospitals and prestigious units were removed from their posts and reassigned to construction battalions in the far north (the lowest paid positions in places with the harshest climates).

And then on March 5, 1953, the radio announced the death of the "Leader of the Peoples, the Genius Josef Vissarionovich Stalin." (He had in fact died on March 3, the day of the joyful Jewish holiday of Purim.[8]) The so-called "thaw" that began soon afterward took a while to reach places remote from the capital.

After the tyrant's burial on March 9, my wife and young daughter were permitted for the first time to visit me in Arkhangelsk. Their arrival, which in ordinary times would have made me happy, was this time an occasion for sadness because of my inability, despite every effort, to overcome my anxiety about being removed from my post and assigned to one of the remote places to which the other Jewish doctors had been sent. After Susanna and Nadya left, I was summoned by the head of the medical department, the same Colonel Beryozkin, a rabid anti-Semite. Fortunately, Colonel Sokolov was still in command of the district military medical board. When he heard about the summons, he called me into his office for some advice. "Don't agree to a transfer to any another position. And don't sign anything without my permission! Understood?!"

Without any preamble, Colonel Beryozkin handed me an order stating that as of the next morning I was relieved of my post on the district military medical board, transferred to remote Mezen, and reassigned to the post of doctor in a worker's battalion. "Sign here to acknowledge that you have been informed of my order!"

I refused to sign and informed him that I had been appointed to my present post by order of the Main Military Medical Administration and was subject only to its command. Beryozkin lost his temper and started to shout, threatening me with court martial for failing to carry out a direct order. "Get out of here and submit a report to me about your refusal." I left. But since all reports that were to be forwarded to a higher level had to pass through the chain of command, that is, had to be given to one's immediate superior officer, I addressed mine to the district military medical board. In it I stated that during my service on the board, I had not only never received a single reprimand but on the contrary had been given commendations by the district headquarters chief of staff, Major General Stavenkov, and by the head of the political department, Colonel Medinsky, for conducting a seminar for the doctors of the district Military Registration and Enlistment Office. I also pointed out that according to service regulations, as well as for other reasons I mentioned, no one had the right to demote an officer to a lesser duty. I showed the report to my superior, Colonel Sokolov. After reading it, he used some strong Russian words to characterize Beryozkin's order and then wrote on the report in red, "I completely agree with the content of Senior-Lieutenant M. Sh. Wolf's report. Especially since you yourself recommended him to the district commander-in-chief, Colonel-General Comrade Popov, for promotion to the rank of captain." And he signed it, "Colonel Sokolov."

"Register the report in the dispatch book and then send it by courier. Let them sign for it," my guardian angel angrily instructed me.

Such a response from his subordinate, Colonel Sokolov, had not been expected by Colonel Beryozkin, and it left him confused and enraged. After consulting with his aides, he sent the report up the chain of command to the district commander-in-chief, Colonel-General Popov. The latter ordered a member of the military council (the Communist Party chairman, in fact, though I don't remember his name) to look into the matter. The council member then summoned my own commanding officer, Colonel Sokolov.

Anticipating a severe dressing-down, Colonel Sokolov presented himself on March 20 to the high command with more than a little trepidation. The military council member asked just one question: "Under whose influence did you write these provocative comments on the report of Senior-Lieutenant Wolf?"

Colonel Sokolov replied, "Comrade Lieutenant-General and esteemed member of the military council, I wrote them under the influence of the doctrines of the Communist Party of the Soviet Union, of which I have been a member for more than thirty years, as well as under that of the upbringing given me by my father, a well-known *zemstvo* doctor. And both the Party and my father taught me to defend the truth and to stand up against any unjust action."

The military council member made no response, but after he had dismissed Colonel Sokolov, he shook his hand and said, "You had very good teachers!" Colonel Sokolov was so delighted by that happy turn of events that, as he later informed me, he treated himself to an extra quarter liter of vodka.

At 6:00 a.m. on April 1, 1953, the first day of Passover, an armed soldier banged on my window. He shouted that I must accompany him at once to district headquarters. I was certain that the fateful hour had arrived. Once outside I asked him, "With my things? What's the reason?" He replied, "I don't know anything. Let's go, Comrade Senior-Lieutenant. The orders said at once!"

The district commandant's reception room was full of men—all Jewish officers who had been discharged or reduced in rank, or who were awaiting transfers. They sat quietly, expecting the entrance at any moment of a representative of the high command. Finally, the same lieutenant-general and military council member who had called in Colonel Sokolov appeared. We all leapt to our feet in anxious anticipation of the next event, whatever it might be. The general immediately asked us to sit down. "Comrade officers! By order of the Central Committee of the Communist Party and the district commander-in-chief, Colonel-General Popov, I am authorized to convey to you what I suspect will be very happy news. A group of malefactors from the organs of state security was exposed a few days ago. Intent on destroying the national unity of the Soviet people, they had arrested a group of celebrated doctors, primarily of Jewish nationality. Subsequent investigation by the Central Committee and other competent bodies has revealed that the arrested doctors were *completely innocent.* The investigation that led to their arrest had used unacceptable methods. All the doctors have now been released from their places of incarceration, and the parties who slandered them have been arrested and handed over to a military high tribunal for immediate trial."

All those in the hall leapt from their seats again. There was long, noisy applause. Many had tears in their eyes. The general asked us several times to return to our seats. After the room was quiet again, he continued. "The exposure of this plot of anti-Soviet elements has shown that the national unity of the peoples of our homeland is indestructible. Nor may there be any doubt about Soviet legality.

Therefore, the district commander-in-chief, Colonel-General Popov, has issued the following orders, in keeping with the findings of the Central Committee.

"1. To convey his apology to all who were affected.

"2. To end without delay all discriminatory acts against doctors.

"3. To return without fail to their former places of service all officers who were reduced in rank or reasssigned to less responsible positions.

"4. To repay within seven days all those who suffered a reduction in salary.

"On my own behalf, I would ask all of you to remain calm and, after you have returned to your former places of service, to work just as selflessly as you did before. Dismissed!"

We filed out, overcome with joy. People embraced each other or quietly wept. In my mind flashed the thought that it had been no accident that the former rabbi, now barber, Reb Moishe-Modest Litunsky had, when I met him the day before, whispered, "Tomorrow is Passover—*Pesach*." Yes! For Soviet Jews, it truly had been *Pesach* and a salvation from calamity.

Soon after, the White Nights began in Arkhangelsk, and the days were long and bright.[9]

Feelings, especially bad ones, even those with roots in the remote past, are retained long afterward, sometimes for years—significantly longer, in any case, than the events or circumstances that provoked them (I recall the Russian nurse who had never seen a Jew in her life, yet who announced that she could love anyone but such a person). The order of the district commander-in-chief was carried out by the district's officials, and many reassigned officers were returned to their previous posts. But the climate of Judophobia could not be swept away by a single order. Hostility lingered, poisoning life and producing a counter tendency: an active desire by Jewish officers to obtain an immediate discharge from the service. Many were successful. My family and I also renewed our efforts to bring my military career to an end. We finally managed to do so at the end of 1955 after the new ruler of the Soviet Union, Nikita Sergeyevich Khrushchev, announced that the armed forces would be reduced by six hundred thousand men.[10] The reduction maintly affected officers who had already served twenty-five years, as well as those whose service had in some way been compromised— who had been frequently ill or had abused alcohol, for example, or who had been actively trying to return to civilian life. I belonged to the last category. My wife, who had managed to see someone in Khrushchev's administration, was finally informed that her petition had been granted and that I would be included in the list of those who were to be demobilized.

After receiving my discharge on December 25, 1955, I began to turn over my files and various other service documents. I shipped all my belongings—up to one hundred kilograms were permitted—home by military travel warrant as separate baggage. On December 28, the eve of my departure, Lyubov Evdokimovna arranged a farewell dinner for all the members of the district military medical board with whom I had become friends during my time in Arkhangelsk. My colleagues, expecting to be discharged soon themselves, envied me in a friendly way and assured me that I was blazing the path for them to civilian life. And so it truly was, with General Stavenkov and Major Avdeyev being the first to be discharged after me, followed by Colonel Maidanov and then Colonel Sokolov. They all stopped in Moscow on their way home and stayed with us several days like relatives.

Saying goodbye to the person who had for more than four years devoted all her time and love to my sinful self was sad and painful. She had known for a while that we would soon be parting and had become quite withdrawn and frequently got up in the middle of the night and walked around her room sighing. During breakfast, dinner, and supper she would not sit down to eat with me as she always had before. Instead, she stood next to me, saying nothing but with her eyes fixed on me. During the last days it was she and not I who packed my things and took them to the station and shipped them to Moscow. I suggested several times to her that she come to live with us. My wife added her own request to mine over the phone. In response, Lyubov Evdokimovna would stop, look down, and say in a mournful voice, "No! No! No! I don't want to be a burden in my old age!" and then go off to another room. At the station she accompanied me to my coach and, after insisting that I not remain outside in the cold, stood by the window until the train left. She made the sign of the cross over me and began to sob. She was still standing there as the platform passed from view.

Part Three

♪♪♪

1956–1992

Up the Down Staircase

♪♪♪

In 2003 I published an article in the Yiddish magazine *Di Tsukunft* (The Future) about Sholem Aleichem's granddaughter Bel Kaufman, the author of the well-known autobiographical novel *Up the Down Staircase*.[1] Although my own movement up was more arduous than Bel Kaufman's, the title I have borrowed from her for this section characterizes better than anything else the period after my demobilization. That period is, in essence, the third part of my life, and although it lasted longer than the first two, it will take less space to write about and may thus prove less tedious to any readers who have remained with me.

And so in 1956, for the first time after all my travels and the lengthy periods of separation, my family and I celebrated the New Year together and with it the beginning of our new life. Nadya was already eleven and attending two schools, both a regular one and a music academy. Convinced that she was "another Mozart," her grandfather had enrolled her in the second and made sure that a piano was installed in the cramped nine-square-meter apartment we occupied at the time. My frequent requests for new lodging to the Military Registration and Enlistment Office, which was supposed to provide for me as one of the six hundred thousand discharged by the order of the Ministry of Defense, had all been unsuccessful.

Returning to my previous place of work in the October Psychoneurological Cinic in the Timiryazev district proved problematic too. After the death of Andre Mikhailovich Barkov and the retirement of the other senior doctors on his staff, the clinic had been taken over by a graduate of the Serbsky Institute of Forensic Psychiatry, a pedantic, callous man with little regard for his patients' lives. In any case, all the staff positions were filled. According to the order of the Ministry of Defense, however, the new clinic head was required to reinstate me in my former position, even if that meant reducing the hours of the other physicians. Faced with that unhappy alternative, I turned down the clinic head's "generous" offer and at the recommendation of an old friend took another position in Moscow at the Kalinin district psychiatric clinic, which had been headed for fifteen years by a cultivated doctor of the old school, Vladimir Alexandrovich Finkelstein. We had a good and trusting relationship from the start. It turned out that he had heard about me even before I had been called back into the service. He was able to give me full-time work, plus an additional half-time appointment as a psychotherapist, a position that had been vacant in his clinic for some time. With his blessing, I returned to hypnotherapy, a technique that I had begun to forget. It proved, in combination with other therapies, to be a very effective treatment for alcoholism in young patients (eighteen to twenty-five years old). I later included the results of that work in an anthology of articles on psychotherapy published by the Gorky State Medical Institute. It was in 1956 too that the psychoactive drug Aminazin first appeared in Moscow.[2] Because of side effects, including some deaths, the older doctors were reluctant to use it on an outpatient basis. I, however, decided to risk it, a decision supported by Dr. Finkelstein.

My old teacher, Professor Dmitry Evgenievich Melekhov, eventually heard about my demobilization and new psychotherapy practice. He called and gave me a proper dressing down and asked why I had not come to him at once after my discharge, adding that if I did not wish to remain an ignoramus, a semiliterate "magician," I would have to transfer to a psychiatric hospital. I reported the conversation to Dr. Finkelstein. He completely agreed with Professor Melekhov but asked me to remain at the clinic part-time. His request was prompted not only by the difficulty of finding a quick replacement for me, but also by the fact that there were a number of patients I had been helping. If I did not remain in some capacity, they would be deprived of that help, and I would lose the experience and standing that my work at the clinic provided. Dr. Finkelstein's offer was not only flattering but also very helpful in addressing my family's material needs.

In January 1957 I started work in Ward No. 7 of the Gannushkin Psychiatric Hospital in Moscow. The ward was headed by Nadezhda Glebovna Kholzakova, one of Professor Tikhon Alexandrovich Geyer's most senior pupils, while its chief of research was Professor Melekhov, who, as I mentioned before, had studied with Professor Gannushkin and had been Professor Geyer's assistant.

Nadezhda Glebovna differed from the hospital's other doctors in her diminutive size and childlike physique, which forced her, as everyone knew, to buy her clothes and shoes at the Children's World department store. Always serious and rarely ever smiling, she remained stern and emotionally vulnerable till the end of her days. Only her face, wrinkled like a prune, the puckered skin of her little hands, and the whiteness of her hair and eyebrows revealed her age, for although she was eighty when I arrived in the ward, she had a remarkably lucid mind and a superb memory of both remote and recent events. Except for Dmitry Evgenievich, who also headed the clinic of the Institute of Psychiatry, there were no other men in the ward. None had been able to tolerate Nadezhda Glebovna's dark moods and gruff disposition, and after a month or two had transferred to other wards. The only person she herself tolerated was the ward's staff physician, the seventy-five-year-old Varvara Afanasieva, who had also been trained by Professor Geyer and who was a highly cultivated aristocrat with a subtle understanding of people and an ability to get along even with the devil. The other women in the ward Nadezhda Glebovna either ignored or treated with disdain. She could not tolerate the junior and senior research fellows either. She believed that they had a "very poor understanding" of their patients and what might happen to them, and were only interested in and cared about themselves. "They look in the mirror every half hour," she would mutter. She moved about silently and spoke softly. Her orders were carried out at once. The only woman she completely trusted was the head nurse, Zinaida Mikhailovna Sukhosad, whom she had raised up from orderly to nurse, and then from nurse to head nurse.

Despite her peculiarities, Nadezhda Glebovna enjoyed great prestige among the senior doctors at the hospital. They said that she had been the most capable of Professor Geyer's pupils. Dmitry Evgenievich had great respect for her too. After every clinical review (patient evaluation and diagnosis), he would ask if she agreed with his assessments. She would answer with a nod if she did or a doubtful shrug if she did not. In the case of a shrug, Dmitry Evgenievich would say, "Have we missed something? We'd better take another look at the patient's condition." And the next week he would announce, "Nadezhda Glebovna was right!"

I cannot pass over in silence that complicated old woman's attitude toward me personally or her influence on the development of my psychiatric views.

I shall always be grateful for her kindness to me, a kindness that astonished not only me but the rest of the staff too. It was she who had approved my choice of Ward No. 7. Unlike the others, I would after my initial patient evaluation give her a summary of the case history and discuss my treatment plan. I would in every matter that was unclear to me first of all ask her. I would also obtain her agreement when discharging patients. All that flattered her, apparently, and she would answer all my questions clearly and succinctly. I never failed to accompany her on her rounds. She only made them on Sundays when there were no other doctors in the ward. When the time came for that weekly event, all the patients were expected to be in their beds. She would then quietly appear in the ward. After checking the cleanliness of the patients' bed linen and underwear, she would lean over each one with a smile and say just one word, "Well?"

And then a miracle would happen. Even the most autistic patients would start to speak and tell her what they had never disclosed in the persistent daily questioning of the attending physicians. In response to those disclosures she would take from a pocket of her snow-white coat a little packet containing an inert powder, a placebo, which the patients would then swallow in her presence. After wishing them well, she would proceed to the next bay.

I would always thank her for her instruction when I received it, and in reply she would quietly follow me to the door as I was on my way out of the ward and put a piece of candy or a paradise apple in the pocket of my coat as an expression of her regard. In time she started to give me tasks that were outside my normal duties. Instead of going herself, she would send me to the "five-minuters"—the meetings of the ward heads that took place every Monday in the office of Valentina Nikolaevna Rybalko, the hospital's chief physician, whom Nadezhda Glebovna did not like and with whom she would not even shake hands. That led to the general conclusion that Nadezhda Glebovna was grooming me as her deputy. And in fact during Nadezhda Glebovna's annual two-month vacations, the chief physician appointed me acting ward head.

Nadezhda Glebovna later entrusted me to implement the new staff instructional program mandated by the hospital methodology committee, and then whenever the head nurse, Zinaida Mikhailovna, or one of the other nurses came to her with an administrative question of one kind or another, Nadezhda Glebovna would without replying simply wave in my direction. The staff members were at first astonished by her attitude toward me but then got used to it.

Dmitry Evgenievich Melekhov had been keeping an eye on me too, just as before. In addition to conducting clinical discussions of my patients in the presence of the other doctors, he would frequently take home the case histories I had prepared and subject them to rigorous scrutiny, returning them the next morning with his comments. With time those comments decreased in number and in the end entailed only the substitution of individual words.

Dmitry Evgenievich later introduced me to Doctor of Medical Sciences Asya Savishna Remezova, the secretary for research of the the Institute of

Psychiatry, with the recommendation that she assign me a thesis topic for the degree of Candidate of Medical Sciences.[3] Taking into account the instruction in psychotherapy I had received from my first teacher, Semyon Isidorovich Konstorum, and my psychotherapeutic practice at the Timiryazev district clinic, she gave me, with Dmitry Evgenievich's approval, the topic, "Psychotherapy as a Component in the Treatment of Epilepsy: A Clinical and Electroencephalographic (EEG) Investigation." The topic involved a study of the basis and dynamics of electroencephalography before and during treatment and then over the course of an extended catamnesis (follow-up medical history). Esfir Semyonovna Tolmasskaya, a Doctor of Medical Sciences and head of the hospital's electroencephalographic laboratory, gladly agreed to direct my thesis research.

The above individuals contributed a great deal to my clinical and scientific development. In addition to my thesis, I published under their auspices over some thirty-five years more than one hundred and twenty scientific articles and reports, five methodological manuals, and a monograph on the treatment of epilepsy. Without false modesty or exaggeration either, I can say that thanks to my teachers I had by the end of the 1970s firmly established myself as a leading Moscow epileptologist.

In 1964, on the recommendation of Dmitry Evgenievich and the Gannushkin Psychiatric Hospital's new chief physician, Olga Vasilievna Kondrashkova, I was appointed a consulting psychiatrist at the psychiatric hospital in Kostroma, northeast of Moscow on the Upper Volga. I spent three days a month there examining in the presence of the hospital's doctors those patients whose symptoms presented particularly difficult diagnostic issues. I organized scientific conferences there too, and assisted individual doctors as a consultant in their research. Under my supervision, two of them, Yury Nikolaevich Titov and V. N. Vinogradov, worked on and successfully defended Candidate theses.

I should stress that my scientific activities were never an end in themselves. All my research, and that of the two thesis writers under my supervision, was organically linked to the clinical and administrative work I did under the direction of Nadezhda Glebovna in Ward No. 7 of the Gannushkin Psychiatric Hospital, and later in Ward No. 20, when I became its head. I received much help in the clinical study, diagnosis, treatment, and rehabilitation of my patients from Professer Melekhov and Asya Savishna Remezova, as well as from Professor Iosef Grigorievich Ravkin (a walking pharmacological encyclopedia), Samuil Gregorievich Zhislin, and Rakhil Grigorievna Golodets. Nor was I ever refused a consultation by one of the most talented of Professor Gannushkin's pupils, Andrei Vladimirovich Snezhnevsky, the founder of clinical psychopharmacology in the Soviet Union and a full member of the Academy of Medical Sciences.[4]

With the support of those distinguished men and women, I was in 1959 appointed chair of the Methodological Resources Committee of the Gannushkin Psychiatric Hospital. From then until my emigration to the United States in 1992, it was the only committee of its kind not only in Moscow but in the entire Soviet Union. The committee's principal task was first to improve the knowledge of the hospital's nurses through lectures on every aspect of the care, treatment, and rehabilitation of psychiatric patients, and then to organize both city-wide and national conferences

Moisey in the 1980s

for nurses in which they themselves played a leading role. I succeeded in publishing the conference proceedings in several anthologies of articles and reports by the nurses who took part. The conferences were attended not only by the nursing staff of Moscow's hospitals, but also by the doctors and research staff of its psychiatric institutes.

The success of the conferences allowed me to extend them to the entire hospital staff and that of the different institutes under its aegis, with the new sessions attracting a broad range of doctors from Moscow and other Russian cities. Over a period of thirty years (1961-91), the Methodological Resources Committee published under my direction and editorship thirteen collections of scientific articles and reports that remain relevant to this day.

Among the other events and activities in which I was involved, I should recall the founding of a museum dedicated to the memory of P. B. Gannushkin and a conference in 1975 celebrating both the museum's inauguration and the centenary of his birth. For the museum opening, the sculptor husband of one of my patients fashioned a bust of Professor Gannushkin for me, which I then donated to the museum. There was a comparable interest in the conferences I organized in memory of Semyon Isidorovich Konstorum and Samuil Zhislin, and for Dmitry Evgenievich Melekhov's eightieth birthday in 1979. Those events saw the participation not only of doctors but also of hospital administrators and their deputies, institute directors, professors, and members of the research staffs of Moscow's many scientific and therapeutic centers.

But let me return to my main work at the hospital as an attending physician and ward head.

In 1962, a new four-story six-hundred-bed hospital was completed. In addition to the two wards that had been moved from older buildings that had fallen into significant disrepair, four new wards were to be opened in the new structure, including what would eventually become my own Ward No. 20. Up to my neck with work in Ward No. 7, my duties at the district clinic, and my pedagogical activities with the Methodological Resources Committee, I could not even think of a possible appointment in one of the new wards. It turned out, however, that I got engaged in spite of myself. I found out about it from the head of our ward, Nadezhda Glebovna. She called me into her office one afternoon and observed in an offended tone, "It seems that you've decided to leave us without saying anything to me about it."

"What do you mean?" I quickly replied. "How could you think so badly of me? I swear by all that's holy that I have no intention of going anywhere else!"

"All right, I believe you. But our own Zinaida Mikhailovna told me today that she's been appointed head nurse of Ward No. 20 with you in charge. How can that be?"

"I repeat that I know nothing about it and am not planning to go anywhere. I like it just fine with you, Nadezhda Glebovna!"

"Well, don't make promises you can't keep," she said, softening and beginning to speak in her normal voice. "You need to grow. I was planning to turn the ward over to you anyway, since I'll be retiring soon. And Dmitry Evgenievich may not know anything about your new appointment either. What will he say?"

We set off for his office at once. He was quite taken aback by our joint arrival. "What's happened?" he asked in alarm. Neither I nor Nadezhda Glebovna had the courage to tell him. "Why don't you say something? Nadezhda Glebovna! Is it serious?"

"Our . . . young man . . . is leaving us!" she finally said.

"I heard something about that. But since your . . . um . . . young man didn't mention it himself, I thought it was just gossip."

"Alas, it isn't gossip."

"Well, what about it? What have you got to say?" he asked, addressing me.

I repeated everything I had said to Nadezhda Glebovna.

Dmitry Evgenievich indignantly picked up his phone and after drily greeting Valentina Nikolayevna, the chief physician, he immediately voiced his complaint. How she responded, I am unable to say, but he replied, "All right, in that case I'll come up there myself."

It turned out that my appointment as the head of the new ward had to some degree been engineered for me by the head nurse, Zinaida Mikhailovna, and by the housekeeping nurse, Lydia Dmitrievna, both of whom wanted to leave Ward No. 7 and had agreed to a transfer to Ward No. 20 to help set it up, but only if I served as its head. The administration agreed to their condition but felt that until the new ward had been provided with beds and other inventory and a full complement of doctors and other junior and senior medical personnel, there was no reason to say anything to me or to Dmitry Evgenievich or to Nadezhda Glebovna.

Dmitry Evgenievich returned from his visit to the chief physician satisfied with their conversation. Both he and Nadezhda Glebovna called me back in and gave me their blessing to embark on my own independent path in patient treatment. Dmitry Evgenievich promised to continue providing help as a diagnostic and treatment consultant.

When the new ward was completely staffed and supplied, Valentina Nikolayevna instructed me to take twenty-five patients from Ward No. 7 and begin work the next day with a one-and-a-half-time appointment—full-time as the ward head and half-time as its attending physician. My selection of patients, which included all those diagnosed with epilepsy, was approved by Nadezhda Glebovna. They were my own patients anyway and were attached to me and had no wish to be reassigned to other doctors.

Because of my research interests, all new epilepsy patients were thenceforth sent to me in Ward No. 20. Their daily average was only fifteen to twenty out of a hundred and twenty patients, but that was enough to establish Ward No. 20 as the "epilepsy ward," as it came to be known to the hospital and psychiatric institute staff and the doctors of Moscow's many clinics.

It is well known that epilepsy patients are difficult to lodge and care for. The hospital's doctors liked to say that it is easier to treat ten patients of any other profile than one with epilepsy, and were surprised by my ability to manage such a high concentration. The answer to their understandable surprise was that I was the first doctor in the country to combine psychoactive drugs with psychotherapy in the treatment of epileptics. I was the first to use intravenous Seduxen[5] to treat *status epilepticus*, or persistent seizures, and to establish in clinical conditions its complete safety—its lack of side effects—as well as to demonstrate the effectiveness of a combined approach not only for the treatment of epilepsy but, through the intravenous administration of other psychoactive medications, of manic-depressive psychosis, schizophrenia, reactive states, and other pathologies.

Moreover, I was also the first in the country to use the French drug Neuleptil[6] to suppress aggressive, impulsive, and antisocial patient behavior. I believed then and do now that Neuleptil is the most effective way to regulate behavior, a drug that indeed allows a high concentration of epileptics in a single ward. Regular dosage with Neuleptil and other psychoactive medications not only ended patient disruption of the ward's essential routines but even allowed the patients to become self-disciplined helpers of the staff in maintaining exemplary harmony in the ward. Our achievements in that regard were reflected in my published articles and methodological guides, *Psychotherapy and Epilepsy* (1964) and *The Psychopharmacological Treatment of Epilepsy* (1981), as well as in my monograph, *Epilepsy: Clinical Diagnosis, Treatment, Electroencephalography, Pathomorphosis, and Therapy Management* (1991).[7]

Another special feature of Ward No. 20 was its emphasis on patient rehabilitation. That rehabilitation was achieved, after the suppression of psychotic impulses by means of psychopharmacological therapy, through the use of various kinds of occupational therapy and the encouragement in the patients of self-sufficiency in maintaining the ward's high standard of hygeine and assisting in the care of other patients. That approach eventually resulted in the hospital administration's allocating to the ward another area of the same size on the same floor, allowing me to open a second, *self-governing* rehabilitation unit. All the patients from the "acute" unit were transferred there as soon as their behavior was regulated and they became critically self-aware of it and their underlying condition.

There were no junior personnel in the rehabilitation unit. The nurses only went there to administer medications or to see how the patients themselves were managing the distribution of food. Everything else was done by the patients themselves. The patients in the rehabilitation unit wore their own clothing from home and had their own cabinets for it and for their personal hygiene articles and cosmetics. They prepared very conscientiously for my daily rounds and during them were given ample opportunity to share their concerns and experiences.

A large place in the treatment regime was devoted to occupational therapy, music therapy, and cultural therapy. A piano and television were obtained to that end. Activity groups were also organized: drawing, sewing, and choral singing. Special garments were given to the patients for public performances. In keeping with the ward's program, the patients celebrated all the Soviet holidays and even organized New Year's parties. During the whole time of the rehabilitation unit's existence there were no unusual disruptions or conspicuous violations of order.

The parents' council I organized was a great help in looking after the condition of the units, the dining area, and the so-called Red (or Beautiful) Corner, a large room in which the social activities and events took place.

In 1962, the Ministry of Health designated me a Doctor of the Highest Grade.[8] During the time of my work at the Gannushkin hospital, I was given various certificates and other awards by the Ministry of Health and the regional organizations. In 1972 and 1982, the hospital staff and members of the Institute of Psychiatry organized celebrations in honor of my fiftieth and sixtieth birthdays.

It would be unjust not to mention the enormous help given to me by the hospital staff—the orderlies, nurses, and doctors—in the implementation of the ward's treatment and rehabilitation methodologies and procedures.

I have mentioned the role of the head nurse, Zinaida Mikhailovna Sukhosad, in the initial organization of the ward. I would like to add that in the seventeen years that she and I worked together, I never had to repeat a single order. A couple of words were all that was necessary for her to understand. Sometimes she would come into my office for the solution of some problem that we had not completely resolved and find outsiders there in the presence of whom it would have been awkward or tactless to resume our discussion. She would open the door and wait for an indication from me. I had only to look in her direction with an attentive gaze or a movement of my eyebrows or a nod for the problem's solution to be clear.

Zinaida Mikhailovna tirelessly trained the medical staff in a spirit of dedication to the life of the ward and of respect for each other and the doctors. If misunderstandings or conflicts arose, she would settle them at once on her own, and I would only hear about them later. As a result, I never had to let anyone go during the years that she and I worked together. Zinaida Mikhailovna was not only my right hand but also a devoted friend. She shared with me all her family's misfortunes. And I did all that I could to help her. I hired her daughter, Natalia, as a nurse in the ward after she graduated from nursing school, and then helped her get into medical school. After receiving her degree, she returned to the hospital and soon became its deputy chief physician and then chief physician, her current position.

An important role in managing the life of the ward was played by the housekeeping nurse, Lydia Dmitrievna. She was a devoted helper in all its activities. The other ward heads were envious and referred to her as my "deputy head" for administration. Like Zinaida Mikhailovna, she cultivated in the junior medical staff—the orderlies—a similar devotion to their duties. All the ward employees trusted her and did as she asked. The orderly Ekaterina Timofeevna Mitrofanova especially distinguished herself. She was a tall, stout woman with a pock-marked face, who never complained or objected and indeed rarely even spoke. Paying no attention to the time, she worked in silence, often performing the duties of others who were ill or away on vacation. When I returned to the hospital after unsuccessful treatment for a stomach ulcer, she simply said, "I will cure you." She made soup for me every day from fresh vegetables and gave me an infusion of aloe, honey, grain alcohol, and butter, and then stood outside my office door to make sure no one came in until I had finished eating. In five or six weeks I had fully recovered.

Although these people have all, to my sorrow, departed from our sinful world, they will remain in my grateful memory forever.

To be sure, the principal role in the treatment of our patients was played by the doctors, by my junior and senior colleagues in the ward. There were many of them in the thirty years I spent there. The overwhelming majority were hard-working men and women who regarded our patients with genuine concern and implemented the recommendations of the consulting physicians to the best of their ability. Many of them were also engaged in scientific research. Several of them with the necessary experience, including I. M. Libina, L. N. Markman, and I. Grafova, substituted for me during my annual two-month vacations and were subsequently made heads of newly organized wards or were asked to take the place of ward heads who had retired or departed for other reasons. It is impossible to list all my colleagues here, but I am obliged to mention a few.

One of the first to come to me in Ward No. 20 was Imma Markovna Libina. Imma Markovna, a doctor with five years of psychiatric experience, had transferred from Ward No. 14, which specialized in the treatment of alcoholic psychosis and was headed by Lydia Romanovna Luria, the sister of Alexander

Luria. It was said of Imma Markovna that she had a "masculine" intellect, for her attitude toward the patients was analytical. The only ones who truly enjoyed her sympathy were the "real" psychotics—those who suffered from schizophrenia, manic-depressive psychosis, reactive psychosis, and so forth. She had little patience with alcoholics or psychopaths of the hysterical type and was fairly cool toward other kinds of psychopathology. Her case histories, however, were distinguished by a thorough exposition of the data, succinct, lucid formulations, and the pedantic inclusion of all her journal notes and prescriptions. She really did not need my help, but she made it a matter of policy to present all her patients to me before devising their treatments, and insisted that I dictate to her a provisional diagnosis, "in case of an extreme emergency," as she put it with an ironic grin. Our opinions almost always coincided, and when they did not, she always deferred to my judgment.

She was formally sociable and made no distinctions with anyone, and her relations with her colleagues and the staff were always kind with a "cool warmth." She worked in the ward six years, after which she was appointed head of Ward No. 10. She retired in 1976 because of a persistent illness and died shortly afterward. We heard about her diagnosis and death from her relatives. She herself never mentioned her illness or asked for any help.

I must also mention Lyudmila Fyodorovna Chebysheva, an alumna of Ward No. 12, where she had worked for three years before coming to me. It would be hard to find another doctor like her: short, willowy, vivacious, always hurrying somewhere (where and why, no one could say), loquacious, egocentric, energetic, uncompromising, impatient, and madly devoted to her patients. If one of them needed something and Lyudmila Fyodorovna decided that it was possible to help him, nothing could prevent her from taking immediate action. If I happened to be busy with something when she came into my office, I would have to interrupt my conversation or whatever else I was doing and listen to her demands. She was sensitive and outspoken, and you could read her thoughts and feelings in her face during her interviews with her patients. But they loved her and were drawn to her. She was, moreover, very kind and always ready to come to anyone's aid, and she got along superbly with the rest of the staff, who carried out all her orders and recommendations at once "because she was fair."

Perhaps as a result of her constant hurrying, she managed to acccomplish a great deal, successfully completing her research and defending her Candidate thesis in two years. She consulted with me but chose a research adviser from her old Ward No. 12. Her case histories were exceptionally thorough and precise. After five years in Ward No. 20, she resigned her position and went to work as a consulting psychiatrist at the Institute of Neurosurgery, where she remains today.

Klavdia Vasilievna Borisova left a special mark on my life. She was born in 1935 in a village in the Tambov province southeast of Moscow and raised without a father, the only daughter of a devoted mother. After graduating from high school, she came to Moscow in 1953 on her own. Responding to a public announcement, she applied for work at the Gannushkin Psychiatric Hospital. She was hired as an orderly in Ward No. 12 and given a bed and afterward a small room in the hospital dormitory, where she remained until 1964. When the regional executive committee scheduled the dormitory for major renovation, she was through the efforts of the hospital and other organizations provided with a room in a communal apartment, where she lived until 1990. After that she bought the cooperative apartment where she lives today.

While working as a orderly she attended the nursing school located in the hospital complex. After completing the curriculum with distinction, she entered the 3rd Moscow Medical Institute and after graduation was appointed a doctor in the same Ward No. 12. She remained there until 1986, when Inna Grigorievna Tyklina, the ward head and her mentor, teacher, and friend, was appointed chief physician of the hospital. Since 1987 Klavdia Vasilievna has served in the outpatient clinic of the Institute of Psychiatry. While still a beginning physician in Ward No. 12 she began, for personal reasons, to combine that work with part-time employment in Ward No. 20 under my tutelage. For she had, in the years before she herself became a doctor, formed many lasting friendships there with both the orderlies and the nurses.

Despite all the hardships she had endured in her village and the difficulties of her subsequent life in Moscow, she not only did not complain but on the contrary was a solace to others and an inspiration. She brought a bright smile and goodness to the ward's life. Everyone who knew her story was amazed by her cultivation and aristocratic manners and her ability to dress modestly yet elegantly. She bought inexpensive but beautiful material and designed original dresses, which she cut out and sewed herself. She did not, as a matter of principle, use cosmetics or go to a hairdresser. She continued to wear the chestnut braids she had worn in her village, wrapping them around her head in various attractive ways.

She had compensated for any defects in her education and culture with great industry and a love for Russian literature and poetry. She knew by heart and could expressively recite whole chapters of Alexander Pushkin's *Eugene Onegin*, as well as the verse of Mikhail Lermontov and of Anna Akhmatova and other contemporaries.[9] That ability to compensate benefited her medical and psychiatric preparation too. Sensing her weakness in differential diagnostics and clinical psychopharmacology, she, more than the others and without being the least shy about it, turned to her colleagues for help and naturally to me as the ward head, and to the other consulting physicians. Everyone liked and respected her for that.

Her greatest sympathy was for women suffering from alcoholism, and that had in fact been a motive for her coming to Ward No. 20. Unlike many others, she always stood up for those unfortunates and never judged them, always finding objective circumstances and reasons for their abuse of alcohol, regarding it as a means of easing their difficult lot and seeking oblivion. That sympathy determined her research interests and, since I had devoted many years to the problem, her choice of me as the research adviser for her Candidate thesis, "Special Features of the Pathogenesis, Clinical Character, and Treatment of Chronic Alcoholism in Women." During her time in the ward, she published three articles on the subject that were given high marks by leading specialists, including the head of the alcoholism clinic, Professor A. Gofman.

Klavdia Vasilievna was well aware of my impending departure from the hospital and Russia in 1992, although, through no choice of my own, I was unable even to say goodbye to her. It was not until eleven years later on my birthday in 2003 that I received my first letter from her. And on my birthday this year I received a greeting from her addressed as much to my wife, Susanna, and the other members of my family as to me. It was accompanied by an ancient prayer of the Optina Pustyn monks and a large photo, a portrait of the tender beauty she was when she first came to work in the ward.[10]

Finally, I am obliged to say a few warm words about the chief physician, Inna Grigorievna Tyklina, who in difficult situations treated my family, my son, and me with kind considerateness. I tried to repay her the same way. At a stressful time for her daughter, whose husband had left her and their little girl and was insisting that their tiny cooperative apartment be divided in two, I testified as a witness in defense of her interests and those of her little girl. The court sided with me. Among other services, I was also able to find the burial place of

Inna Grigorievna's father, who had been killed in the liberation of Poland from German occupation.

In the thirty years I headed it, thousands of patients passed through Ward No. 20 and through my heart. It would be impossible to speak of them all, but I am compelled to write about one who to this day remembers me too.

Lydia, or Lida, not quite seventeen at the time and a student in her last year of high school, was admitted to Ward No. 7 when I was in temporary charge of it during one of Nadezhda Glebovna's two-month vacations. According to her teachers and the information in the referral, the story of her young life and illness came down to the following.

A childless couple, both engineers, had adopted her from an orphanage when she was three. Shortly afterward she began having epileptic seizures for which she was treated with intermittent success by a pediatric psychiatrist. When she was fifteen, her adoptive parents decided to divorce, her adoptive mother having become pregnant by another man she wanted to marry. During the divorce hearing, the judge asked which parent would take Lida. Her father said that he was prepared to do so, but that he would need time to find a suitable apartment for them, and that in the meantime she would have to stay where she was registered and living. Her so-called mother, however, categorically refused to allow it, justifying her refusal by the fact that Lida was ill and "might during a seizure kill the baby" that was expected a week later. The judge interviewed Lida and asked whom she would prefer to live with. It was then that she first learned that she had been adopted, and that her mother had refused to take her. Enraged, she ran out of the courtroom, went home, broke all the dishes, and attacked her grandmother, giving her a severe beating.

Finding the apartment a shambles and her mother beaten, the daughter called the police, who put Lida in a detention center for minors while the case was investigated. She remained there two weeks. For several days she refused to eat. The out-patient psychiatric panel called in to examine her concluded that she was suffering from "a chronic illness that would require long-term treatment" in an exurban psychiatric facility for the severely disturbed. When the principal of Lida's school learned of the panel's recommendation, the school's administrative council granted her, as "an exceptional student," a diploma without the usual examinations, at the same time appealing to the chief municipal psychiatrist to transfer her to a local hospital where her fate could be decided after a proper assessment of her condition. The psychiatrist agreed with the council and transferred Lida to the Gannushkin Psychiatric Hospital, and thus to Ward No. 7 and my temporary care.

Placed in the observation room for several days, she refused to socialize or answer any questions. She took the medications she was given and appeared to swallow them. In fact, she was hiding the pills under her tongue and spitting them into a tissue as soon as the medical staff left. After a careful search, the staff found the pills and informed her that her medications would henceforth be adminstered by injection. When Lida saw the syringe, she started to talk and asked that the pills be given to her only by the head nurse. She swallowed them in the latter's presence and lifted her tongue to show that she had done so. Then she agreed to be examined, but only by the head of the ward.

She and I hit it off the first time we spoke. She recounted in detail everything that had happened and described her relationship with her parents, defending her father and providing, as it turned out, an accurate characterization of her mother, and promised to obey the ward rules and assist the orderlies and the head nurse. "I've been keeping an eye on her," Lida said. "She's very honest and hasn't been deceiving you." Evident in her at the time were a certain listlessness of speech and stiffness of thought, characteristic of the ill.

She kept her promise, meticulously following the daily schedule and revealing an exceptional memory. Unlike the other patients, she performed all the occupational therapy activities with extraordinary accuracy and even helped those who were lagging behind to complete the tasks. After she had finished her own activities, she would remain behind to help the occupational therapist collect and sort whatever had been produced. When the therapist was ill, she performed her duties for her. After that, the chief physician agreed to give Lida the temporary status of "acting occupational therapist."

Her seizures stopped. Her behavior remained normal the whole time she was with us and she became sociable and cooperative. It was clear that Lida not only did not need to be transferred to a hospital for the chronically ill but that she did not need to be hospitalized at all and could be discharged for out-patient treatment. But to whom to discharge her? Her mother did not want her, and her father was unable to take her. So I discharged her to the ward, lodging her in the electroencephalography (EEG) unit. And then I summoned her adoptive parents. The conversation was brief. I demanded that they buy Lida a one-room cooperative apartment without delay and obtain the necessary furniture.

If they refused, the hospital would sue them. They agreed and asked that the hospital inercede with the regional administrative office so Lida would be given priority in receiving an apartment. That assistance was provided. A week later the answer came that her parents had made the required down-payment and that an apartment would be assigned to Lida in due course.

Until that happened, however, Lida continued to live in the EEG unit and perform the duties of occupational therapist. She also revealed an aptitude for the specialty of EEG technician. She quickly mastered the procedure for making recordings, and hers, to my astonishment, were better than those of the strapping laboratory assistant who normally did the work. To be officially taken on in that capacity, however, she would need a diploma from a nursing school. She refused to enroll. By force in the literal sense, the head nurse and I managed to get her to the office of the director of the nursing school on the hospital grounds. After we provided a brief explanation of her situation, the school director, based on our word, enrolled Lida as a first-year student and promised to obtain her diploma from her high school. Two years later she graduated from the nursing school with distinction and was given the position of EEG technician.

Before Lida graduated we were informed that she had at last been assigned a apartment. Her father called her to say that it had been fully furnished, as agreed. The head nurse, Zinaida Mikhailovna; the housekeeping nurse, Lydia Dmitrievna; and the union organizer all went to inspect the apartment with Lida. They came back very happy. It was bright and had every convenience. The only thing lacking was bed linen. It was provided by the hospital and Lida moved into her new apartment at once.

I had in the meantime decided that the education of the very capable Lida should not end there. After a lengthy effort of persuasion on my part, she agreed to prepare for admission to night school at the 3rd Moscow Medical Institute. She graduated five years later, in 1970, while continuing to work in our ward as a laboratory technician. She was then at my request hired as a psychiatrist by the head of one my former clinics, where she remains to this day.

I have told her story in such detail because Lida was my greatest triumph in the battle for the welfare of my patients—for the rehabilitation of the insulted and the injured. Her story also shows the lengths that a doctor must be prepared to go in the struggle for his patients' health and welfare. Lida has remained a devoted friend. She calls me more often than all the others do, remembers my birthday, takes an interest in my life, tracks down my former students, passes on all the news about Ward No. 20, and would be prepared to come to my aid, even flying to Portland, if I should ask her.

On February 20, 1992, in connection with my emigration to the United States, I said good-bye with great pain in my heart to Ward No. 20, that creation to which I had devoted thirty years of my professional life.

Everything in this section so far has concerned my movement up the staircase. In the following I will touch briefly on a few events that concerned movement down it.

First, I should stress that the successes I have described here were achieved at the cost of a great effort to overcome obstacles that were often intentionally placed in my path, some by those in the hospital administration who questioned the "soundness" and effectiveness of the projects I undertook, others by anti-Semites who hated me merely because I was a Jew. I will cite a few typical instances of obstacles of both kinds.

When I first thought of organizing a New Year's party for the patients of our ward, the administration was aghast: "He's completely lost his mind!" And on New Year's Eve, the chief physician's deputies for therapy and management, Lydia Romanovna Luria and Dmitry Nikolaevich Zonov, and the hospital's director of nursing, Klavdia Sidorovna Chizhikova, came running. In one voice they began to plead, attempting to frighten me. "Don't do this. You're risking a great deal—your professional standing, your livelihood. The patients will start a fire, which you'll be able to put out yourself only in the best of circumstances. But what if you have to call the fire department? There will be a lawsuit. People are already laughing at you, as it is!" When I assured them that every precaution against fire had been taken; that during the lighting of the candles on the New Year's tree, the family council members would be present with the fire department chief at their head, since his daughter was being treated in the ward; and that Dmitry Evgenievich Melekhov himself had promised to come—when I assured them of all those things, the adversaries who had come running were forced to concede that I had not in fact completely lost my mind. It is unnecessary to describe the toll on me that little downstairs tumble took.

Of the chief physician's two deputies, Lydia Romanovna came to that first New Year's party in the history of the hospital. She spent the whole evening with us and left satisfied. The next year there were New Year's parties of the same kind in many of the hospital's wards, and of course no fires.

In 1965, I received my first direct anti-Semitic blow. It involved the defense of my Candidate thesis. My research advisers were impatient for me to finish so that they could themselves, by producing a student, obtain the coveted rank of professor. There were long waiting lists at all the Moscow medical institutes authorized to accept thesis students—a wait as long as two years. My advisors therefore looked for a place without a waiting list. The State Medical Institute of the city of Gorky (now Nizhny Novgorod), about four hundred and thirty kilometers east of Moscow, turned out to be one. Nikolai Pavlovich Ivanov, head of its Department of Psychiatry and a psychotherapist of national reputation, knew of me from my publications and gladly consented to be my official first reader. Professor Rozhnov, the head of the Department of Psychotherapy of the local branch of the Central Institute for the Advanced Training of Physicians, was appointed my second reader. The defense took place at the Central Institute's offices in Gorky. Both readers had assured my advisers that my thesis would be approved by an overwhelming majority. The exact opposite proved to be the case. Neither my research advisers nor my thesis readers had accounted for the anti-Semitic character of a majority of the local membership of the institute's science council.

Besides my wife and one of her brothers, I had been accompanied to Gorky by my chief research adviser, Asya Savishna Remezova, and by my old teacher, Dmitry Evgenievich Melekhov. Asya Savishna introduced me to the council and praised my scientific work and my scrupulous handling of the statistical data and research results. I then explained the substance of the thesis, after which my official readers gave their own high assessments.

And then it began, one provocative question after another, all of which I answered exhaustively, in my committee's opinion. And then a series of unofficial readers stood up to make presentations with an anti-Semitic reek. All of them were opposed, since in their view the thesis was fundamentally "anti-Marxist and anti-Leninist" in its affirmation of "the primacy of the psychic and spiritual over the material." Dmitry Evgenievich responded. He cited compelling facts to counter the pseudo-science of the Leninist materialists and gave his own high assessment of the thesis's conclusions. But even his authoritative support was not enough, and the thesis was rejected by a majority of thirteen against and ten for. Exactly one year later, however, the science council of the Institute of Psychiatry of the Ministry of Health of the Russian Soviet Socialist Republic, which had in the meantime acquired the right to sponsor thesis research, *unanimously* approved the thesis without changes and conferred on me the academic degree of Candidate of Medical Sciences.

In 1979, three months after his eightieth birthday, Dmitry Evgenievich suddenly died of a cerebral embolism while recovering from an operation. His death was a painful loss to me. His wife, who has since passed away, long retained friendly feelings for me and assured me that she would edit his last but for obvious reasons still unpublished work, an unfinished study of the role of religion in psychiatry. I tried to convince the Moscow Orthodox Patriarchate to publish that interesting monograph, but without success. It was, however, later excerpted in the psychiatric journal *Synapse* (1991) and then published in the compendium, *Psychiatry and Current Issues of Spiritual Life* (1995).[11]

After the retirement of Asya Savishna Remezova, the special epilepsy clinic created on the grounds of the hospital in the Institute of Psychiatry came to be headed by the secretary of the institute's Communist Party bureau, Doctor of Medical Sciences Ivan Ivanovich Boldyrev, a semi-literate Leninist and inveterate anti-Semite. He could in no way reconcile himself to the fact that the ward I headed had its own EEG unit. Through various insinuations ("Ward No. 20 is a hotbed of Zionism") and noisy rows, he secured the transfer of the splendid eight-channel EEG apparatus from my ward to his, despite the fact that he was incapable of using it, since he was unfamiliar either with the technology of electroencephalography or with the technique of interpreting the recordings. And so the apparatus sat on the floor under his desk and gathered dust. As a result I was forced to suspend my on-going study of electroencephalography. I banged my head against the wall for a year until the father of one of my patients, who worked in the office of the Central Committee of the Communist Party, helped me to obtain and set up new equipment of even better quality and design.

In 1988, after sharing all the joys and frustrations of its life with me for seventeen years, Ward No. 20's head nurse, Zinaida Mikhailovna Sukhosad, retired. She had, in essence, been forced out, so that an obvious agent and informer (I've forgotten her first and last name) could be installed in her place. The new nurse tracked my every step. At her instigation, the so-called Department for the Struggle against the Misappropriation of Soviet Property—the Soviet financial police—started an investigation of "crimes" I had allegedly committed: the distribution to patients for bribes of expensive medications unavailable in the pharmacies, the use of the patients' relatives to obtain building materials for my *dacha*, and the acceptance of bribes for the treatment in the ward of patients from outside the Moscow region.

The Kuibishev district office of the anti-misappropriation department seized the ward's ledgers and for six months conducted its investigation behind my back, summoning former patients and their relatives and insisting that they corroborate the allegations against me. The interrogated were required to sign the usual non-disclosure form, but knowing that the help I had given them was disinterested, they told me of the encounters at once. For six months my family and I were subjected to the malicious slanders of that informer, the ward's head nurse. The business ended with my complete exoneration, a formal apology from the anti-misappropriation investigator, and the expulsion from the ward of the ill-fated slanderer.

Acts of ill-concealed anti-Semitism were also directed against my son, both when he entered medical school and after he graduated and joined the Institute of Psychiatry, where I had worked for many years without compensation. But more of that below.

1990 saw the retirement of the hospital's chief physician, Inna Grigorievna Tyklina, with whom I had enjoyed warm relations. She was replaced by the envious upstart, anti-Semite, and ignoramus P. P. Papsuev. Despite the many services I had rendered him, he took part of my life from me—the ward's rehabilitation unit. I was forced to return all its patients to the "acute" unit.

All those setbacks and the many others received on the stairway down took a heavy toll on my health. I became ill with diabetes, one reason for the abrupt end of my work at the hospital and departure for the United States in March 1992.

Family and Children.
The Return of Relatives "from the Other Side."
Our Son's Wedding. Our first Granddaughter, Lyubochka.

$$\text{ۇ ۇ ۇ}$$

Naturally, there was more to my life than work, although, for reasons that did not depend on me, I was, like all Soviet civilian doctors (those in the army and other privileged sectors were much better off), obliged to devote most of my day not only to my main job, but also to my secondary one and to my private practice (forbidden by the authorities), my research, and my various other endeavors. That did not mean, however, that my family was thrust into the background— quite the contrary. My work load, like that of every other Soviet doctor, had been assumed for my family's sake, for its welfare. No ordinary Soviet civilian doctor could have fed his family on his base salary, let alone provide for their minimal welfare. Even in the years of relative Soviet prosperity (the period of Khrushchev and the leaders who came immediately after him), a doctor, even one with an advanced research degree, could not have lived more than ten days on the meager income provided by a single full-time appointment. That is why doctors who had no outside help, whether from their parents or some other source, were obliged to put on the harness and, as they used to say in my "broad native land," plow from morning till night.

When I was in the army I sent most of my pay home to Susanna, her parents, and her aunt Sara, since the allowance I got for official trips and earned as a staff physician was more than enough for my own needs. As I indicated before, as soon as I was demobilized and returned home, I immediately obtained full- plus half-time employment. Later, in addition to the income I got from what had by then become two full-time appointments, I received fees for consulting within the hospital network and for articles and from private patients, who also helped me to obtain so-called "deficit" goods—those in short supply. Susanna also had full- plus half-time employment. The combination of our two incomes assured us a fairly comfortable life for the times.

To my bitter regret, I was unable for reasons beyond my control to give enough attention to our daughter, Nadezhda. As I mentioned, because of my military wanderings, she was raised from 1949 until 1956 without my participation and under the influence not only of her mother but of her grandfather and

*Moisey, Susanna, and
Nadezhda*

grandmother, who indulged her every whim and desire. Her grandfather, a stout, burly man, fed her whatever she wanted whenever she wanted it. After my return, I tried to modify her behavior but unfortunately was not always able to do so.

She had an exceptional ear for music. Her grandfather bought records and played them for her, and she was able to learn the words and melodies in one listening. That led him to the conclusion that his granddaughter was a genius. When she was five he took her to the district music school. When the school's principal and teachers told him that his little girl was too young (the usual enrollment age was seven), he said in a tone that allowed no objection, "I've brought you another Mozart and you say she's too young!" And they accepted her! For a long time she took no particular interest in her music studies. It was only in her sixth year under the influence of a conservatory professor, Lydia Abramovna Averbukh, the mother of one of my patients, that she at last got serious and passed the entrance examinations for a special pre-university music school and then for the Gnesin Institute of Music Pedagogy.[1]

Her music training entailed considerable expense. In order to ease her way along the thorny path of music education, I also had to treat a number of her teachers and their relatives. In 1969 she passed her comprehensive examinations at the Gnesin Institute and was awarded a diploma in piano accompaniment and solo performance. After some effort, she managed to obtain a place with the Moscow Regional Philharmonic, and also had success as a soloist in various Russian cities and as a composer, writing a number of fine romances and a children's opera and making several recordings.[2] In the United States, to our great regret, she was unable to put her musical abilities to any practical use or even to fashion a personal life for herself.

On October 5, 1957, on Yom Kippur, the holiest day of the year for Jews, when God is supposed to forgive all our sins, our son was born. As the Torah prescribes, his *brit milah* (circumcision) was performed on the eighth day after his birth, and he was given the name of my lost father, Shloyme. The question then arose of how to register him with the Bureau of Civil Registrations of the Ministry of Internal Affairs, and I struggled for a long time with the answer. We had given our daughter the name of my lost mother, Noemi, which Susanna then changed to Nadezhda, partly from a concern about anti-Semitism. To register our son as "Shloyme" or "Solomon," its Russian equivalent, would have involved the same risk. We were afraid that he would be teased at school and made fun of. After a long search for an appropriate Russian substitute, I found the corresponding "Miroslav." Shloyme comes from "*she'ha shalom shelo*" ("to whom peace belongs"), and Miroslav, an ancient Russian name, combines the Russian words for "peace" and "glory," with the second part providing the diminutive, "Slava." Knowing of my love for Jewish tradition and my pain at the loss of my family, upon his arrival in the United States and Portland in 1990, he immediately changed his first name from Miroslav to Solomon, and his last one from his mother's Ukrainian Kozlovsky (Kozlovskaya in the feminine form) to my own Wolf.

We brought him from the maternity hospital to our nine-square-meter pencil box of an apartment and laid him in a cupboard drawer. The new family circumstance forced us to take urgent measures to move from that one-room residence. And God helped us—along with a few other expedients. In recognition of Susanna's service as a pediatrician, the head of the Shcherbakov district department of health assigned us two rooms in a three-room apartment, and then, thanks to the efforts of the second secretary of the Party district council (whose niece I had treated), the Kuibishev district housing committee traded those rooms for a separate two-room apartment near the Deer Ponds in Sokolniki Park and my main workplace. I have a special memory of the ponds, since to a certain extent they determined my mode of life and the state of my health. Thanks to their proximity, I became a "walrus," that is, someone who swims in the fresh air everyday all year round, even during the most severe frosts when a hole has to be chopped in the ice.

After two years in that location, we were given a three-room apartment in the same district a mere five-minute walk from my workplace. We also bought a two-room cooperative apartment for the eventual use of our growing daughter. And then the chairman of the Kuibishev district administrative council helped me to acquire a luxurious two-room cooperative apartment in a prestigious area of Moscow, which we eventually gave to our son and his family. Our heavy work load allowed us to maintain a large *dacha*, too, and ultimately to build a second cottage on our plot, where we also laid out an orchard and planted a vegetable garden. Several years before we emigrated, we bought with the help of relatives of my patients three cars in succession and built a co-op garage for them, as well.

Fortunately, the lot of our only son, Miroslav—Solomon—Slava—Slavichka—was far better than mine at his young age. From early childhood he was distinguished by a gentle, cheerful personality, sociability, curiosity, and a fine memory. Because of our strapped circumstances in the first years after he was born, he attended nursery schools and then a kindergarten where Susanna worked as the pediatrician, and he enjoyed the universal affection of the staff. I used to take him to kindergarten myself. It was a ten-minute walk to the streetcar. Along the way he would ask me various "whys." Once in the winter during a thaw he asked me, addressing me the same way he does now, "Papa, why is the snow covered with pee like a diaper?" I was so startled that for a long time I was unable to give him an intelligible answer.

But I did not remain in his debt long. During our walks to the trolley, I taught him his multiplication tables, one set per day. In ten days he had completely mastered them. Then came tin soldiers and building blocks. He could sit for hours constructing little houses. When he entered English-language school, he was one of the best students in the first through the fourth grades and knew everything, but was restless and not very diligent. In response to the questions addressed by his teacher, Maria Andreyevna, to other students, he would jump up from his place and say, "Me, ask me, Maria Andreyevna!" and was often a disruptive presence in the classroom. In his fifth year, however, he settled down and became not only an excellent student but a favorite of the teachers. It was then too that he revealed a talent for art. At the teachers' request, he covered the walls of the classrooms with his pictures. His musical ability also declared itself—along with impatience and a reluctance to practice. It was only at his sister's and mother's urging that we kept him playing. At the age of fourteen, he became more serious and started to spend hours at a time at the piano, playing things by ear and improvising. To be sure, he does that much less often now. Thanks to his own love for art and music, he has devoted a lot of time to making his oldest daughter musically literate and is doing the same with his middle one,

Emilia (Tsilya Rivka), and his youngest, Julia (Shulamit). But let me return to that subject later.

Solomon's poetic nature was noticed by one of my patients, Tatyana

"At the Piano"
by Tatyana Alexandrovna Oranskaya

Alexandrovna Oranskaya, a Merited Artist of the Russian Soviet Socialist Republic.[3] Her paintings were exhibited at the State Tretyakov Gallery and the Pushkin Museum of Fine Arts in Moscow. In 1971 she produced a remarkable pastel of my son at the age of fourteen called, "At the Piano." Unlike the other paintings given to me that hang in my son's home, that portrait now hangs on the wall over my own desk. I gaze at it, and it arouses in me warm memories of the happy days granted me by my son and by Tatyana Alexandrovna, who caught and rendered his human essence so precisely.

Solomon attended the same English-language school for ten years, despite the fact that it was much farther away from our home after our change of addrees than another just across the street. He categorically refused to "betray" his old school and the friends he had made there, many of whom he has kept in touch with to this day and helped.

As established by tradition, he celebrated his *bar mitzvah* at the age of thirteen. The celebration took place privately, with only close relatives from Susanna's family taking part. From that time on Solomon became an active helper in our home. When I returned from work, he and no one else would help me off with my coat and fix me something to eat, and he has ever since always tried to carry out the Fifth Commandment to "honor thy father and thy mother" and has regarded himself as a Jew with a strong allegiance to Jewish traditions, Jewish history, literature, and music, and the Jewish state. And he has endeavored to pass all that on to his own children.

He graduated from high school with the highest marks, although he failed to win the gold medal usually given to the best student in the graduating class. When he entered the medical institute, however, he was made conscious of his affiliation with the "Chosen People," and even the change of his last name from my Wolf to his mother's Kozlovsky had been of little help. He suffered the most direct attack during the institute entrance examination in biology. He answered all the questions thoroughly and received the highest possible mark from the teacher conducting the examination, but when she handed over his student record book to the chairman of the examination committee to cosign, the latter announced that he wanted to verify my son's knowledge himself to see how well it corresponded to the mark given to him by the examiner. My anxious son then had to wait until after the entire group had been examined, at which point that "vigilant guardian of order," a confirmed anti-Semite, began to ask him questions that had nothing at all to do with what was on the prescribed examination cards, and that went far beyond the limits of any school biology course. That special examination lasted an hour. But my son prevailed that time too. The committee chairman confirmed the correctness of the mark given by the first examiner, offered his hand in congratulation, and declared that my son's answers had given him "aesthetic pleasure."

Solomon was then enrolled in the 2nd Moscow State Medical Institute. As before, his studies were easy for him and he devoted himself to them with enthusiasm. He had time for everything. Against our wishes, in his third year he even began to work part-time in the evenings as an emergency medical technician. Later he even made voluntary house calls.

In 1977 a momentous event occurred that would have a profound affect on all our lives. At the end of January, S. I., a patient I had successfully treated for epilepsy, called to tell me that she had retired and was planning to visit an uncle in Los Angeles whom she had not seen in over fifty years. She asked me what I would like her to bring back. I thanked her, wished her a safe trip, and said that there was nothing I needed. She insisted—perhaps a pair of jeans for my son, which were in fashion then . . . I politely turned down that offer too. But she continued to insist. To put an end to it, I jokingly replied, "You know what? Why don't you bring back my Aunt Pesya?" I told her that Pesya had lived in Portugal but after the war had gone to America. Even though I didn't believe in such miracles, I told her, just in case, Pesya's married name—Katzan, as well as the first name of her husband—Fishel, and those of her children—Zeilik and Rokhl.

Several months later, after I had completely forgotten about the conversation and my facetious request, I got a phone call out of the blue. "It's me, S. I., calling from Los Angeles. I found your aunt. She'll call you herself later today." I was thunderstruck and for a moment unable to speak. But the familiar voice in the phone went on, "It's me, it's me, S. I.! I'm quite serious! It's true! I found your aunt and uncle and their children! The children came by to see me and assured me that they all remember you, and that their parents will call you today. Wait for their call."

Tears were streaming down my cheeks.

No more than two hours later the phone rang again and I heard the voice of my dear aunt with whom I had had no contact for forty years! It was indeed my favorite Aunt Pesya speaking, along with her husband, Fishel. They asked which of our family were still alive. I said that Polina, the youngest daughter of Pesya's sister, Ronya, had survived. I gave her Polina's phone number in Kiev and heard Fishel say, "*Boruch Hashem, Boruch Hashem!*" ("God be praised, God be praised!"). Pesya and Fishel handled it much better than I did, I have to admit. Before they hung up, they told me that they would submit their documents to the Soviet consulate the next day, and that as soon as they got their visas, they would come for a visit.

I later learned that after her arrival in Los Angeles, S. I. had told her uncle about how I had freed her from her epileptic condition and the frequent seizures from which she had suffered for many years, and about my facetious request. Her uncle, Meier Frenkel, composed a letter the same day, made five hundred copies, and sent them out to American synagogues to see if someone might perhaps reply. Soon afterward a Portland rabbi, Yonah Geller, called them.[4] He told Mr. Frenkel that Fishel Katzan, who sometimes substituted for his synagogue's cantor, and his family were living in Portland. He had asked Fishel to come to see him and shown him Mr. Frenkel's letter. Dizzy with joy and "almost falling down," as he later told us, Fishel rushed home to share the joyful news with Aunt Pesya.

The two of them arrived in Moscow that July, if I remember correctly. Our mutual joy is impossible to describe. It was against Soviet rules for them to reside with us, so they stayed at an Intourist hotel, which was under the KGB's vigilant eye twenty-four hours a day. We could visit them there, of course, but anyone entering the hotel would be subject to surveillance. It was not a risk I wished to take. My intrepid Susanna, however, stopped by the hotel to pick them up in our car for a drive around Moscow before bringing them back to our home.

They had several meals with us, since I had assured Uncle Fishel that everything would be kosher. Pesya told us that among those still alive in our family was my great-uncle Shimon's son Berl, who had lain in the same grave with my brother, Yankel, but escaped. We also learned from Pesya that Miriam, the younger daughter of my mother's sister, Hannah, was living in Israel, while Ruvim, the son of my mother's brother, Yosele, was in Brazil. Pesya gave us their addresses and we were able to get in touch with them too. As soon as he heard from us, Ruvim flew to Moscow to meet the cousin his father had told him about. Ruvim's wife and son and daughter-in-law soon came to visit too. They returned home through Frankfurt, where at our request they called on Berl. Our conversations with them all when they visited went on until midnight, and more often than not came down to the need for us to emigrate as soon as possible, with promises from the visitors to send invitations, help us find work, and provide material support. The same promises were made to my cousin Polina in Kiev and to her husband, Mikhail Krell, and their son, Alik.

I had my doubts. First, my family and I were not ready to emigrate—our son was only in his third year of medical school. If we had applied to leave, he would have been expelled from the institute at once and drafted into the Soviet army. Second, my age (fifty-five at the time) and my professional and social circumstances, and Susanna's too, would not allow us to break with everything in one stroke to enter water where, as Grandmother Rivka would have said, you "cannot see the bottom"—that is, leave with no prospects whatever for an independent life. And so I listened politely but kept my own counsel.

Besides those issues, there was the question of Susanna's aged mother, whom we could not simply abandon to the mercy of fate. Susanna's mother had, since the death of her husband, Moishe-Boaz, in 1960, already been living with us for more than sixteen years. Because of her frailty and growing senility, it would have been impossible to take her with us. She in fact died ten years later in 1987 at the age of ninety-two. Her passing was felt most keenly by our children, who at the end had been her primary caregivers.

The first to emigrate were therefore my cousin Polina and her husband and son. Even though Pesya kept her promises and gave them every sort of material assistance, their first letters from the United States were not very hopeful. Aunt Pesya and Uncle Fishel's own letters, however, continued to urge us not to delay, since the "situation could change," making emigration impossible. Their son, Zeilik, came to see us the following year. He was more realistic and sensibly advised us that before undertaking such a momentous step, Susanna and I should first come for a visit to make a sober assessment of the situation and to see what we could truly rely on. As for our son, Zeilik persuaded us that it would indeed be possible for him to make a life for himself in America, once he had completed medical school. As it turned out, Zeilik was quite right about that.

In 1980 Solomon graduated from medical school and was, at my request, given a residency at the Psychiatric Institute of our hospital. When the Institute's new director, the anti-Semitic professor V. V. Kovalyov, learned that Miroslav Kozlovsky, that is, Solomon, was the son of Moisey Wolf, he immediately cancelled Solomon's appointment and gave him a new assignment as a clerk in the records department, where he would file medical histories. Solomon immediately informed me of the change. The information plunged me into a state verging on shock. Enraged, I went to see the chief physician, Inna Grivorievna Tyklina, intending to submit my resignation. She was completely taken aback by that idea and by my distraught demeanor. "What happened?" she asked.

I told her the bitter story and ended by saying that if I had not earned the right to have my son work in the institute on the same footing as the children of many other colleagues of hers and mine, then there was nothing more for me to do there. At that point certain qualities of her character that had been hidden from me revealed themselves: her strong sense of fair play and her ability without superfluous words to answer good with good. She leapt to her feet, tore up my letter of resignation, removed her white coat, and in a loud, angry voice, said, "Enough of this nonsense! Go back to your ward and let me to take care of this myself."

And she strode off at a quick pace to the office of the Party regional committee. Thirty minutes later she called me in my office and said with characteristic brusqueness, "It's been taken care of. Your son will work at the institute as a physician!" And without waiting for me to answer, she hung up.

The next morning the head of the Department of Organic Psychosis, Professor Rakhil Grigorievna Golodets, called Solomon to inform him that he had been assigned to her as a junior research fellow. Three years later he brilliantly defended his thesis and was awarded the degree of Candidate of Medical Sciences.

The time had come to attend to his personal life. As wise King Solomon said, "For everything there is a season, . . . a time to love . . . and a time to build."[5] The shift to the independent life of a husband and father from that of someone who had been attached and devoted to the life of his parents' home had its difficulties. But after overcoming various obstacles—the disappointments and sufferings of Goethe's young Werther[6]—Solomon passed that examination with honors too. At the end of 1981, the institute's chief resident, Valentin Alexandrovich Raisky, dropped by my office to talk about what he said was an important matter. "You have a fine son. Rakhil Grigorievna and all his colleagues at the institute like him and hold him in high regard. I think it's time he got married. A friend of mine has a wonderful daughter. Her name is Margarita—Rita—Leytes. If you have no objection, I can help with the introductions. Maybe your son would like to spend New Year's with her? Here's her number. Let him call her."

To the suggestion that they spend the New Year together, the pleasant (according to Solomon) voice of the young woman in question replied that she had already made plans to spend it with friends of her brother, who lived in the United States, but that she would be happy to meet after New Year's. A bit crestfallen, Solomon went to spend New Year's with his own friends at our new cooperative apartment. Susanna had prepared a delicious supper with wine for them. His friends came in couples. Only he was alone—without a young woman.

Susanna and I waited at home for his New Year's greeting. Around five minutes to twelve he called, happily conveying his greetings, and then adding in delight, "Papa! Guess who I met an hour ago! The girl Valentin Alexandrovich mentioned to you! It turned out that she'd been invited by a mutual friend who hadn't told her where they were going. When she got here and heard my name, she realized I was the one she was supposed to meet—as she loudly told her girlfriends . . ."

After a courtship of some eight months, Solomon announced that he had proposed to Margarita, and that her parents had invited us for supper. He asked us to accept their invitation. Could we even have considered refusing? Obviously not, and for so many reasons! We agreed on a time. Susanna, as a sign of our approval of Solomon's choice, gave his future bride the watch hanging from her neck (as I have already mentioned in a note). The obligations of each side in regard to the planning and execution of the wedding were agreed on, with the duties and costs to be shared equally, including hiring the hall, finding people to help, and ordering the food and drink.

The young people registered their union at the marriage registry office as required by Soviet law and then, in the fully furnished apartment we gave them, they celebrated their marriage according to the laws of Jewish tradition under a *chuppah* with the appropriate ceremonies and Jewish musical accompaniment. It was videotaped, but to our enormous chagrin, the Soviet exit-customs officer confiscated the tape when Rita's parents departed for the United States ahead of Solomon and his family.

Solomon and Margarita

A new stage began in the life of our son and in ours too. A beautiful offshoot broke loose from the tree. We had mixed feelings about his move to the new apartment. It was hardest on Susanna. It took us a long time to fall asleep that first night. Early the next morning I heard sobbing. I ran to the other room. Susanna was standing by the window. She was weeping bitter tears, and not just weeping, but howling in pain.

From that day forth Solomon would, before going home to his own apartment, drop by to see his mother. I myself saw him often during the day, since by then he was working in my ward. Susanna would revive when he came by and for a long time would not let him go. Gradually, however, she and I got used to the fact that he had left us. "We stole him from you," his mother-in-law would boast.

Rita soon got pregnant. We, and I in particular, greeted that event with joy. "God has heard my prayers," I thought, "and a new limb, a new extension, has sprung from the Wolf family tree." The pregnancy was uneventful, and that summer I took Solomon and Rita with me to a resort in the Crimea. And then they stayed with us in the cottage we had built next to our *dacha*. A month before the baby was due, I got the future mother a place in a rest home for expectant mothers in Sokolniki not far from the hospital where Solomon and I worked. That allowed us to visit her every day. I also managed to make an arrangement with the chief physician of Obstetric Hospital No. 9 for Rita to give birth there, since it was next door to her parents' home. A few weeks later, while I was on leave for treatment at a diabetic clinic outside Moscow, I got an urgent call informing me that Hospital No. 9 had been closed and placed under quarantine for a streptococcus outbreak. I needed to find an alternative quickly with facilities no worse than the first. Fortunately, I was able to make new arrangements over the phone, registering Rita at another hospital.

On December 25, 1984, *in a mazldiker sho* (at a lucky hour), our granddaughter was born. We named her—*ir tsu lange yorn*: may she live long!—Lyubov or Ahavah ("Love" in Russian and Hebrew, respectively) after my lost sister, Libche. She bears that name with unfeigned pride to this day. From the moment of her birth she became, just like her two sisters after her, the meaning of my life: Lyuba, Lyubochka, Lyubochka-Golubochka (my sweetheart), Lyubka—Love. She earned that name not only because she inherited the best qualities of her ancestors and our son, but also because a love has been instilled in her for the Jewish people and its traditions and for the Hebrew language and Israel and its future (a topic to which I will return). Lyubochka, God be thanked, grew and made everyone happy, even old grandmother Tsilya, who because of her great age no longer recognized her or any of the rest of the family. Tsilya would notice her and say, "See what a beautiful child has come to visit us!"

Lyubochka spent every spring and summer with her parents at our *dacha*, a circumstance that made me love that plot of land all the more and want to replant the vegetable garden every year. Lyubochka started to talk around one. Her first word was *"pugaga"*—*pugovitsa,* or "button." Later that spring when I was planting seedlings or sewing seeds, she would walk behind me and take a seedling and put it in the hole that had been dug for it and ask, "Grandpa, Grandpa, with the little bud up or down?" And then she would do just as I told her.

And after that? After that came walks to the woods near our *dacha*. When, following a rain, puddles formed on the unpaved road leading to the woods, I would take her hand and help her over them. Once while doing so I said something like, "Op-pa!" Whenever we came to a puddle after that, she would, depending on its size, say "big op-pa" or "little op-pa," and then with obvious joy take my hand and jump over it. In the woods she liked to climb onto stumps and jump from them into my arms. There was a small pond there and she would insist on our walking all the way around it.

She liked the story "with continuations" I used to make up about a hunter. Each time I was supposed to repeat the previous episodes but could not always do so exactly. Lyubochka would immediately point out, "Grandpa! That isn't right! Yesterday you told it a different way!" And I would have to correct my mistake. Returning home, she would run ahead, triumphantly looking back from time to time to show me how well she knew the way. She would stop only when she came to a big or little "op-pa." My thoughts were so filled with her in my leisure that I started to write poems that, it goes without saying, were dedicated to her, to "*Tayer* (Darling) Lyubochka."

Time flew by and soon she was enrolled in a kindergarten near our home, and then later on in the winter she would go skiing, and in the summer, horseback riding. She liked to be told stories and to sing Russian ditties, such as "In the Forest Grew a Little Spruce," "Grandpa and Grandma Together," "A Birthday Happens Only Once a Year," and so on.

Once, on my birthday, she brought me flowers.

Around that time, the Leyteses—Rita's parents—were getting ready to emigrate to the United States, to Palo Alto, California, where their son had been living for eight years. They urged Solomon and his family to join them there. Susanna and I were not ready for such a move, as I have already indicated. And naturally we did not want our only son to leave us. He realized that. Moreover, he himself did not want to be supported by anyone in the first years before he had passed the examinations that would allow him to practice medicine in America. A certain tension about that had emerged in his relationship with Rita and her parents, and between the latter and Susanna and me. I wrote to Aunt Pesya about it. She at once took the situation in hand. "You must stop putting it off and come visit and have a look at everything yourself," she said. "We'll send an invitation at once. You can meet Morris Wolf's children and the descendants of your grandfather's brothers, Sheiya (Sam) and Osher (Harry). They're very prosperous and prominent people in Portland. It isn't out of the question that they'll be able to help Solomon find work, and we ourselves will also help to get him established."

A month later I received a formal invitation to visit from Morris's son Leslie, sent by him instead of Pesya because of complications she had run into in regard to the change of her maiden name; and in August 1987 I flew to New York.

Told of my visit, Miriam, the surviving daughter of my mother's sister, came to New York from Israel with her husband, Zulya. Even though we had not seen each other in over fifty years, we had no trouble recognizing each other. I also met another cousin on my mother's side who had lived in New York since 1930, along with his daughters and some other members of Miriam's family. All of them greeted me with open arms. Five days later I left for Portland.

Although Aunt Pesya and Uncle Fishel had after their visit to Moscow moved from Portland to Los Angeles along with their son, Zeilik, and his wife, Rena, and their daughter, Rakhil, and Rakhil's own two daughters, they had done everything to ensure that my other Portland relatives would receive me in a fitting way. Zcilik and Rena even came from Los Angeles to Portland to act as interpreters, since I had no English at the time. It is essential to emphasize that all my Portland relatives were magnificently hospitable. Each of them—Morris's sons, Martin and Leslie, and his daughter, Maureen; and Harry's daughter, Blossom, and her children, especially her son, Jeffrey L. Grayson—all of them devoted a day to a reception in my honor, and all showed in various ways how glad they were that I had come and that we were at last meeting each other.

Uncle Fishel and my beloved Aunt Pesya also provided a great deal of material and moral support, just as they had promised to do. Fishel died in 1999 and Pesya in 2000—*zichronam livracha* (may God bless their memories). And eternal memory as well to their son, Zeilik, who passed away a year before his father died.

After Portland, I visited Los Angeles and not only Aunt Pesya and Uncle Fishel but also the family of Ronya's daughter, Polina. Thanks to the efforts and unceasing support of Pesya and Zeilik, Polina and her family were decently established in a subsidized furnished apartment in the Fairfax area, the city's Jewish neighborhood. Their son, Alik, was working as a staff electrician and earning good money and had raised both a son, the brilliant Marc, who had graduated from university at the age of eighteen and was a college professor, and a daughter, Ronya, named after her great-grandmother. Polina and Mikhail no longer regretted leaving Kiev, although they had been comfortable there too.

I also managed during that summer of 1987 to meet Professor Daniel Friedman, the director of the Neuropsychiatric Institute at UCLA.[7] He had promised to give me twenty minutes, but we ended up talking for two hours. He was not, however, able to offer any work ("It's too late and you don't know the language"). A few of his younger Russian-speaking colleagues, whom he had hired after they got their American licenses, confirmed that in order to obtain work as doctors in America, they had had to relearn everything and work like dogs for five or six years. A bit more encouraging was a visit in Vancouver, Washington, with a professor I had been introduced to by Martin Wolf. When, at the end of our conversation, he learned that my son spoke English, he promised to give him work after his arrival, although not, until he got his license, as a physician.

I did not return home from America entirely empty handed, either. Aunt Pesya had, along with an official invitation for our daughter, given me $5,000 to spend on gifts, a sum that would go a long, long way in Moscow.

But I was still torn about emigrating. I was overjoyed by Aunt Pesya's family feeling, which had not diminished during the long period of our separation; on the contrary, in everything she did, she showed time and again her devotion to and sense of responsibility for all of us, the remnants of a clan that had been nearly wiped out by the Holocaust. And I was confident that with God's help and that of Aunt Pesya and her son, and perhaps even of the other members of the Wolf clan, Solomon, at least, would be able to find his way in America. The rest, however, filled me with alarm. I had during my brief stay become acquainted with American culture, with the mode of thought of its people, their behavior, their rules, their beliefs, and I took no comfort in any of it. It was obvious that neither I nor Susanna would be able to work, that we would have to assume the unenviable role of pensioners. And I was dubious about our daughter's future too.

Nevertheless, our son's emigration seemed more and more likely. He asked me how he should proceed: submit his own application along with those of his wife and her parents or refuse to go with them. I replied that he was an adult and entitled to make up his own mind, but that his daughter must not grow up orphaned by her living father, that he must be with her. As for us—his mother and I and his sister, who had no wish to emigrate—life would show us what to do.

With heavy hearts, we said our farewells, and in August 1990 Solomon and his family departed for America. Several of our Portland relatives met them on their arrival. The Jewish Federation of Greater Portland provided them with a subsidized furnished apartment, and with the help of God and the short-term aid of our relatives, both our son and daughter-in-law landed on their feet. Lyubochka was enrolled in the Portland Jewish Academy. The first two months, as her parents told us, were very hard for her as she struggled to get used to completely different surroundings, but soon she started to speak English and then quickly adapted.

For us, however, the separation from Solomon but especially from Lyubochka, was very hard to bear. Not a day went by when we were not in tears. Life without our son and granddaughter seemed meaningless, and in the end we too decided to emigrate. It took a year and a half to receive the invitation, submit the necessary documents, and obtain the airline ticket through the Hebrew Immigrant Aid Society or HIAS. On March 1, 1992, we left Moscow early in the morning and arrived in Portland later the same day with two carry-ons each and two more checked bags. I should add that I also managed to bring a Torah scroll that never left my hands the whole way. We were met at the airport in Portland by our son and daughter-in-law and by Martin Wolf.

With the assistance of the Jewish Federation of Greater Portland, an apartment was rented for us near our son and his family. Thus did a new life begin. *Vayeired Yaakov Mitzrayma* (And Jacob went down into Egypt) [8] . . .

Part Four

♪♪♪

1992–2006

Return to Cheremoshno and Melnitsa. Portland. Israel. Nadezhda. Grandchildren.

♪♪♪

I finished the preceding part of this book two years ago.[1] There was in the interim a bitter event in the life of my family that took from me my desire to write—that took my will and my ability to concentrate. But time has played its healing role, gradually easing the pain and clearing the mind, even an aged one like my own. But before I speak of that event and tell the rest of my story, I need to return to the last part.

It ended with my "going down into" America just as our ancient ancestor Jacob had gone down into Egypt. Many Torah commentators have wondered why in the account of the patriarch Jacob's departure from Canaan to join his favorite son, Joseph, the verb "went down" (*vayeired*) was used instead of "came." The most authoritative commentator on the Bible and Talmud, the eleventh-century Rashi,[2] explains the choice of *vayeired* this way: "went down" means that Jacob "descended many steps below." Rashi adds that whenever someone leaves a place of established residence, he "goes down" and his splendor, wealth, and fame are reduced to nothing.

I cite Rashi here to indicate the kind of thoughts and feelings that were troubling me, an old man of seventy, as I considered whether to emigrate or stay where I was. To emigrate would mean leaving our apartments and *dacha*, my hospital ward created at an enormous expense of effort, the work I loved, the patients whom I had treated and who trusted and respected me and who gave me my standing as a doctor, and my colleagues and the other scientists at the institute who had nurtured my scientific career. Would abandoning all that be right? It was a very hard and painful decision. Most emigrants make a similar one. The young, however, are encouraged by faith that they will master the new country's language, customs, and culture. They are confident that they will be able to continue working in their professions or else will find new ones, and so on. In the end, it will seem to them that they have lost nothing by the change of residence.

There was another issue, too.

Around that time an Israeli couple had entered our lives—Tzvi Tal and his wife, Hannah. Tzvi was a short, stocky, broad-shouldered man who said little but knew how to listen and was a *shofet* (justice) of the Supreme Court of Israel.[3] Hannah taught Hebrew and headed the Machanayim Society's placement bureau for women "repatriated" from the Soviet Union.[4] Both Tzvi and Hannah were *vatikim* (old-timers)—native-born residents of Israel who had never left. They had two sons, one of whom was killed in the 1973 Yom Kippur War, while the other was a professor at the Hebrew University of Jerusalem. Tzvi and Hannah had been sent to Moscow in 1991 by the Machanayim Society (the word means "two camps") to promote through the newly organized Moscow Yeshiva the renewal of Jewish spiritual life after the capital's liberation from the Communist regime.

Both Tzvi and Hannah became friends and of course urged us to come to Israel, promising to use their great authority in the country to help us and our daughter obtain work in our professions and find good apartments. I was ready "even tomorrow" to realize my old dream of returning to my ancestral land. Nadya, however, having secured a place in the Moscow music world as a soloist, accompanist, and composer, was opposed to emigrating anywhere, but especially to Israel, which was full of unemployed musicians. Her ignorance of Hebrew, the state language, also alarmed her. She resisted for a long time, refusing to go to any new country. In the end, however, she yielded to my insistent pleas to emigrate to America, putting off a final decision until she had conducted her own reconnaissance.

Two months before we left I underwent my last Soviet (or Russian) humiliation. Those departing the country were permitted to take no more than one hundred kilograms of baggage, which would be subject to demeaning inspection by the exit-customs authorities as it crossed the border. Naturally, that restriction was a tremendous obstacle. Of everyday items (clothing, footwear, bed linen, kitchenware, family pictures, and the like) no more than forty-eight kilograms were allowed. The rest—antiques and cultural and artistic treasures—could only be taken out of the country with special permission.

To avoid conflicts, it was necessary to get rid of everything "extra." For me, that above all meant my rich psychiatric, literary, and religious library of over two thousand volumes. I gave most of it to the Lvov Jewish Library and the library of the Gannushkin Psychiatric Hospital, with the rest going to colleagues and friends. I had been collecting and using the books for such a long time that parting with them was very distressing. They had been my helpers and my consultants, and now I suddenly had to get rid of them. There was nothing

I could do about it, however, and I took comfort in the thought that many other old psychiatrists had done the same thing, donating their own books and archives to libraries or friends.

It was even more painful to part with my personal archive and its unpublished articles, abstracts, lectures, extracts and excerpts, copies of case histories, letters from patients and friends, and a great deal else besides. All of it had to be put to the torch. One of my friends spent a day helping me with that sinful business. Each burned file of documents seared my brain and heart. Fifteen years have passed since then, and still the flame and ash of that little bonfire often rise up before me. It left a significant scar on my soul.

Getting permission to take works of art and literature of particular value was also difficult. Especially precious to me were two antique objects of religious significance—parchment scrolls of the Torah and the Megillah (Book of Esther)—and several paintings by a former patient of mine, the well-known artist Tatyana Oranskaya, already mentioned in regard to her portrait of my son. The scrolls required authorization not only from the Ministry of Culture but also from the Moscow Rabbinate and the director of the Central Jewish Museum. I was helped in dealing with all three institutions by well-connected friends.

I think everything that could be saved, however reduced in size, was saved and taken with us. But the main and most essential thing in my soul, the memory of my lost family, remained and tore at me ever more painfully the closer our departure came. That I would be unable to bid farewell to the graves and remains of my family shot and burned by German thugs (*Yemach shemo vezichro*: May their names and memory be obliterated!) gave me no peace. I had no clear idea where my family members were buried, nor did we or anyone else even know to whom to turn for help. That tormented me terribly. For it meant a failure to carry out the ancient commandment to honor thy father and thy mother all the days of thy life. It seemed that the sin would lie upon me like a heavy stone for the rest of my life. "A grievous sin for the rest of my life! For the rest of my life! For the rest of my life!" constantly, relentlessly throbbed in my mind.

And then something happened that cannot be called anything other than a miracle.

Before we left for America, Susanna and I made a last holiday visit to a health spa in the Crimea. One afternoon, by sheer accident, I happened to notice an envelope left on a cafeteria table with the return address of Cheremoshno! My head started to spin and I set off at a run. I quickly found the man to whom the envelope had been addressed and asked him who in Cheremoshno had written to him. He said that the letter had come from the principal of the village school, and he told me his last name, Kovalchuk, which I recalled hearing as a child. It emerged from our conversation that the old people of the village still remembered my grandfather and grandmother and the rest of our relatives who had lived there. My very kind interlocutor understood from my agitated state how important it was for me to see my family's grave and he immediately invited Susanna and me to visit him, an offer we gratefully accepted. We were treated to genuinely warm hospitality when we got there. The school principal, who had been in his teens at the time, told us the details of the shooting and mass burial of the victims of Nazism fifty years before and offered to take us to the site in his car. He came by for us the next morning.

The burial ground turned out to be near Melnitsa, where my grandfather and grandmother had spent their last years, as I mentioned in Part One of this account. Deep within a dense pine wood we found a glade about one hundred and fifty meters long and one hundred wide overgrown with tall, yellowing grass and surrounded by a low, ramshackle fence. In the center of the glade was a little wooden post with a plywood board lying next to it. On the board were some words in Ukrainian: "*Tut zakhoroneny dvinadtsat tysiach radianskikh gromodian, znishchennykh nimitskimi okkupantami*" ("Buried here are twelve thousand Soviet citizens killed by German invaders"). And that was all! No date, no names, no ethnic identity!

I stood speechless for a few moments. My throat turned dry and then I fell over onto the fence, probably fainting for a few seconds. I opened my eyes in the embrace of the school principal. I do not remember his comforting words, but the ones that raised me from my swoon rang out like a command: "Pray! Pray, I tell you!" Leaning on his shoulder, I started to recite with a thick tongue the words of the Jewish prayer for the dead: "*El malei rachamim . . .*" ("God full of mercy . . ."). Tears were streaming down my face. Susanna stood beside me and wept too. Then with the principal's help she pulled me away from that mass killing ground and put me in the car, and we returned to the home of our host.

Thus passed my farewell to the grave of my beloved, never to be forgotten mama and my sisters (my father and brother were killed elsewhere, as I have told), my grandfather, my grandmother, and the rest of my relatives, some thirty in all. I returned to Moscow with a heavy heart and a sense of having performed only part of my duty, and the words "for I shall never go there again" ringing in my mind.

The day of our departure for America, the three of us—Susanna, Nadya, and I— were accompanied to the airport by Susanna's brothers and their sons and a number of other relatives of hers, along with two guards from among my most trusted friends. The latter were necessary because of the robberies that at the time had been taking place along the airport access roads. We reached our destination safely, and the inspection of our things also passed without complications. But when it came to the Torah scroll I had been carrying in my arms the whole time, the airport officials insisted that I check it as baggage. We were forced to make a direct appeal to the supervisor for special authorization from him. I explained that according to the laws of the Jewish faith, it was forbidden to keep the Torah with things that lay on the floor, and even more so in a hold under an area where people walk. The supervisor turned out to be a good-natured, inquisitive fellow. To his question about what Jews would do if a Torah scroll should accidentally fall on the floor, I replied that anyone present at such a lamentable event would be required to fast for a month. He smiled and said, "Oh, in that case, it's a serious business. I can't take such a sin on myself. Here's a permit allowing the scroll on board, and may God bless you. Hold on tight to your Torah!"

As indeed I did.

We arrived in Portland late the same night. We were met, as I have mentioned, by my cousin Martin Wolf and by Solomon and Margarita, who took us directly from the airport to a modestly furnished two-bedroom apartment that had already been rented for us. There were other Jews living in the building who had fled Russia just as we had, and we enjoyed good relations with them all from the start.

We were helped into the American rhythm of life by our son and our neighbors, as well as by the Jewish Federation of Greater Portland, led by its executive director, Charlie Schiffman; by the prominent philanthropist and public figure Jerry Stern; and by a number of other righteous Jews who had settled in Portland many years before our arrival, such as the retired barber Yasha Berenshtein and his wife, Maria, and the computer expert Mihail Elisman.

A special role in my adaptation was played by Charlie, a man of moral principles recalling those of Uncle Vassil in the story by the famous Yiddish writer I. L. Peretz.[5] Charlie has sustained us with his warm, considerate heart, and to this day has been an unselfish friend of our and many other Jewish families. A separate story could and should be written about him. No one who has turned to him in need has ever gone without help, although most of what he does for believers and nonbelievers alike is done *beseter*—secretly. He speaks Hebrew fluently. His father was a member of the Israeli police force until old age. Charlie has helped scores of Russian Jews find work and obtain necessary material and medical assistance. In difficult times he is wherever he is needed most.

He played a special role in my life in another way, as well.

To convey how, I will have to return to my early childhood. Even before I was three, Grandmother Rivka, herself the daughter of a rabbi, as I have said, would make me recite a short prayer every morning when I woke, the *Modeh ani:* *"Modeh ani le'fanecha melech chai v'kayom shehechezarta bi nishmati b'chemla, raba emunatecha"* ("I offer thanks to Thee, living eternal King, for Thou hast mercifully returned my soul to me, great is Thy belief in me").[6] According to Judaism, sleep resembles nonexistence, a vanishing of our souls, which God returns to us each morning when we wake. That is why everyone on waking must first thank God for the "return of his soul."

It was in fact Charlie Schiffman who gave me back my own Jewish soul, nearly lost after fifty years in the Soviet "paradise"; for there I could neither speak Hebrew, nor pray openly, nor freely read Jewish literature, nor, because of my profession, publicly honor our holy days and other traditions. All I had been taught for seventeen years by my parents and my grandfathers and grandmother, by my teachers at the Tarbut Hebrew Gymnasium, and especially by Rabbi Maisel, who had instructed me in Warsaw, had largely been put aside.

After our first ten-minute conversation, Charlie both believed me and had faith in me. He was instrumental in arranging for me to publish articles in the Portland English-language *Jewish Review* about the weekly Torah chapter, the history of the Jewish people, the reborn state of Israel, and so forth, all of the articles in Russian to provide a way for Jews newly arrived from Russia to become familiar with Jewish history, culture, and traditions. Charlie wrote a letter about me to the numerous local Jewish federations in the United States and Canada, suggesting that they invite me to lecture in Yiddish. Thanks to his letter, I received requests from Jewish institutions and organizations in a number of American and Canadian cities, including Washington, New York, Chicago, Los Angeles, Palm Beach, Vancouver, and Toronto.

Thanks to Charlie, too, I was able to prepare two reference works for Soviet Jewish immigrants, the first a Hebrew-Yiddish, and the second a Hebrew-Yiddish-Russian-English lexicon.[7] My kind "Uncle Vassil" also introduced me to Portland religious life. I had the honor of taking part in reading the weekly chapters of the Torah and Megillah at the city's main synagogues, thereby becoming acquainted with the spiritual (religious) development of American Jewry. The preceding are only the main things that Charlie has done for me personally. Besides them, he has also done a great deal for my family. When things have been hard for us, we have had a tested friend to whom we could turn, knowing that help would come.

I have been given no less happiness by the well-known Portland businessman and philanthropist Jerry Stern. His shining eyes, reserved yet warm smile, and the friendly accessibility he communicates in his first meetings with people mark him as an exceptional man. Our first conversation created the impression that he had come into the world to do good for others, and that impression has never been disappointed. He and his charitable activities are known throughout the city.

Before I met Jerry, I had been told how after the liberalizing reforms of *Glasnost* and *Perestroika* introduced in the Soviet Union in 1985,[8] he had, following an instruction in his father's will, tracked down in the Volga city of Saratov three families of until then unknown relatives and brought them to Portland. He had bought each family a home, given them a monthly allowance, hired English teachers for them, and found them work. I was told too that during a visit to Russia he had arranged to send two hundred and fifty indigent Jews to Israel by charter airline at his own expense. Here in Portland, and also in Palm Springs, California, where he has another home, he has been a stalwart of the local synagogues and philanthropic organizations. In the annual lists published in the *Jewish Review* of those who have given financial support to various organizations, Jerry and his family have been preeminent.

Our first meeting took place in Charlie Schiffman's office. I had dropped by to greet Charlie on the 5,754th Jewish New Year (1994). While I was there, a smiling, modestly dressed man of medium height came in. It was obvious from his casual demeanor that he and Charlie were old friends. He greeted Charlie and then turned to me. Charlie made the introductions. "A true Jew, Dr. Moishe Wolf, recently arrived on our shores from Moscow."

The newcomer shook my hand and held it a bit longer than usual in his own soft, wide, warm one and said, "Jerry Stern!" And then with a broad, good-natured smile, he said, "How are you?" adding in Yiddish in a slightly ironical echo of Charlie's words, *"Vus macht an emeser yid?"* ("How's a true Jew doing?").

Charlie, not wanting to leave the matter there, proceeded to give his smiling friend an explanation. "We were comparing our knowledge of New Year's prayers and melodies."

"Well?"

"It's amazing! He hasn't prayed in over fifty years, yet he remembers everything. He could be a cantor in one of our synagogues."

With a sigh, Jerry turned serious. "Yes! I just got back from there. I saw and heard everything. The Soviets tore everything Jewish from the souls of our brothers." And then he asked me, "How did you manage to learn all that and not forget?"

"It's a long story. If you like, we'll get together some time and I'll tell you."

"Of course! We must do that!" And in fractured Yiddish he ended the conversation, said goodbye, and left.

A few days later our telephone rang. "Good morning, Moishe! This is Jerry. Would you like to have breakfast together? There's a little Jewish restaurant nearby that serves only kosher. It's a comfortable place where we can have a quiet meal and chat."

I thanked him and of course agreed, giving him my address. He came by shortly afterward in his car. He opened the door for me from the inside and with a friendly smile invited me to get in. The restaurant's owner, an old friend of his, was waiting for us in front and took us to a table for two. After seating us, he asked Jerry, "The usual?"

Jerry nodded. A heartfelt conversation then followed over our meal. That time I did most of the talking. I told him about what I had experienced in my two previous worlds—free Poland and Bolshevik Russia—and then about what seemed to await me here in rich, democratic America. I could tell from the questions he asked for clarification and from the responsive expression on his face that he was listening with care and empathy. When I had finished, he sighed deeply and said, "It's all quite clear. I understand and sympathize. But you have to realize that you are not alone. I know all your relatives, both those who have already passed away and those who are still alive and flourishing. The latter will help you. And more than anyone, your deceased father's sister, Pesya, and her husband, Fishel, will do so. That they're no longer in Portland but in Los

Angeles doesn't matter. Your son will soon finish his residency and have his own practice and won't need help anymore but will be able to help you. And there will be others who will help you and your wife and daughter. And finally, what am I in this world for? You can always turn to me if things get hard. We're not about to go away!"

But I never did have to turn to him, for he himself would come by from time to time to see if there was anything we needed. I would of course express my appreciation but say that, thanks to God, we had everything we wanted; we weren't starving or sleeping on the street. Jeffrey Grayson, a grandson of my great-uncle Harry Wolf and a well-known millionaire in the city, had agreed to pay our rent for a year. After that God and the Section 8 program would see us through.[9]

Jerry, however, had been informed of the actual state of our affairs and of the fact that Nadya still had not found work and that living with us had been hard for her. Without injuring her pride, he quickly found a way to help her buy the house in which Susanna and I now live, and in which he continues to visit us. Once he asked me if I would like to see an essay written by his father in Yiddish after the death of Jerry's mother. And there the remarkable source of his goodness was revealed to me. In all my life I had never read such a touching elegy. With inimitable love the author described in simple Yiddish words the noble, radiant qualities of his departed wife and his own grief and sense of loss. No one, not even his kind, loving children, was able to fill the void within him or assuage his grief. Reading autobiographical works of that kind had never brought me to tears before, but this time they ran down my cheeks unbidden. Although he cannot read Yiddish, Jerry has held onto that handwritten avowal (and its English translation) as the apple of his eye. It evidently stands as a model for him of how one should act, and of his love for his own wife, Helen, love she so richly deserves.

On another occasion, Jerry asked me how I regarded the state of Israel. I said that I had been raised from early childhood to love our ancestral homeland, and that it had been my life's dream to move one day to the land of our ancient forebears, where my cousin and her children and grandchildren were already living. I also told him how that cousin, upon learning of my first visit to America in 1987, had made special a trip to New York to meet my flight, and after the usual kisses and embraces had started to make me feel ashamed that I, who was such a "passionate patriot" of Israel and who knew Hebrew perfectly, had nonetheless been sitting in anti-Semitic Russia instead of making *aliyah*, that is, emigrating to Israel. She had ended her speech with the words, "I feel certain that you and your family will come to us. *Leshana haba'ah b'Yerushalayim!* Next year in Jerusalem!"

"We-e-ll?" Jerry asked. Implied in that drawled response were all the questions that I had failed to answer.

"As you see, I'm here. And I think you understand very well why my children and grandchild and my wife and I have come to this country. If I were younger, I might perhaps be of some use to our state. But to go there as a pensioner and a burden . . . There are already too many such people in Israel, even without me."

"You may be right about that. But wouldn't you at least like to visit Israel?"

"Wanting and being able are two big differences, as they say in Odessa."

"True!" Realizing that the topic was awkward for me, Jerry dropped it, apparently for good—or so it seemed.

Two or three months passed and then the phone rang again. "It's Jerry! Are you free? I have something important I want to talk to you about."

Ten minutes later he was sitting in front of me with his usual warm smile. After making sure that I still wanted to go to Israel, he told me to get ready to do so—to submit my documents to the appropriate office and call him when I had a reply. The gist was that he was going to buy me a round-trip ticket and give me a small fund for expenses, so that I would not have to rely on anyone else but could simply be a tourist in Israel for a month. Can my feelings at that moment be imagined? I was dumbstruck. A few moments passed and then I embraced him with tears running down my cheeks. He at once started to calm me down and said in a gently reproving voice, "Stop it! Get a hold of yourself! You aren't the first and I hope you won't be the last either. Get ready for the trip and give your thanks not to me but to God! When you return, we'll get together and you can tell me all about it." And with that we parted.

I arrived in Israel on the eve of *Pesach*—Passover. And I did indeed spend a month there, three weeks of it in Haifa with the families of my cousin, Miriam, and her children. They all gave generously of their time and attention, acquainting me with various historic places and prominent figures in the country and relating their critical views of the foreign and domestic policies of the Jewish state, all the while stressing their love of and devotion to the country: "*Ein li eretz acharet*" ("There is no other land for us"). Hoping to convince me, they constantly repeated how essential it was for us not to put it off, but to make the decision to join them.

I met many old acquaintances there—colleagues, students, and former Communists who while still in the Soviet Union had condemned with unfeigned indignation the "Zionist grovelers and traitors" who were abandoning their homeland for Israel. Along with such people, I found others who described themselves as *marranos*[10] who in the Soviet Union had been forced to "dine with the wolves" to avoid persecution.

I spent the last week in Jerusalem with the family of our friends Tzvi and Hannah Tal. During the last week of her and Tzvi's visit to Moscow, Hannah had grown close to Susanna, who had helped her get ready for her return home. Thanks to Tzvi, I was able to visit the Israeli Supreme Court or Bagatz, the parliament or Knesset, built with funds from James de Rothschild as a gift to the state of Israel, along with many other places that would have been closed to an ordinary tourist. Susanna and I have remained in phone and e-mail contact with Tzvi and Hannah ever since.

I will say one more thing. There in the Holy Land I became convinced of just how capable the Jewish people is, despite its colossal recent losses—the six million murdered in World War II by Hitler's thugs, and those lost in the on-going struggle with the neighboring Arab countries and the terrorist gangs that have taken refuge in them. I became convinced too of the ancient Aramaic saying that "*avira d'Israeil machkima mavra*" ("the air of the land of Israel makes one wise").[11] Everything that our long-suffering people has achieved in such a short period in the areas of culture, the economy, building, science, scholarship, and defensive strength brings delight and a profound belief that *am Yisrael hai le'olam va'ed* (the Jewish people will live forever). I would have included here a more complete account of my trip to Israel, had it not been beyond the scope of this book.[12]

I returned refreshed, tanned, strengthened, and, it may well be, even a little wiser. And of course I called Jerry Stern the moment I got back.

Over the course of our twelve-year acquaintance, I have had the pleasure of seeing Jerry and his wife, Helen, many times and have always been delighted by their tender affection and respect for each another. I was fortunate to be present at the celebration of their golden wedding anniversary. I put my own sincere feelings in verse. A few years ago Jerry and Helen changed their main place of residence, giving more time to their home in California but spending holidays in Portland, where their son and two daughters and their families still live. And when they are in town they never fail to call or visit us.

Besides those prominent individuals and their wives, our life in Portland has been blessed by a number of other less well-known people who stood by us in difficult times and helped in whatever way they could. I want to say a few words about the most remarkable of them.

Above all, I cannot fail to mention the lively, colorful Yasha Berenshtein, a long-retired barber who was a gifted reciter of the works of famous Russian poets and a devotee of performance whistling, as well as an organizer of artistic entertainments for the elderly residents of the Robison Jewish Home (now Cedar Sinai Park) in Portland. I was introduced to that extraordinary man by my relative Jeffrey Grayson, the son of Grandfather Yeruchim's niece Blossom, as I mentioned in the account of my first visit to the United States in 1987. Jeffrey organized a reception in my honor then and invited all my local relatives, along with Yasha, as toastmaster, and his wife, Maria, as an interpreter, since I had no English then. Yasha's talents were immediately apparent. He masterfully recited poetry, danced, whistled, told humorous stories, and was the life of the party. We became fast friends and remained in touch after my return to Moscow. He was among those who met Solomon and his family at the airport when they arrived in Portland three years later. Yasha took them under his wing, and then after Susanna and Nadya and I came, he got involved in our lives too. He and I remained close until his passing in 1998.

Many other Portland immigrants have warm memories of him, since he was one of several volunteers who met new arrivals at the airport and took them to the apartments that the Jewish Federation of Greater Portland had rented for them. He then kept a close eye on them for a good while afterward, providing various services as needed. Everyone in the city knew and respected Yasha. His wife, Maria, was just like him. He would arrive at social events dressed like a London dandy, escorting her by the arm with conspicuous pride. He would frequently drop by to see us unannounced but always with intriguing propositions that it was impossible to turn down. He introduced us to interesting people and picturesque places in the city and to its synagogues and other social institutions. He had humorous opinions about them all, which he happily shared.

A very interesting person named Mihail (or Misha) Elisman also became a close friend of ours. A taciturn, soft-spoken engineer and master computer programmer, he is not only a lover of music but a talented musician who plays the flute and the piano. He is a regular participant in orchestral programs and also performs as a soloist. His specialty, however, is *goodness*. You never have to ask twice. He hurries to be of service at the first sign. He is an exceptionally devoted father, and does everything he possibly can for his daughter. I myself have been the happy beneficiary of his goodness more than once. His life is not easy, but he never complains, and that may be why it is so hard to help him in return.

Let me say a few words about two other people who from the first days of my time in Portland have helped to keep me afloat: Paul Haist, the editor of the *Jewish Review*, and Deborah Moon, the city editor and his deputy. Thanks to Paul, I have for the past thirteen years had my own Russian column, twelve years in the biweekly paper and this year in the Internet edition. No other English-language Jewish newspaper in the United States hosts a Russian column, although I would not by that remark wish to imply that mine is anything special; indeed, it is only thanks to Paul's stubbornness and Deborah's assistance that the *Jewish Review* continues to publish it in the Internet edition.

Despite all the efforts of my friends, I remained unemployed. My volunteer work at the Portland State University library, the Portland Jewish Academy, and the Oregon Health and Science University (OHSU) sleep clinic and electroencephalography laboratory led to nothing secure, which depressed my general mood. It was only later through the efforts of my son that I was able to work as a consultant at the OHSU Intercultural Psychiatry Clinic. For various financial reasons, I refused to accept a fee, but the work considerably improved my outlook. The chance to be useful again, to give patients medical and social assistance, inspired me. I even presumed to co-author with my son an article on the treatment of schizophrenia in Russia with Clozaril (clozapine), published in the journal *Psychiatric Services* in 1995.[13] Over the years I established my own niche at the clinic. Many patients got used to me and I to them, and some of them even became friends and now visit me at home. I have also been enriched by my trips to other cities to lecture. The opportunity to publish in various magazines and newspapers has also occupied a good deal of my time and flattered my self-esteem, however falsely it may have done so.

My greatest joy, however, has come from our son's family. Solomon and Margarita have good, secure jobs and their own home on a plot of green land, and he enjoys the respect of his patients and the hospital administration. He is surrounded by friends and, thank God, he and his children are well provided for. He has fulfilled all my hopes for him, and despite the burdens of his work, he is for us, his aged parents, our only support, even though he may not always be immediately available. But I understand that he is busy not only with his work but also at home. His children will not go to bed without him, and he has other responsibilities there too. I fully understand that, and it would be far better to say nothing (my policy, in fact), but resentment, however groundless, accumulates and then finds an outlet, naturally producing a pained reaction. But he forgives my elderly irritability and discontent. And I? I have always forgiven him and do forgive him and have asked God to forgive him too.

Our grandchildren have also given us much joy. Of the eldest, Lyuba, who will soon be twenty-two (may she live to be 120!), I have already written above. I only want to add that she has inherited the best qualities of her father and imbibed Jewishness from the first days of her life. As I mentioned earlier, she attended the Portland Jewish Academy, where she was one of its best students. She celebrated her *bat mitzvah* at twelve, just as a young girl should. At the Shaarie Torah synagogue in Portland she conducted the evening and morning services by herself, including the main part, reading the Torah chapter *Ha'azinu* (Harken) in its entirety, as well as the *Maftir* and *Haftarah* (further selections from the Nevi'im or Prophets).[14] After blessing, Portland's most senior rabbi, Yonah Geller, remarked that no girl in his memory had ever led the service and read the Torah with such precision and beauty.

After finishing the Portland Jewish Academy, Lyuba went to Lake Oswego High School, from which she graduated with distinction in 2003. She was also named a Presidential Scholar as one of the best high-school students in the country and went to Washington to receive a gold medal from the First Lady.[15] She then entered Stanford University, where she has also been an exceptional student, from her first year providing tutoring in Hebrew and mathematics and taking an active part in campus Jewish social life. The Hillel rabbi has often invited her to read the Torah and lead the service, and she enjoys the respect of the faculty and her fellow students. Last summer she spent a month in Israel and charmed both our relatives and our friends, communicating with them in Hebrew. She came home tanned and invigorated and spoke with enthusiasm of the country and its people, and then after spending a few days with us in Portland, she returned to California.

I miss her very much and naturally worry about her. Understanding that, she always calls on Sabbath eve to greet us: "*Shabbat shalom*, Grandpa! *Shabbat shalom*, Grandma!" But every call from her is a great joy, and she is always in my thoughts. Every night before I go to sleep, I sing in my mind, just as I used to when she was a little girl,

> Lyubo, Lyubochka! Lyubochka, little dove,
> Be happy, my darling!

Life goes on and it must be lived. After Lyubochka, two other doves came into God's world, Emilia (Emma or Emochka), born May 31, 1998, and Julia (Shulya or Shulenka), the little one (so far), born July 24, 2000. These two are my healing balm, my best medicine. Emochka, the first, differs from the rest of the Wolf clan in being blond and blue-eyed. Perhaps she inherited those traits from her great-grandmother Tsilya, Susanna's mother. She has from early childhood been very lively and inquisitive. When she was born eight years ago and I was healthier, I would visit her every day and rock her to sleep in her carriage, and later, after she had learned to walk, take her for strolls in the woods. She quickly learned how to cross the street: "First you have to look to the left and then to the right, and if there aren't any cars, then you can cross." After that we learned the names of the flowers and trees and to recognize the latter by the shape of their leaves. Emochka proved to be very capable and to have an excellent memory. She was fond of looking under trees for "gifts that airplanes dropped especially for Grandma." She also liked to hide behind Grandpa and "wake him up." And then he would make a startled search for the "imp" who had dared to pull his ear and interrupt his nap. And Emochka, after helping him look for a long time, would admit with a giggle on the way home that she was the culprit. She later taught her little sister the game, and then it was doubly amusing.

Long before starting first grade, Emochka learned to read Russian children's books and the Roman and Hebrew alphabets, do basic arithmetic, play some chords on the piano, and recite verses by heart. Certain features of Emma's personality revealed themselves early on: stubborness and a tendency to imitate others. When she does not agree with something, she fiercely clenches her little fists, her angry indignation expressed in her dilated pupils. The anger is short-lived, however, since she is easy to distract. In general, she is good and obedient and likes to help me, whether with watering the flowers in our garden with the hose or picking fruit from the trees. But most of all, she likes to help her grandmother make things in the kitchen. When she visits, she immediately puts on an apron and says, "Let me do it by myself! Let me do it by myself!" And imagine, that little eight-year-old lady makes complicated dishes and beats her grandfather at chess and her grandmother at cards. She enjoys dancing and swimming classes, and is of course a very good student, now in third grade.

For the past two years, our whole family has gathered in our home every week to celebrate *Kabbalat Shabbat* (greeting or receiving the Sabbath), with the honor of leading it and singing the hymn *Lecha Dodi* ("Come, my beloved") given to Emma.[16] She has herself served those at the table, putting a place setting and a *kippah* or yarmulke in front of each. And although it has been repeated every Friday, and all of us are quite used to it, tears of joy and sadness still well in the eyes of her grandfather who did the same in his own childhood and youth, and then before him rises the image of his own Grandmother Rivka, who selflessly loved her children and grandchildren, and our mama, innocently murdered by Nazi thugs.

I am unable to remember who taught Emochka the traditional ceremony in its entirety, but without her performance of it, the whole feast would have had lost much of its charm and festive meaning. It was only after she had concluded the ceremony with its prayer of thanksgiving that the anguished soul of her grandfather (mine, that is) would at last find peace. And besides the Sabbath ceremony, she very quickly mastered the recitative of the Megillah and the ceremony of the Passover Seder: the Four Questions from the *Haggadah* or "telling" of the story of the Exodus of the Jews from Egypt.[17]

Shulenka is not merely my love (all three of them are, and it would be impossible to say which of them is dearer) but a *continuation* of my first love. She (may she be happy and live to 120!) is blue-eyed like Emma. She returns her love not to me but to her papa. She may not even be aware of it, but when he is home she does not leave his arms. She senses his arrival even as he approaches the doorway and runs to meet him, delightedly crying "Papa, Papa!" and then leaps into his arms and hugs him and—no, no, she does not kiss him but instead rests her little face against his shoulder and lies still from happiness. She loves her mama no less, but in a different way. She puts her face in her dress or her breast. That is the only difference, but to me it speaks volumes.

Shulenka, like Emochka, is fond of television. It is difficult to distract her from it. She starts to cry, a weapon against which I am helpless. Nevertheless, I manage with various blandishments to sit her down at her notebook and we work for ten minutes or so. More she will not tolerate. Then we declare a *hafsoke* (break) for . . . a week. She explains that she "is very busy," for they are all worried about what they will do for their Aunt Nadya's upcoming birthday. There was never for any reason a year when we did not celebrate that important event.

Only here in Portland did such a thing happen!

It should be noted that from early childhood Nadya's health had never been very good. She was often depressed or sick with one childhood disease or another that seemed to hit her harder than it did the other children. She had gotten used to being looked after, and her mother and grandparents did so unstintingly.

She was not allowed to do any work at home, "lest, God forbid, she should injure her fingers and be unable to play the piano." We hired the best tutors for her while she was in school. One way or another, she studied well, and in 1969 graduated from the Gnesin Institute of Music Pedagogy, as I have already said. Besides the piano, she played the accordion, and performed as a piano soloist and accompanyist with the Moscow Regional Philharmonic, successfully touring in the Moscow area and in various other cities of the USSR, as I have also mentioned. She was an avid composer and wrote a number of songs to the words of well-known poets. For her composition "A Song for Women of Different Lands," she received an award in Berlin at the 1975 world congress commemorating International Women's Year. She also composed an opera, *The Inaccessible Princess*, based on a children's tale by the French writer Christian Pineau.[18] It was premièred at the Theater for Young Audiences in Moscow, recorded in 1983, and successfully performed at other theaters in Moscow and abroad, eventually leading Pineau to invite her to Paris in 1990. Her recitals were also very well received, although she herself was rarely satisfied with her playing.

It was hard for Nadya to adapt to her new life in Portland. Unlike in Moscow, she had to organize her concerts herself, which she found difficult, and that left her fragile and despondent. On the advice of friends, she started a music education and performance company (Apollon Artists Corporation) from her home. But her hopes for the enterprise were soon disappointed. There were not enough students, and the high cost of upkeep on her house and the expense of printing the methodological materials, programs, and tickets undermined her plan, as did her poor health.

The absence of a personal life and the approach and then arrival of menopause brought a worsening of Nadya's health and state of mind. In April 2003 her physical condition began to deteriorate in a clearly progressive fashion, and she lost weight and grew weaker. She did not trust doctors, preferring instead to treat herself with naturopathic nostrums and responding with a categorical refusal to our frequent urging that

Nadezhda

she see an internist. It was only after she had almost completely lost her strength that we were able to persuade her to check into a hospital. She called several times a day from there, pleading with us to bring her home and promising to submit to all the required tests and procedures on an out-patient basis.

Against my better judgment, I agreed, and with Susanna's consent arranged for Nadya's discharge and return home. And for that decision I carry a great and terrible guilt!

Once home, Nadya continued to refuse ordinary methods of treatment, resorting instead to practitioners of alternative medicine. But instead of improving, her condition got worse. She was no longer able to walk or stand unsupported. At the insistence of our son, she was returned almost by force to the hospital and the gynecological ward, where she was diagnosed with a malignant uterine tumor and told that she needed immediate surgery. But even under the threat of forced hospitalization, Nadya adamantly refused to undergo the surgery. In such circumstances, a court-ordered psychiatric evaluation is called for, and one was scheduled in early June 2004. The judge called to the hospital interviewed her doctors and the patient herself and then ruled that she could, if she wished, be discharged and returned home to the care of her family. Her fate was from that moment irrevocably decided. Her irrational behavior naturally had an enormous affect on us—on all the members of her family.

It is well known that everyone experiences things in his own particular way, that even identical twins may react differently to the same event. But all of us, and especially the members of Nadya's immediate family, that is, her mother, her brother, and I, took her suffering and impending death very hard. Susanna quietly moaned and wept, Solomon turned pale and morose and remained stubbornly silent. As for me, it was as if I had lost the capacity to feel. I moved about like a mindless, insensate automaton. Fragmentary, intertwined memories swarmed relentlessly in my mind. They were especially harrowing when I sat up with Nadya at night, while she, poor thing, moaned continuously. She answered questions only after they had been repeated several times. She stopped eating, asking only for water, and was aware that she was dying. The last days she would call for me and beg me to stay with her and not leave her. She was unable even to turn over by herself, but would ask me to help her stand and then put her arms around my neck, trying to hold on to me but not having the strength to do so. Only by placing my arms behind her back was I able to lift her. Once back in bed she would not let go of me for a long time. Breathing hard in my face, she pleaded with me not to leave her.

I held her head in my hands as she was dying, and she stared up at me with a sad, heavy expression grown dim and yet, as it seemed to me, filled with *compassion.* "Don't leave me alone, Papa!" were her last audible words. And then for a while she whispered something. Then her breathing became intermittent, shallow, and faint, and then she fell back and was still.

Thus did she pass out of our sinful world and from us without ever regaining consciousness.

That happened around two in the morning on July 8, 2004, one month and seven days before her fifty-ninth birthday. *BeGan-Eden tehe Menuchata*—May her resting place be in Paradise. For she has truly deserved it.

I will not describe the funeral. Our son said a moving farewell, but the rest of it is in a haze. I do not remember returning home. Nor do I remember the funeral supper. I came to only the next morning with a face turned to stone and a weight on my heart and an inner emptiness. I did not weep, but the saddest part is that I was unable to smile at our granddaughters, from whom we had kept everything. Now, more than two years later, I can smile at them once again and hug and kiss them. But as before the muscles of my face are stiff and sluggish. I cannot watch movies or musical programs. I cannot read. I walk with my head bowed. A terrible feeling of guilt weighs on it and forces it down. Most of the time I am silent. I have only to close my eyes and her image, her dull *compassionate* gaze, appears before me.

Since the time of her passing I have been afflicted with listlessness and a daytime lethargy, even now nodding off whenever I am left alone, and then sitting motionlessly in my chair asleep for hours. But at night I am tormented by insomnia and vivid, fragmentary images of her. It has become harder to move about, since my arthritis has grown worse, as has a wheezing shortness of breath . . .

My story is nearing its end, but I may not conclude without a word of thanks to the editors of the magazines and newspapers to which I have been a contributor, including Moshe Shklar of *Kheshbn* in Los Angeles, Israel Rudnitsky of *Toplpunkt* (*Colon*) in Tel Aviv, Boris Sandler of *Forverts* (*Forward*) in New York, and Paul Haist of the *Jewish Review* in Portland, all of whom published sympathetic obituaries of Nadya. Lilka Maisner and Sidney Resnick, the leaders of literary clubs in Los Angeles and Hamden, Connecticut, sent me warm letters of condolence. Lilka, as everyone calls her, continues to this day to gather friends at her home every Saturday and does not forget to write warm letters to me from time to time to stress that her club and editorial board need me as much as they ever did, and that I should not stop writing my articles. Especially warm and friendly have been the letters and calls from the very kind Sid, who continues to send me needed literature and to share his views on events in Israel. I should point out that those views were and are those of a confirmed Communist, and that he has not altered them to this day, despite the fact that many of his party's own leaders rejected those ideas a long time ago. His warm attitude toward his old friends has remained no less firm and unalterable. He likes to repeat that "true friends are never former." He has given material aid to many people, even though his own resources are modest.

I must also mention my favorite Yiddish (and English and Hebrew) poet, the world renowned Simcha Simchovitch, who was born a year before me, in 1921, and who also lived in Poland (in Otwock) before the war, although he is now in Toronto. Fate brought us together ten years ago when the Jewish Federation of Greater Portland sent me to Toronto to take part as a guest speaker in the celebration of Simcha's seventy-fifth birthday. We have been friends ever since. Since then he has produced five more collections of verse, and it has been my honor to publish a critical essay on each of them. Of particular interest, I think, are the editions of his Yiddish poetry with his own facing English translations. The translations have great importance, perhaps even greater than the originals do.

I have mentioned only the closest people here. There were many others whom I did not even know. They sent letters to convey the warm feelings evoked in them by the performances of our unforgettable daughter, departed from life so early. Such letters have helped to ease our pain, however briefly. Relief has also been provided by former patients of mine, some of whom continue to come to me for psychotherapy sessions. I am revived when I talk to them, especially if it seems to me that I have managed to engage them somehow. But, understanding my own state of mind, they come less and less often.

I think it is unnecessary to write here of the importance that our son—our sole support—has for us. We pester him day and night, whether he is at home or at work. Although I understand that he is up to his neck in work and burdened with many professional and domestic responsibilities, if I need him for some reason, I immediately pick up the phone and call him. I am aware that he has long grown tired of it, yet he calls me every evening at bedtime to say good night. Actually, I am slandering him. He has much to do and works very hard.

"My family, three children," is his customary answer when I grumble and plead like a beggar with him to visit more often. But unless he has other things he has to do, he comes every Friday with his family to spend the evening and celebrate the arrival of the Sabbath. On Saturday, after their music lessons, he brings the children to see us for several hours. He usually sets out my medications for the week then (there are so many—a whole pharmacy). Lately, his children, my chief medication, have been helping with that task. Sometimes he leaves them with us to spend the night.

For they are our comfort and joy. They naturally spend more time with their grandmother, who spoils them and plays cards or checkers with them or lets them watch television. I try to divert them from that "baneful" activity, forbidden by their parents. I ask them to study Hebrew or mathematics but am having less and less success with that. Yet I try not to show my disappointment, for the important thing is that they are with us. There was a time when their mischievousness and squealing and laughter annoyed me, but now I find it soothing. If I ask them to do something, they immediately carry out my request.

I no longer remember how the Christian rather than Jewish world became aware of our grief and my virtual isolation. Perhaps it was the cancellation of Nadya's concerts and the explanation that was given. Or perhaps the information was passed on by the non-Jewish clergy, immigrants from Russia and Ukraine who, not knowing English, came to me in the first years of our time in Portland with various purposes, but mainly to seek new adherents to their own faith. Even after they had convinced themselves of my steadfastness and skeptical attitude—if not toward Jesus Christ in every respect, then at least toward any other creed—those men continued to visit me and to show a genuine interest in Hebrew and in certain controversial questions of Judaism. They and others even asked me to serve as their teacher. I thus acquired pupils and friends who to this day have continued to do kind deeds for us. Among them are Alex Mihaylov, David Summer, and Warren Dean and his wife, Shirel. David especially distinguished himself, visiting me twice a week. He spent a month in Israel as a tourist and returned inspired, not least by the discovery that he could, after just eight months of study, interact with the local people in Hebrew. He gladdened me with his deep interest in the Torah and in various Jewish prayers and traditions.

The people mentioned here have shown compassion for our grief and tried in every way they could to comfort us and distract me from my terrible suffering.

I have to admit that when they come to talk, they really do put my mind at ease and make it less difficult to suffer the ailments that have become ever more severe for both Susanna and me.

The last few years two Russian women have helped to care for us, their work paid for by Medicaid. Both of them, Anya Brichak and Zhenya Snegur, have done everything necessary to keep our home clean and neat, prepare meals, and help me get around. They too are my guardian angels. They never have to be asked for anything. Anya, may God grant her health, bathes me in the tub every day, getting soaked herself, and then puts clean underwear on me. She comes to my room several times a day to bring me some "tasty treat" and ask how I am feeling and if there is anything I want. It would be difficult to list all the good turns done by her every day, even though her own life, as far as I can tell, is not an easy one and I am unable to help her in return. May God grant her long, happy years. She has earned them. Every night before I go to sleep I say a prayer for her welfare and that of her family.

Zhenya, my other guardian angel, treats us the same way. She also enlisted the help of her husband, a taciturn man who needs only half a word to understand. Seeing how hard it was for me to move about, and my almost twenty-four-hour confinement to the house ("like a prison"), Zhenya decided that her husband might, through his work, be able to obtain a motorized wheelchair for me. A month later he brought one at no cost, and thanks to it I can now go outside. Before my forays, Zhenya wraps me up, and then she follows behind to make sure I am operating the vehicle safely.

As a man of faith, I believe that both Anya and Zhenya have been sent by God to carry out his Holy Will by helping people in need—by helping us, my wife and me. Every night before I go to sleep I pray for Zhenya's welfare too and that of her family. Both she and Anya take care of us not for money but by the grace of God and their own kind hearts.

My dolorous tale has at last reached an end. It may be that I should have written more about my life companion, Susanna, with whom I have lived and shared our joys and grief equally for almost sixty-two years. A separate story could be written about that. But I no longer have the strength for it. Our loss has for her, poor soul, been even harder to bear than it has been for me. She loved Nadyenka very much. Unlike me, she had never been separated from her. And as her mother, she was better informed about Nadya's intimate experiences. Moreover, in spite of everything and her own infirmities, she has continued to manage our household and at times has looked after me too. Her emotional reserve may produce the impression in some that our shared grief has been easier for her, but in fact it has not.

It may be fitting here to repeat the words of the Yiddish poet Avrom Reyzen.[19]

> The sun sets, blazing,
> It sets, slipping from view,
> And then the last beams fade.
> Soon darkness will descend,
> And the last dream vanish.
> Thus will my own life end.

"What?! How dare you? Blasphemer!" I hear the indignant voice of my son.

"What?! Grandpa, how can you believe such a thing? Is that what you taught me?" I hear the distant, tearful voice of my eldest granddaughter, Lyubochka.

My saviors, my younger granddaughters, Emochka and Shulenka, stare up at me, their eyes wide in astonishment. Shulenka has in her little hands a heavy book, which she holds out to me.

"It's for you. Here. Read!" she says.

A passage has been marked in it. I open the book to the page and read. It is the last verse of the Book of Job: "So Job died, being old and full of days."

And then I open my eyes. Dawn was breaking!

Notes

♪♪♪

Editor's Introduction

1 In 1931, the Jewish population of Warsaw was about three hundred and fifty thousand, the largest urban concentration in Europe and 30 percent of the city's total. The vast majority (almost 90 percent) identified Yiddish as their first language, with the rest indicating Modern Hebrew and Polish. Most of the Yiddish-speaking respondents, however, would have been comfortable in Polish too, with many, like Dr. Wolf and his father, also conversant with Modern Hebrew and perhaps German. See Ezra Mendelsohn, *The Jews of East Central Europe*, 23, 31, for the statistical details.

2 Because of the shifts in national control of the various cities, towns, and villages of Volhynia and the other territories of the Polish-Ukrainian borderlands (or *kresy*), most are known by at least three different names: the Russian one used when they were part of the Russian empire until the First World War, the Polish one when they were part of the free Polish Republic from 1918-1939, the Russian one again after the partition of Poland and their incorporation into the Soviet Union until its collapse in 1991, and the Ukrainian one they have today as part of the independent state of Ukraine. Thus, the name of the village of Moisey's grandparents is *Cheremoshno* in Russian, *Czeremoszno* in Polish, and *Cheremoshne* in Ukrainian. Similarly, the now western Ukrainian city where he was enrolled for his second year of medical school is *Lvov* in Russian, *Lwów* in Polish, *Lemberg* in German (when it was part of the Habsburg empire from 1772-1918), and *Lviv* in Ukrainian today. While there may be a certain misleading (and, for some, even politically unsatisfactory) awkwardness in the solution I have chosen, the place names in the following discussion and in the translation of the narrative have all been rendered in a Roman transliteration of their Cyrillic Russian form, since that is the form used for much of their modern history and also the one preferred by Dr. Wolf himself in his manuscript.

3 Iu. S. Savenko, "Nekrolog. Moisei Solomonovich Vol'f (1922-2007)" [Obituary. Moisei Solomonovich Wolf], *Nezavisimyi psikhiatricheskii zhurnal* 2 (2007): 92-94.

Author's Preface

1 *Pirkei Avot* (Ethics of the Fathers) 4:29: "for despite yourself you were made, and despite yourself you were born, and despite yourself you live, and despite yourself you die, and despite yourself you are destined to give an account and reckoning before the supreme King of kings, the Holy One, blessed be He."

2 The great Russian memoirist Sergey Aksakov (1791-1859), author of *A Family Chronicle* (1856) and *The Childhood Years of the Bagrov Grandson* (1858), had several sons. The oldest, Konstantin (1817-60), himself a writer, is the likely source of the

quotation, a twist on the Latin maxim, *De mortuis aut bene aut nihil:* Of the dead either good or nothing.

Ancestors

1 Dr. Wolf naturally uses the Hebrew names for the books of the Tanach or Hebrew Bible. The interpolated English translations here and elsewhere are from the King James Version.

2 Dr. Wolf mentions only the records of the male members of the community, but the *pinkassim* would have included comparable, if perhaps less detailed, information about the female members too.

3 The Yad Vashem complex in Jerusalem (the phrase, from Isaiah 56: 5, means "a memorial and a name") was established in 1953 by the Holocaust Martyrs' and Heroes' Remembrance Authority. It is Israel's official monument to the victims of the Holocaust and includes a historical museum and publishing arm, among other components.

4 Babi Yar is a ravine on the outskirts of Kiev and the site of the largest single mass killing of the Holocaust. On September 29-30, 1941, 33,761 people were shot there, with at least ninety-six thousand more executed in the following months. The overwhelming majority of the victims were Jews. In 1976 a monument was built to "all" the victims by the Soviet government, and in 1991, on the massacre's fiftieth anniversary, a second monument to the "Jewish" victims was erected. In June 2013 it was announced in Kiev by the World Forum of Russian-Speaking Jews that a robust new memorial complex will be built at Babi Yar that will include a historical museum, a Jewish center, and a synagogue—a long overdue expression of recovery and remembrance.

5 The Gulag (an abbreviated acronym for Main Directorate of Corrective Labor Camps and Colonies) was at its zenith a vast network of more than 475 often enormous forced-labor prison complexes and settlements, through which at least eighteen million people passed between its full-scale establishment in 1929 and curtailment in 1953 after the death of Stalin. The majority of convicts were men and women who had been arrested for their social or political identities, or else convicted of vague, trivial, or imaginary political offenses, such as the expression of "anti-Soviet" attitudes. Prison terms of ten years were common and the conditions were harsh, if not homicidal.

6 At the time of the author's childhood a mixed village of Poles, Ukrainians, and Jews in Volhynia (Wołyń) in eastern Poland, Cheremoshno is now in northwestern Ukraine.

7 After the passage in the Russian empire of the Jewish Statute of 1804, Jews did, without conversion to Orthodox Christianity, the state religion, have the right, at least in principle, to buy or lease land and establish enterprises, providing they were within the so-called Pale of Settlement, the territory designated in 1791 for restricted Jewish residence that included what would become present-day Lithuania, Belarus,

Poland, Moldova, and Ukraine. In the 1880s, however, that right was, along with others, withdrawn even in the Pale. Mechl could thus have purchased the property, although his heirs' subsequent claim to it might well have been contested.

8 Samuel Wolf (1881-1958). Harry J. Wolf (1884-1948) was the co-founder with Sam Schnitzer in 1911 of the Alaska Junk Company, which eventually became the highly successful Schnitzer and Wolf Machinery Company and then, after the Schnitzers bought out the Wolfs in the 1950s, Schnitzer Industries.

9 Melnitsa (Mielnice) is a Volhynian town nineteen kilometers south-southeast of Cheremoshno.

10 Hannah (or Anna) Wolf-Chusid (1888-1988). Morris Chusid (1886-1957).

11 Morris Wolf (1896-1981).

12 The August 25, 1939, "non-aggression" pact signed by the German foreign minister, Joachim von Ribbentrop, and his Soviet counterpart, Vyacheslav Molotov, secretly divided Poland between the Third Reich and the Soviet Union. In keeping with its terms, the Germans invaded Poland on September 1, 1939, annexing the western part of the country and placing the central part, including Warsaw, under its "protection" as a nominally independent territory. The Soviets then invaded Poland from the opposite direction on September 17, annexing Polish Ukraine (Volhynia and Galicia) as far west as the Bug River. Less than two years later, on June 22, 1941, the Germans would renege on the agreement and invade the Soviet Union itself, quickly overrunning the new territory of western Ukraine and with it the towns and villages of Volhynia and Galicia.

13 The Kaddish, its opening words inspired by Ezekiel 38:23 glorifying the name of God ("May His great Name be exalted and sanctified"), is a central prayer in the Jewish liturgy and, with the funeral prayer beginning "*El malei rachamim*" ("God full of mercy"), an integral part of the mourning ritual.

14 *Kulak*, meaning "fist" in Russian, was a derogatory Soviet term for a prosperous peasant and then, by extension, sometimes a term of abuse for any successful small holder, however innocent or useful his enterprise. Established as a fictive social category or class with the Stalinist collectivization of agriculture begun in 1928, the term justified the terror-starvation, Gulag incarceration, and execution of millions of innocent people.

15 Kovel (Kowel) is a regional center in Volhynia about thirty kilometers southwest of Cheremoshno. At the time of the narrative, its Jewish population was about 46 percent of the total.

16 The date may, despite Berl Wolf's attestation, seem late, but the Jews living closest to the Molotov-Ribbentrop line separating German and Soviet territory in western Volhynia were among the last to perish in the region, the German forces having passed through before Hitler's decision to murder all Jews everywhere. That does not mean that no Jews were killed in Volhynia as the Germans made their way east in the summer of 1941; there were numerous executions, but the victims tended to be young men of fighting age (who were, along with Poles and Communists and other political activists, eliminated as potential combatants), with Jewish women and

children and the elderly put in ghettos until they were shot over pits in accordance with German racial policy even as late, in the district surrounding Kovel, as the summer and early fall of 1942.

My Immediate Family

1 Zwoleń is a small town some one hundred kilometers south of Warsaw.

2 Ivan Susanin (d. 1613) is perhaps most endurably enshrined in Mikhail Glinka's opera *A Life for the Tsar* (1836). There have been numerous representations of him, always with a long white Santa Claus beard.

3 Pesya Wolf; afterwards, Pesya (Paula) Katzan (1909-2000).

4 *Author's note:* There is a detailed description of this episode in a long sketch I published in the Soviet Yiddish magazine, *Sovetish Heymland.*

5 Translated by Matthew Arnold. Heine's "Prinzessin Sabbat" is included in the *Hebräische Melodien* section of his *Romanzero* (Romances, 1852). The German lines read, "*Mit der Frau Prinzessin Sabbat,/ Die man nennt die stille Fürstin./ Perl' und Blume aller Schönheit/ Ist die Fürstin. Schöner war/ Nicht die Königin von Saba,/ Salomonis Busenfreundin.*" Dr. Wolf has tactfully omitted the poem's sarcastic continuation.

6 The Zionist Tarbut (the word means "culture" in Hebrew) movement, founded in Warsaw in 1922, sponsored a network of Hebrew-language schools and academies in Poland (where they had modest state support), Lithuania, and Romania. The institution from which the author would graduate in 1938 was a European-style gymnasium, that is, a rigorous combined elementary and secondary school that emphasized modern languages and the humanities and natural sciences, with the key difference that virtually all the instruction was in Modern Hebrew. See the description of the curriculum later in the text.

7 Symon Petliura (1879-1926), a Ukrainian journalist, writer, and politician, was a leader of the Ukrainian independence movement following the 1917 Russian revolution and, after 1919, an active ally of Polish republican forces. Petliura's own role in the pogroms that took between thirty-five and fifty thousand Jewish lives in the Ukraine after the revolution remains in dispute, but the case can at least be made that he did not do nearly enough to prevent them. Nestor Makhno (1888-1934) also fought for Ukrainian independence, with the forces under his command, mostly irregular peasant bands, committing numerous atrocities against Jews. Marshal Semyon Budyonny (1883-1973) was the commander of the Bolshevik Cossack First Cavalry Army that fought against Polish and Ukrainian forces in western Ukraine after the revolution. His campaign (vividly depicted in Isaac Babel's classic 1927 story cycle *Red Cavalry*) to recover the Ukraine for the new Soviet empire was only partly successful, with the contested territory ultimately divided between Poland (Galicia and Volhynia) and the Soviet Union (eastern Ukraine) in the 1921 Treaty of Riga.

8 *Author's note:* During our first dinner at the home of the parents of the future wife of our son, my wife repeated Grandmother Rivka's gesture. After expressing our approval of our son's choice of their daughter, she removed the gold watch hanging

from her own neck and put it around that of the bride-to-be, Margarita Samuilovna Leytes.

9 The Socialist Józef Piłsudski (1867-1935) was the leader of Polish republican forces after the collapse in 1917 of the Russian empire of which Poland had been a part, and then head of state (1918-22 and 1926-1935) after the establishment of the Second Polish Republic (1918-39). He was well regarded by many Jews for his resistance to anti-Semitism and, as they saw it, his defense of their interests.

10 Later in his professional life, Dr. Wolf would prefer the Russian equivalent of his first name and patronymic, Moisey Solomonovich, the form used (without the patronymic) on the title page of this book and in his many other publications.

11 The first twentieth-century *Birkat Hachama* was in 1925, when the author was three.

12 A *britzka* is a light open carriage resembling a phaeton, with two opposing seats.

13 Dr. Wolf seems to have misremembered the Tarbut tuition fee by at least a factor of ten, since the 1929 value of the złoty was about thirty-five to the dollar.

14 The *Hashomer Hatzair*, the *Hehalutz*, and the Betar movement were Jewish youth organizations spanning a wide range of Zionist ideology and activity, from left to right. The Boy Scout-like *Hashomer Hatzair*, founded in Austro-Hungarian Galicia in 1913, advocated the liberation of Jewish youth through *aliyah* ("going up" in Hebrew), that is, emigration to Palestine and residence there in *kibbutzim*, and was quite secular in its orientation, seeking to fashion a self-reliant modern Jewish identity free of the constraints of Orthodox Jewish life. The *Hehalutz*, founded in Poland in 1916, also sought to promote *aliyah*, but with a greater emphasis on practical agricultural training in preparation for residence in Palestine in *kibbutzim* and *moshavim*, or cooperative farming settlements. The Betar movement, founded in Riga in 1923, was, in contrast, a militant, even militarist, right-wing organization stressing courage, self-respect, military training (sometimes with the help of the Polish army), and, in the face of growing anti-Semitism, Jewish self-defense. As a Zionist group, it also advocated *aliyah* and strove to cultivate a cadre of strong young men and women who would secure the future state of Israel. It was enormously popular among Jewish youth in Poland in the years before World War II.

15 The words are from Psalms 22:1.

16 If the Hungarian Theodor Herzl (1860-1904) was not actually the founder of political Zionism, he certainly became its leading spokesman with the publication of his book *Der Judenstaat* (*The Jewish State*) in 1896; his founding of the leading Zionist paper, the weekly *Die Welt* (*The World*) in 1897; and his organization of the first international Zionist congress in Basel, Switzerland, the same year.

17 The Balfour Declaration, named for the British foreign secretary Arthur Balfour, was a formal statement by his government expressing "sympathy with Jewish Zionist aspirations" and favoring the establishment of "a homeland for the Jewish people" in Palestine after the end of World War I.

18 Adam Mickiewicz (1798-1855) was Poland's greatest romantic poet. His patriotic *Oda do Młodości* was published in 1820.

19 The verse epic *Pan Tadeusz* (1834) is Mickiewicz's greatest work. The Jewish innkeeper Jankiel Korczmar, a very positive character, remains true to his own traditions yet still loves Poland as his homeland. At the poem's conclusion, he gives an account of recent Polish history while accompanying himself on a dulcimer-like zither.

20 It was customary in Poland and in the Soviet Union, just as it is in Russia today, for students to begin their medical studies in their first year of undergraduate enrollment, and to be examined for admission not to a university but to a department, be it medicine, law, philology, mathematics, or a science. The medical curriculum typically consisted of five years of concentrated study, with a set of rigorous examinations at the end. While students like Dr. Wolf thus began their medical training much earlier than is typical in the United States (Dr. Wolf was sixteen), their level of knowledge could, at the end of their term of study and according to their talent and seriousness, still have been at a high level and provided adequate preparation for a graduate internship or residency.

21 The so-called *Kristallnacht* (Night of Broken Glass) nationwide Nazi pogrom of November 9-10, 1938, resulted in the murder of ninety-one Jews, the arrest and deportation to concentration camps of thirty thousand more, and the destruction of over two thousand synagogues, among many other atrocities.

22 The distinguished conductor and composer Stanisław Moniuszko (1819-72) wrote songs, operettas, and operas featuring Polish folk themes, including his major work, *Halka* (Helen), which premièred in 1848.

New Ordeals and a Refuge

1 Most of the tens of thousands of Jews who fled east to Soviet territory just as Dr. Wolf did were offered Soviet citizenship with, for those sixteen and older, an appropriate internal passport or identity document (the principal means of population control). If they refused the offer, they could be returned to German-occupied Poland or, more commonly, immediately deported to the Gulag in Kazakhstan or Siberia.

2 Bessarabia, as the eastern half of the principality of Moldavia was called after it was ceded to the Russian empire by the Ottoman Turks in 1812, declared independence in 1918 and soon afterward joined the kingdom of Romania, with which it had close linguistic and ethnic ties (the western half of Moldavia had in 1859 already become part of the kingdom of Wallachia, the predecessor of Romania). In 1940, Bessarabia was reoccupied by the Soviet Union as a delayed consequence of the Molotov-Ribbentrop Pact and thus made available for rapid Soviet-style resettlement of the kind described by Dr. Wolf. With the collapse of the Soviet Union in 1991, the territory largely became independent again as the new state of Moldova.

3 Manevichi (Maniewicze) is a Volhynian town sixty kilometers northeast of Kovel.

4 *Shavuot* (Celebration of the Weeks) commences seven weeks (fifty days) from the second day of Passover and commemorates the giving of the Ten Commandments to Moses on Mt. Sinai.

5 Soon after the Soviet annexation of southeastern Poland on September 17, 1939, all

private agricultural holdings were expropriated and consolidated in collective farms or *kolkhozy*. Since these were state enterprises and the students of public universities and institutes were obliged to serve the state, they were assigned at the end of the school year as temporary harvest labor to facilitate (or mitigate) the radical change the new arrangements entailed.

6 Running toward a dive-bomber (*Stuka*) might have taken one out from under its trajectory and away from the target, but if the attack was a strafing run by a Messerschmitt, the tactic would probably have been suicidal.

Dubovka. A Collective Farm. A Hospital. A Factory

1 Stalingrad, renamed Volgograd in 1961, is a major industrial center on the Volga River in southern Russia. From August 23, 1942, until February 2, 1943, it was the site of arguably the most important single engagement of World War II and one of the costliest in human history, with military and civilian deaths of perhaps as many as two million. It ended with the destruction of the German army group sent against the city and marked the beginning of the German retreat and defeat.

2 Although barred from the Soviet Communist Party and anticipating a suspicious, if not very dangerous reception farther east, most Polish political convicts would have fled the invading Germans anyway, since the latter would have shot them at once, whatever their stripe or standing.

3 In the history of the Communist Party of the Soviet Union, "Bolsheviks" (Majoritarians) and "Mensheviks" (Minoritarians) were factions with different views of the conduct of the Russian revolution and the nature of the world "cataclysm" that was expected to follow. "Trotskyites," on the other hand, were followers of Lev (or Leon) Trotsky, the exiled Bolshevik leader whom Stalin had murdered in Mexican exile in 1940. Needless to say, the Bolsheviks, led first by Lenin and then by Stalin, had prevailed and were ruthless in maintaining their ideological authority.

4 The so-called Finnish or Winter War began with a Soviet attack on Finland on November 30, 1939, and ended with the expulsion of Soviet forces on March 13, 1940, despite their enormous advantage in troop strength and materiel.

5 *Kvass* is a mildly alcoholic (1% or less) beverage popular in Russia and Ukraine. It is typically made from naturally fermented dark rye bread.

6 Now in Belarus, Brest, or Brest-Litovsk (Brześę-Litewski), is an industrial city on the Bug river. It was overrun in the first hours of the June 22, 1941, invasion.

Stalingrad. Medical School. Work as a Loader. Trenches. Bombardment and the Front.

1 Toviy Davidovich Epstein (or Epshtein, 1895-1969) was the deputy director of the People's Commissariat of Public Health of the Tatar Autonomous Republic from 1935 to 1938 and again from 1942; chairman of the Department of Social Medicine of the Stalingrad Medical Institute from 1939 to 1942; and head of the Department

of the History of Medicine (1949-53) and the Department of Public Health (1954-66) of the Kazan Medical Institute.

2 A *budyonovka* was a soft wool hat with a short bill and pointed crown worn in the Soviet Army from 1918 until the late 1930s. In this case it should be seen as a variety of cheap army-surplus headgear.

3 Vladimir Mayakovsky (1893-1930) was a leading Russian Futurist poet who, like many in the pre revolutionary literary avant-garde, greeted the 1917 Bolshevik revolution with enthusiasm. In the 1920s he wrote verse of an often crudely patriotic variety quite unlike the bold modernist experimentation of his earlier period. He killed himself, perhaps by accident, perhaps because he was depressed by a failed love affair, or perhaps from his disappointment and shame at the brutally totalitarian turn the revolution had taken under Stalin. The phrase "love boat smashed against everyday life" is from his "Unfinished" (1930). The sentimental picture of him holding a kitten to his face described by Dr. Wolf is highly improbable. There is, however, a well-known photograph of him by Alexander Rodchenko with a Scottish terrier in his arms, a copy of which which the librarian might easily have owned.

4 "A Conversation with Comrade Lenin" (1929).

5 "Lines about My Soviet Passport" (1929).

6 The great nineteenth-century novelist Ivan Turgenev (1818-83) published the fifty-one brief "Poems in Prose" in his anthology *Senilia* (1877-82). Their limpid clarity, simplicity, and purity of language make them excellent and oft-used pedagogical tools.

7 1937 was the height of the political and social purges instigated by Stalin and carried out by the NKVD, a predecessor of the KGB. Many victims were summarily executed and buried in mass graves, others were sent to the Gulag, while still others, the most fortunate, were sentenced to "permanent internal exile," that is, to forced relocation in towns and cities on the remote periphery of the Soviet state, such as Arkhangelsk on the White Sea in the far north, where Dr. Wolf would himself be transferred in 1951.

8 The German air wing involved in the battle of Stalingrad consisted of over twelve hundred planes, which carried out more than three thousand largely uncontested sorties per day and dropped over two thousand tons of bombs.

9 Field Marshal Friedrich Paulus (1890-1957) was after his surrender imprisoned by the Soviets until 1953, when he was allowed to return to Germany.

10 The complete text, from Proverbs 24: 17, reads, "Rejoice not when thine enemy falleth, and let not thine heart be glad when he stumbleth."

Kazan. The Magarils. The Military Commissariat. The Naval Medical Academy. Septic Angina. The Mogilevskys and Epsteins.

1 The Aramaic phrase is from the beginning of the Passover Seder *Haggadah* or liturgy: "*Kol dichfin yeitei v'yeichol*" ("Let all who are hungry come eat").

2 Gershon Sirota (1874-1943), the "Jewish Caruso," was a leading European cantor with an international performance career, including a sold-out concert at Carnegie

Hall in 1912 and several recordings. He began in Odessa and later sang in synagogues in Vilnius (Wilno) in Lithuania and then in Warsaw, where he was killed in the Ghetto uprising.

3 Septic angina or alimentary toxic aleukia is caused by a mold found in overwintered millet, rye, wheat, and oats. The mold's toxin produces necrotic lesions in the mouth, esophagus, and stomach that may lead to severe hemorrhaging and death. There were several serious outbreaks in the Soviet Union from 1942 to 1947, probably because of relatively mild winters and a severe shortage of grain and the labor to harvest what little there was.

4 Menzelinsk is a town about 240 kilometers east of Kazan on the Menzelya River, a tributary of the Kama, which itself empties into the Volga.

5 In the Soviet Union, Jews were considered a "nationality," that is, a distinct ethnic group like Russians or Tatars, and were permanently identified as such in their internal passports or identity papers.

6 Academician Leon A. Orbeli (1882-1956) was a distinguished Soviet physiologist and founder of evolutionary physiology, and, during the war, a high-ranking officer in the medical corps. He served as vice-chairman of the Academy of Medical Sciences from 1942 to 1946.

7 The neuropsychologist and Moscow University professor Alexander Luria (1902-1977) was a founder of cultural-historical psychology and a scholar of international standing.

The 2nd Moscow Medical Institute. The Kozlovsky Family. Marriage. Our Daughter Noemi (Nadezhda).

1 Soviet citizens were required to obtain permits for residence in towns and cities and to register with the police within a specified period, wherever they happened to be lodged.

2 The feast of *Simchat Torah* ("Rejoice in the Law") marks the last (and simultaneously the first) day of the annual cycle of Torah readings.

3 The Zionist poet Chaim Nahman Bialik (1873-1934) wrote in both Hebrew and Yiddish.

4 Shloyme Mikhelevich Shlifer served from 1944-1957 as chief rabbi of the Moscow Choral Synagogue, the main synagogue of the Soviet Union, just as it is of Russia today.

5 Konotop, first mentioned in 1635 as a Cossack settlement, is a small industrial town in north central Ukraine.

6 The distinguished actor, director, and producer Solomon Mikhailovich Mikhoels (1890-1948) was a member of the Moscow State Yiddish Theater from 1919 until 1948, and its director from 1928. The Jewish Anti-Fascist Committee, meant to influence international public opinion and organize financial and political support abroad during the war, was active from 1942 until 1948, when it was dissolved by the authorities and many of its members arrested.

7 The Soviet Union declared war on Japan on August 8, 1945. The unconditional Japanese surrender to the Allies occurred on August 14, 1945, and its formal surrender, on September 2, 1945.

8 The MVD filtration camps' purpose was the internment, interrogation, and almost certain summary deportation to the Gulag for "treason" of prisoners of war and other Soviet citizens who had been trapped behind enemy lines, their crime no more than having failed to avoid capture.

9 The Serbsky State Research Institute for Social and Forensic Psychiatry, as it is officially known today, was founded in 1921 as the main center of forensic psychiatry in the Soviet Union, and was intended to serve as an adjunct of the criminal court system, a role it still plays, conducting some twenty-five hundred court-ordered mental-health evaluations a year. During the later Soviet period, it had a second, more sinister role: assisting the state in suppressing dissent by declaring dissenters mentally ill, collaborating in their forced hospitalization, and then subjecting them to shameful and destructive "treatment." Dr. Wolf identifies the director of the Serbsky Institute as a member of the NKVD, although it is more likely that she held officer rank in the MVD, as did many other members of the institute's staff.

10 The *zemstva* were an instrument of rural self-government instituted in Russia and Ukraine in 1864 following the emancipation of the serfs by Tsar Alexander II in 1861. Besides providing a degree of local rule and taxing authority, *zemstvo* assemblies facilitated agrarian reform, elementary education aimed at the newly freed peasantry, and public medical services, among other boons. The *zemstva* were, in their service role, a magnet for the liberal or left-leaning but not necessarily revolutionary intelligentsia at the end of the nineteenth and the beginning of the twentieth century. The citing of Dr. Barkov's service as a *zemstvo* physician may therefore be taken as a sign of his humane, progressive orientation and moral and social integrity. For Dr. Wolf he represents the best Russian liberal tradition and a counterbalance to the Serbsky Institute.

11 The distinguished German psychiatrist Emil Kraepelin (1856-1926) is regarded not only by Dr. Wolf but by many others as the founder of modern scientific psychiatry and psychopharmacology. Kraepelin believed that psychiatric disorders were biological or genetic in origin, a view that, despite its eclipse in the twentieth century by Freudian and other psychoanalytic theories, has re-established itself in recent psychiatric thinking, which generally accepts in refined form Kraepelin's empirical, pattern- and trajectory-oriented classification of the different kinds of psychosis.

12 Under Soviet and current Russian law, a "second-class invalid" (*invalid vtoroi gruppy*) is someone who, while still functional and capable of managing his daily needs, suffers from a persistent illness or incapacity that makes regular work impossible.

13 S. I. Konstorum (1890-1950) and D. E. Melekhov (1899-1979) were, as Dr. Wolf indicates here and in his later descriptions of them, distinguished and highly influential Soviet psychiatrists of an independent, empirical bent. Konstorum was a founder of Russian clinical psychotherapy who had been trained in St. Petersburg, Leipzig, and Jena, while Melekhov was a founder of "social psychiatry," which

stressed the social causes and effects of mental disorders.

14 As the chair of the Department of Psychiatry of Moscow University and head of its psychiatry clinic, P. B. Gannushkin (1875-1933) was a figure of enormous authority and influence during the early Soviet period, and the founder of a school of psychiatrists and clinicians that included, among other distinguished colleagues, the psychoneurologist T. A. Geyer (1875-1955). In 1930 the Moscow University psychiatry clinic was reorganized as the Moscow Municipal Institute of Neuropsychiatry, and in 1936 renamed in honor of Professor Gannushkin. In 1937 it became the Gannushkin Psychiatric Hospital (Moscow Municipal Psychiatric Hospital No. 4) and the chief workplace of Professors Konstorum and Melekhov and later of Dr. Wolf himself.

15 Yu. V. Kannabikh (1872-1939) was a highly respected psychiatrist and historian of world psychiatry and, against the grain of his place and time, an advocate with his wife, S. A. Liozner-Kannabikh, of the psychoanalytic theories of Alfred Adler.

16 A Ravkin preparation is an infusion of motherwort (*Leonurus*) combined with the sedatives sodium bromide (sedoneural) and sodium barbital, while a Bekhterev preparation is an infusion of spring adonis (*Adonis vernalis*) combined with sodium bromide and the analgesic codeine phosphate.

17 The *Kol Nidre* (the phrase means "all vows" in Aramaic and comes from the first words of the prayer) is recited, or sung by a cantor, in the synagogue at the start of the evening service on Yom Kippur.

18 Konstantin Simonov (1915-79) and Ilya Ehrenburg (1891-1967) were very well-known Soviet writers of the day, the first for his poetry, fiction, and drama, the second for his journalism, poetry, translations, and fiction. Obtaining the participation in a local public-lecture series of such prominent and powerful men—Simonov was also editor-in-chief of the literary monthly *Novyi mir* (*New World*) and secretary of the Soviet Writers Union, and both he and Ehrenburg were past winners of the Stalin Prize, among other honors—was a tremendous coup.

A Bureaucratic Odyssey. Khabarovsk. Vladivostok. Korsakov. Yuzhno-Sakhalinsk.

1 Sakhalin is an island in the north Pacific separated from the coast of the Russian Far East by the Tatar Strait and about nine thousand kilometers from Moscow. It had a complex history of dual occupation by the Russians (the northern half) and the Japanese (the southern half) from 1855 until 1945, when Japan ceded its portion to the Soviet Union under the terms of the Allied Yalta Agreement. The capital of Sakhalin is Yuzhno-Sakhalinsk, about nine hundred and fifty kilometers northeast of Vladivostok. To be sent as a Jew from Moscow in 1950 to such a remote place on the Soviet periphery was, as Dr. Wolf implies, tantamount to internal exile and fully in keeping with the broad anti-Semitic campaign of the time.

2 Liberty ships were freighters and transports of a single simple design quickly built in the United States between 1941 and 1945 for use by the American military and

merchant fleets and for provision to American allies, including Great Britain and the Soviet Union, which received some fifty of the more than twenty-seven hundred vessels produced. Lend-Lease was an American program in operation from 1941 until 1945 for distribution of essential materials to Great Britain, the Soviet Union, China, France, and other allies. Of the $50.1 billion spent on the program, the Soviet Union received $11.3 billion in goods that, in addition to Liberty ships, included locomotives, military vehicles, weapons and ammunition, food, and much else.

3   The October 1948 Ashkhabad earthquake in Soviet Turkmenistan, estimated at 7.3 on the Richter scale, took at least one hundred and ten thousand lives in the city and surrounding area.

4   *Pelmeni* are a kind of Siberian tortelloni or wonton stuffed with ground beef and pork and usually served with sour cream.

5   *Yaponets* is the common Russian word for a Japanese male but a conceivable, if highly unlikely, last name of independent East-European derivation. Read from right to left, it becomes *Tsenopay*, with the "ts" rendered as a single letter in Cyrillic. To identify oneself as "Mishka Yaponets" ("Mickey the Jap") would be an expression of extreme insolence.

A Bright Beam of Light in the Kingdom of Darkness

1   Major-General Anatoly Vasilievich Stavenkov (1896-1968) saw action in the Battle of Stalingrad as the commander of the 61st Cavalry Division, and served as military commissar of Volga region from 1949 to 1951.

2   Courses in Marxist-Leninism were commonly taken in the Soviet Union to bolster social and professional résumés, avert political scrutiny, and facilitate promotion. For most people, they were regarded as a tedious but necessary step; for army officers like Dr. Wolf, they were unavoidable, especially in the Stalinist 1940s and 1950s.

3   The huge multi-site forced-labor camp in the tundra town of Vorkuta north of the Arctic Circle and just west of the Ural mountains provided workers for the Vorkuta coal-mining combine and was one of the most notorious installations in the vast Gulag network. After the death of Stalin, hundreds of thousands of Gulag inmates were released all over the Soviet Union and nominally "rehabilitated," as the term had it; that is, they were cleared of the charges that had led to their "illegal" incarceration and usually permitted to return to their original places of residence, if they still existed, or to their families, if they could still be found.

4   The campaign against "rootless cosmopolitans," a cant phrase for Jews (or Zionists), began in earnest on January 28, 1949, with the publication of an article in the Communist Party newspaper, *Pravda*, attacking a prominent Jewish theater critic. Encouraged by Stalin, perhaps in alarmed response to the triumphant arrival in Moscow in 1948 of Golda Meir, Israel's first ambassador to the Soviet Union, the campaign grew louder and ever more menacing over the next four years, culminating in the so-called Night of the Executed Poets in 1952 and the hysteria of the Doctors' Plot in 1953. It came to an end with Stalin's death two months after the last episode.

While the events surrounding the half-baked Lamarckian theories of the agronomist Trofim Lysenko (he maintained that acquired traits were heritable, with genetics dismissed by his supporters, including Stalin himself, as "bourgeois pseudoscience") might not have been anti-Semitic in their initial motivation, their result was still the discrediting of the achievements of legitimate Soviet science and the banning from employment or even arrest of a number of distinguished Jewish biologists.

Black Days and White Nights

1 The town of Pechora in the Komi Republic, although not as far north as Vorkuta, was just as remote and also part of the Gulag network. Colonel Beryozkin's reference to a "field unit" in either place was accordingly a not so veiled threat to send Dr. Wolf to a prison camp.

2 In 1951, two hundred rubles (twenty after the 1961 revaluation) would have been about 12 percent of Dr. Wolf's monthly salary as a senior-lieutenant and extremely reasonable for a well-furnished room.

3 I. I. Lukomsky (1908-1981).

4 Mikhail Zharov (1899-1981) was a prominent stage actor whose screen career began in the era of silent movies and included such classics as Yakov Protazanov's *Aelita* (1924), Nikolai Ekk's *Road to Life* (1931), and Sergey Eisenstein's *Ivan the Terrible* (1942-44).

5 Exodus 14: 15-31.

6 The Yiddish-language actor and director and Jewish Anti-Fascist Committee chairman Solomon Mikhoels was assassinated by the MVD in January 1948. On the Night of the Executed Poets in August 1952, thirteen distinguished Jewish writers, poets, artists, musicians, and actors were arrested and immediately shot on the charge of involvement in a Jewish "cabal." Ten Jewish "engineer-saboteurs" from the Stalin Automobile Factory in Moscow were also arrested the same day and shot.

7 The Doctor's Plot, announced in a January 13, 1953, article in *Pravda*, involved the arrest on Stalin's orders of thirty-seven mostly Jewish physicians who had treated high-ranking members of the government and Communist Party. The physicians were accused of being "Zionist spies" and of having conspired to kill Soviet leaders by poisoning them. The first arrests were followed by hundreds more, as "sabotage" was "unmasked" in ever wider circles of the Soviet medical profession.

8 While the irony of Stalin's death on Purim is certainly an appealing one, it is much more likely that he in fact died on the official date of March 5, 1953, four days after suffering a massive stroke. The period following his fortunate demise is commonly known as the "Thaw," after the title of the adaptable Ilya Ehrenburg's 1954 novel.

9 The weeks of midnight sunshine before and after the summer solstice in the far northern latitudes are known as White Nights in Russian.

10 Nikita Khrushchev (1894-1971; First Secretary of the Communist Party, 1953-64) ordered a reduction in all branches of the military service of approximately 1,840,000 men between 1955 and 1957, including 640,000 announced for August 1955.

Up the Down Staircase

1 "*Di eybik yung Bella Kaufman*" ("The Forever Young Bella Kaufman"), *Di Tsukunft* 108, 1 (May-November 2003): 36-40. Bel Kaufman (b. 1911) published her best-selling autobiographical novel *Up the Down Staircase* in 1965.

2 Dating from 1950, Aminazin (chloropromazine, but commonly known in the United States as Thorazine) is one of the oldest anti-psychotic drugs. It is still used to treat schizophrenia and bipolar disorder.

3 In the Soviet educational system (as in the Russian one today) there were two advanced degrees, the Candidate (*kandidatskaya*), awarded early in a professional career, usually after the completion of a postgraduate academic program and the writing of a thesis under its auspices; and the Doctoral (*doktorskaya*), the highest, usually awarded in mid-career and involving more extensive research and the publication of a book. Because Soviet education did not normally require graduate study for the basic degree of medical doctor (students instead received five years of thorough, highly specialized undergraduate training followed by rigorous state examinations and a one- to two-year residency, as indicated in an earlier note), physicians wishing to raise their professional qualifications and academic standing frequently undertook the kind of research program Dr. Wolf describes.

4 Andrei Mikhailovich Snezhnevsky (1904-1987) was the director of the Institute of Psychiatry of the USSR Academy of Medical Sciences from 1962 to 1982 and an influential specialist in the diagnosis and treatment of schizophrenia, which he believed to be a genetic disorder capable of psycho-pharmacological management. His idea that such illness might be characterized by periods of latency, or "sluggish" presentation, was used by the Soviet authorities to justify their employment of psychiatric hospitals, but especially of the Serbsky Institute of which Dr. Snezhnevsky had himself been the director from 1950 to 1951, to "treat" political dissidents and other non-conformists.

5 Seduxen (diazepam), marketed in the United States as Valium, is a tranquilizer commonly used as a sedative, muscle relaxant, and anticonvulsant.

6 Neuleptil (pericyazine) is a sedative with weak anti-psychotic properties widely used to control hostility, impulsiveness, and aggressiveness by reducing pathological arousal and affective tension.

7 *Psikhoterapiia epilepsii* (Moscow, 1964), *Psikhofarmakoterapiia epilepsii* (Moscow, 1981), and *Epilepsiia (klinika, lechenie, elektroentsefalografiia, patomorfoz i organizatsiia terapii)* (Moscow, 1991), respectively.

8 Soviet medical doctors belonged to one of three categories, depending on the extent of their academic preparation and the nature of their administrative responsibilities. The rank of Doctor of the Highest Grade was as a rule given to those who headed health facilities (Dr. Wolf's epilepsy ward at the Gannushkin Psychiatric Hospital, for example), or had notable clinical or public-health achievements or significant publication records.

9 Alexander Pushkin (1799-1837) published the first complete edition of *Eugene Onegin*, his great novel in verse and one of the foundation works of Russian literature

and culture, in 1833. Mikhail Lermontov (1814-1841) was a leading romantic poet. Anna Akhmatova (1889-1966), harassed by the Soviet authorities for much of the Stalinist period, was one of the greatest Russian poets of the twentieth century.

10 Founded in the early sixteenth century, the Optina Pustyn monastery south of Moscow near Kozelsk was, especially in the nineteenth century, one of the most important spiritual centers of the Russian Orthodox church, a retreat favored by such men as Leo Tolstoy and Fyodor Dostoevsky.

11 See *"Psikhiatriia i problemy dukhovnoi zhizni"* in *Psikhiatriia i aktual'nye problemy dukhovnoi zhizni*, 3rd ed. (Moscow, 2003).

Family and Children. The Return of Relatives "from the Other Side." Our Son's Wedding. Our first Granddaughter, Lyubochka.

1   Founded in 1895 as a secondary school, the Gnesin State Institute of Music Pedagogy quickly became, after its reorganization in 1944 as a post-secondary institution, a leading Soviet academy of music education, offering rigorous training in conducting and performance. It is currently known as the Gnesin Russian Academy of Music.

2   N. M. Kozlovskaya (1945-2004). Her recordings are, as a composer, *The Inaccessible Princess (Nedostupnaia Printsessa*, 1983); as a composer and pianist, *A Starlit Hour*, with Vadim Korshunov, tenor (1991); and as an arranger and pianist, *Russian Folk Songs*, with Vadim Korshunov, tenor (1991).

3   Tatyana Oranskaya (1914-1982) was a distinguished painter known especially for her portraits of children and women. Her work is in the permanent collection of the State Tretyakov Gallery in Moscow, the country's principal home of Russian art.

4   Rabbi Yonah H. Geller (1921-2008) was the long-time rabbi of the Shaarie Torah synagogue in Portland.

5   The quotation is a loose paraphrase of Ecclesiastes 3: 1-9.

6   Goethe, *Sorrows of Young Werther* (*Der Leiden des jungen Werther*, 1774) was an epistolary novel in sentimental style and a precursor of the Romantic movement in literature. It stands here as a sort of arch shorthand for disappointment in love.

7   In addition to directing the Neuropsychiatric Institute at UCLA, Daniel X. Friedman (1921-1993) was the Braun Professor of Psychiatry and Pharmacology and acting chair of the Department of Psychiatry and Bio-Behavioral Sciences. Like Dr. Wolf, he had served as an army psychiatrist, where he was the first in the American military to use electroencephalography as a diagnostic tool, just as Dr. Wolf had been among the first to do so in the Soviet Union.

8   See Bereishit/Genesis 46 and, perhaps most poignantly, even though it is in fact a New Testament reference, Acts 7: 14-15.

Return to Cheremoshno and Melnitsa. Portland. Israel. Nadezhda. Grandchildren

1   This last part of the book was written in the summer and fall of 2006, just months before Dr. Wolf's death in February 2007.

2 The French rabbi Shlomo Yitzhaki (1040-1105), commonly known by his acronym Rashi, was the author of the first comprehensive commentaries to the Torah and the rest of the Hebrew Bible, revered to this day for their concision and clarity.

3 Tsvi Tal (b. 1927), a prominent religious Zionist who was one of the three judges in the first, 1986-88, capital trial of the Ukrainian death-camp guard John Demjanjuk, served as a Justice of the Supreme Court of Israel from 1990 until his mandatory retirement in 1997.

4 Originally founded in the Soviet Union for the covert study of Judaism and Zionist values, the Machanayim Society today focuses on teaching Judaism and Israeli culture to Jewish immigrants and assisting in their resettlement.

5 Isaac Leib Peretz (or Yitzhak Leibush Perets, 1852-1915) brought new expressive power to Yiddish and introduced modernizing techniques from Western European literature. "If Not Still Higher" (*"Oyb nisht noch hecher,"* 1906), the parable-like story alluded to here, is about a Hassidic rabbi who, disguising himself as the peasant Vassil, performs a good deed anonymously and selflessly.

6 See Lamentations 3: 22-23.

7 *A Standard Phonetic and Spelling Dictionary of Hebrew (and Aramaic) Words in the Yiddish Language* (Portland, 1996), and *Hebrew and Aramaic Words in the Yiddish Language: Their Phonetic Spelling and Translation into English and Russian* (Portland, 1998).

8 *Glasnost* ("Openness") and Perestroika ("Restructuring") were the catchwords of Mikhail Gorbachev's policy of liberalization that began with his installation as General Secretary of the Communist Party in 1985 and ended with the collapse and disintegration of the Soviet Union in 1991. The policy permitted much greater access to information than in any previous period, as well as much greater freedom of movement outside the country.

9 The Section 8 program of the Department of Housing and Urban Development (HUD) provides for subsidized housing in designated apartment communities for those families meeting the income standard.

10 In its original Spanish usage, *marrano* meant a Jew who had feigned conversion to Christianity through fear or self-interest, or whose adoption of the new faith, however sincere it may have been, was still regarded as unreliable or impure. In a broader modern sense, the term signifies a politic adaptation or accommodation but with the point of view reversed: not a pretender to another faith but a betrayer of one's own.

11 The expression, oft-repeated, comes from the Talmud: *Bava Batra* 158b (Rabbi Zeira).

12 *Author's note:* For my impressions and thoughts about Israel, her people, and her problems, see my two long articles published in the magazine *Kheshbn*, No. 133 (1998) and No. 134 (1999).

13 M. Wolf, S. Wolf, and W. H. Wilson, "Clozapine Treatment in Russia: A Review of Clinical Research," in *Psychiatric Services* 46, 3 (1995): 256-59.

14 *Ha'azinu* (the Hebrew second-person plural form of "harken" or "listen") is the first word of the fifty-third weekly Torah portion or parashah in the annual cycle of Torah readings. It corresponds to Deuteronomy 32: 1-52 and is typically read on the Sabbath before *Sukkot* (feast of the booths or tabernacles), usually in early fall.

15 The Presidential Scholars program, established by executive order in 1964, is intended to recognize and honor the nation's most talented and accomplished high-school seniors. Up to 141 students are named each year, making the non-monetary award one of the most prestigious.

16 *Kabbalat Shabbat* begins with this hymn, taken from the Song of Solomon (7: 11-13), and includes the recitation or reading of Psalms 24, 29, and 95-99.

17 The *Haggadah* (the word means "telling" in Hebrew) is the text that sets out the order of the Passover Seder or Feast and provides an account of the liberation of the Jews from the Egyptian Captivity. The Four Questions (Mah Nishtanah) pertain to the nature of the ritual procedure and the meaning of its content.

18 Christian Pineau (1904-1995) was a French resistance leader, Buchenwald survivor, and statesman, as well as a writer of memoirs and children's stories. Nadezhda's opera was based on his 1938 tale, "*Le fils du prince consort.*"

19 Avrom Reyzen (Abraham Reisen, 1876-1953) was a well-known Yiddish poet, short-story writer, and editor even before moving to New York from Minsk in 1911. The lines here are adapted from his 1902 collection, *Tsayt-lider* (Seasonal Poems).